Linden Hills Congregational Church
4200 Upton Avenue South
Minneapolis 10, Minnesota

MEN AS TREES WALKING

And he cometh to Bethsaida; and they bring a blind man unto him, and besought him to touch him. And he took the blind man by the hand, and led him out of the town; and when he had spit on his eyes, and put his hands upon him, he asked him if he saw aught. And he looked up, and said, I see men as trees, walking. After that he put his hands again upon his eyes, and made him look up: and he was restored, and saw every man clearly.

MARK 8:22-25

MEN
AS TREES
WALKING

by Margaret T. Applegarth

HARPER & BROTHERS, PUBLISHERS, NEW YORK

Library of Congress Catalog Card Number: 52–8458

CONTENTS

CONTENTS

6

ROOT OUT OF A DRY GROUND
(*Beauty, because of handicaps*)

MEN AS TREES WALKING

1

PILLAR OF STARCH BY DAY, AND
OF SUGAR BY NIGHT

The Lord God who planted a garden eastward in Eden, planted a garden eastward in your town, also. A garden with a tree in it.

And the Lord God who, later, led the Children of Israel out of bondage in Egypt into their promised land, led them all the way with a pillar of cloud by day and a pillar of fire by night. So that even if such knowledge is too wonderful for you, and you cannot attain unto it, still there is that tree in that garden in your town, to lead you out of your bondage, too. For with equally miraculous methods a tree is a daily drama of God at work in nature for the guidance of mankind—since there it stands: a pillar of starch by day! a pillar of sugar by night!

But the man of God is often too blind to see through the trunk to the sap. And too deaf to hear the little leaves clapping their hands, just as the Psalmist said. Not in applause, however. But because each leaf is the kind of economical engine which any manufacturer would give his eyeteeth to know how to build and run from a distant dynamo ninety-three million miles away, without a penny of "overhead"! Each tiny leaf a windmill and a factory—all day creating starch, all night creating sugar; and sending them down the trunk to feed the twigs, the branches, the roots.

In its public life, each leaf is an obvious windmill, innocently twirling away for all the world to see what fun it is to do its tremendous task in this nonchalant merry-go-round. But in its purely private life, it is a starch factory all day, quietly absorbing every particle of sunlight; arranged on its stem for no other purpose than to store the power of the sun, packing it away until darkness falls. Then, without observing union hours, or any night shift of "hands," that same leaf labors till morning converting the starch into sugar by some secret formula which has been in the Family ever since Eden; and shooting the sugar down the stalks and stems and trunk to furnish all the material needed by the growing parts of the tree.

Green chlorophyll is its secret. The only thing on earth with power to trap the sun's energy and use it for the manufacture of foods. And so, on that fragile humble waving piece of greenness all animal life depends. Hundreds of thousands of humble leaves on each tree, no one of which could do it alone, all properly placed for the catching of sunrays.

My soul shall make her boast in the Lord: the humble shall hear thereof and be glad.

Let the man of God hold a leaf in his hands, therefore, if he would think his Maker's thoughts after Him.

O magnify the Lord with me, and let us exalt His name together.

Perhaps the most wonderful way to magnify Him is to use a magnifying glass, and see how excitingly all of God's minutest details have been thought through toward the sole end of feeding the children of men. On the under side of any apparently carefree leaf, the glass will show several thousand pores, arranged to catch carbon dioxide out of the air and to let loose on the air ("transpire" is the word) the water sent up to the leaf from the roots. A chemical process so complicated that no human chemist could make it work. But each debonair dancer-in-green up there on the bough just tosses off the coolness with such quiet ease that only a poet can be lost in wonder, love and praise:

> And then there crept a little noiseless noise among the leaves
> Born of the very sigh that silence heaves.

This was John Keats, perhaps on his knees as vespers were being intoned toward dusk, when the starch factory "hands" were about to begin their second sacred duty of turning starch into sugar and vitamins.

O taste and see that the Lord is good: blessed is the man that trusteth in Him.

And how tell the man of God of the further drama of a tree at work from its lowest roots to its highest leaf, playing all day and all night with the Atlantic and Pacific Oceans, the Great Lakes, and all the seven seas? First, the sun drawing water up from oceans to clouds. Then the clouds emptying, in rain and dew. Next, the clever water cleverly traveling up the trunk and out to the leaf, where all the little pores will regulate the transpiration properly. And the man of God in his ignorance will say: "Odd how much cooler it is under a tree in summer!" But it is not odd; it is God! And the leaf, obeying. How much of the Atlantic and Pacific Oceans or the Great Lakes, etc., does the man of God's tree use up every day? The total is simply staggering: picture this man carrying five hundred buckets of water upstairs in a ten-hour day, and imagine him ready to faint by nightfall. But without union hours or any night shift of "hands," this systematic stream of water is carried up every trunk to become sap, mixed with minerals from the ground, continuously.

O fear the Lord, ye His saints: for there is no want to them that fear Him.

A further spiritual discovery about the sun and the tree is to notice what starts happening after December 21, the shortest day in the year. For the very next morning the sun will begin its annual play with the sleeping tree. One extra minute each new day. Just this brief new touch of gentle warmth, prolonged one more minute day after day, week after week, through January, February and March, until a swift surge and an old-remembered rhythm throbs from lowest root to topmost twig, and buds begin to bulge. The tides of the Atlantic and Pacific are gathered up. They come down in the small rain. They climb invisibly up that visible dead-looking trunk. The tides of spring warmth wrap themselves around the trunk and the twigs. Each new morning after the earth has turned in its orbit, there is more even than the day before. Men call it *Lent:* to lengthen! The tides of the wind toss the branches around. And then suddenly patience has her perfect work. The leaf! The tender leaf! But how will it ever learn its duty, or fulfill its destiny? It is born knowing:

They looked unto Him and were lightened; and their faces were not ashamed.

For when Shakespeare wrote that there were sermons in trees, what more stirring sermon than being "strangely warmed" on May 9? being planted by the rivers of waters? being a leaf for the healing of the nations? bearing fruit every season?

Twenty years before Pitrim Sorokin became a professor at Harvard, or dedicated the rest of his life to a study of altruistic love, he carved on a tree trunk in Russia, far north near Archangel, the words he has lived up to ever since: "LOVE IS THE ONLY CREATIVE FORCE." It is stabilizing to think that such a sentiment still stands visibly on one tree in Russia! But the same sermon is written deep into every tree in every nation on the face of the earth—inscribed by the Lord God, Himself.

But men can and do cut between the root and the trunk for certain public occasions. In much the same puzzling way that kept happening when the British royal family traveled through Africa a few years ago. The Africans themselves would stand around, spell-bound. For in a land where nobody hurried, a truck would dash up; brisk men would jump out; quick hands would unwind big rolls of green grass growing on strips of sod; with swift gestures, where no grass had grown two minutes before, there would be green pastures. Then a rush back to the truck to remove and set up tall trees complete with green leaves, which would be placed where no trees had ever stood in the memory of the oldest man. And people who had been waiting in blazing sunlight for the King and Queen to come, now would find themselves pleasantly stand-ing in the shade. But there would always be some small child with a penetrating voice to pipe up: "But why doesn't the white King want his trees to have roots?" Nobody paid a particle of attention to the unanswerable question, for by this time several collapsible model huts had been set up, clean as a whistle; and other workmen were suddenly draping certain natives in brilliant brand new yards of material, woven in marvelous stitches—so that here was their dull little town charming as could be, with all sorts of local color, and cooler with these spectacular trees. All done just in time for the royal arrival.

The Queen would always be smiling. The King would always be bowing his head and shaking somebody's hand. The Princesses would always be standing around in the the shade, looking shy but friendly. The head man would always make a speech. The blackest little boy in the briefest little snowwhite breeches would always bow over into a loop and offer a bouquet of flowers nobody in town had ever seen before. The Queen would always be standing on the green grass under a green tree to receive them. The King would always be standing beside her, and would make a kind speech in his gentle quiet way. So that it would always be very wonderful. Then royalty would get back into its shining car, and would drive decorously and slowly out of sight. But nobody in town ever watched them go, because of the really alarming activity which had begun to take place—all that green grass would be rolled up again and shoved into the truck; all those tall trees would be tipped over sideways and eased cautiously back into the truck; all those collapsible huts would be promptly collapsed, and tossed up on top of the truck; all the bright yard goods would be unwound from proud bodies. And before anybody could say "Palaver," that truck would be off like the wind by some short cut to the next stop where the King and the Queen must stand on green grass and be shaded by trees.

"But why doesn't the white King want his trees to have roots?" the same embarrassing little boy would pipe up, when everything was over. But no black parents could ever answer, as they stood in the blazing sunshine, remembering how beautiful their village had been when the King was on hand. But white kings were white kings. And white queens were white queens. So how could a black person know how they felt about *roots?* Although up until an hour ago everybody in town had grown up supposing that roots mattered terribly . . .

There had been this same fixing up of the scenery almost a hundred years earlier, when Catherine the Great had traveled two thousand miles up the Dnieper River in a palatial houseboat, to visit her Russian subjects. By night swift couriers hastily preceded her arrival, transporting from place to place tall cardboard fronts of peasants' houses—picturesque and spacious, propped in front of the miserable little old hovels. A few warmly-dressed comfortable peasants would be wrapped up in extra costumes to stand on the shore to bow and dance and sing Russian folksongs to their Empress. Then the same false fronts would be frantically rushed to the next stop; and the next; and the next. So that the Empress might think all her subjects were in excellent condition.

Is God that kind of a ruler? Does He stay so briefly in church on a Sunday morning that a carved altar and a divided chancel and a robed choir, chanting, can easily deceive Him into thinking: "All is well with my people here," before moving down the block to see what the Baptists are doing. But no, deep grow the roots of the Lord God's planting! And He surely would think it idolatrous to carve a tree trunk into pillars and choir stalls, if His people fell on their knees to worship only their handiwork.

Perhaps the time has come when the man of God should repeat the ninth chapter of Judges, about the day when the trees chose a king, and asked the olive tree to rule over them. But the olive said: "Should I leave my fatness, wherewith by me they honor God and man, and go to be promoted over the trees?" So then they asked the fig tree, which refused and said: "Should I forsake my sweetness and my good fruit, and go to be promoted over the trees?"

Next they said to the vine: "Come thou, and reign over us"; but the vine said: "Should I leave my vine which cheereth God and man, and go to be promoted over the trees?" That left only the bramble, which accepted at once, but said "If in truth ye anoint me king over you, then come and put your trust in my shadow; and if not, let fire come out of the bramble, and devour the cedars of Lebanon."

O magnify the Lord with me: and exalt His name together—root! trunk! branch! leaf! Moment by moment. Day after day. Night after night. Year after year. Century after century. Age after age the living Sequoia trees praise Thee, O God, in California, between three and four thousand years old; and that famous old cypress at Mitla, with room for a regiment under its shade; or that giant banyan with the thousand trunks in India, under which nine thousand people once gathered . . .

Who hath seen Him, that he might tell us? and who can magnify Him as He is? There are yet hid greater things than these be, for we have seen but few of His works. (Ecclesiasticus 43:33.)

Perhaps only that exquisite cripple, Katherine Butler Hathaway, can magnify Him as He is, when she read what He wrote in His willows about the way she walked:

I have always loved willows, because they are the only trees that have wantonly escaped the classic idea of a tree; because instead of growing straight up into the air they lean sideways at all sorts of sad and desperate angles, their branches jutting out of them anywhere, like soft green spray, instead of being placed symmetrically on each side of the trunk, and because sometimes even four or five trunks grow fan-wise out of one root. This waywardness in their structure gives willows a wild romantic abandon, as though they were changelings and held the spirits of people who have been crossed in love. I like them, too, because they can be so old, all tumble-down and rotten and apparently dead, and yet when April comes there will rise out of those black crumbling ruins the most tender and youthful green wands, holding new leaves high in the air in great, round, soft billowy bouquets, more expressive of spring than any other tree. Because of this wonderful mingling of agedness and tender youth, willows seem to belong to a race of trees apart, one that is ancient and magic and lorn.

(*The Little Locksmith;* by permission, Coward-McCann, Inc.)

And I saw another angel ascend from the sunrising, having the seal of the living God; and he cried with a great voice to the four angels, saying: "Hurt not the earth, neither the sea, nor the trees."

Revelation 7:2-3

> That mortal man most happy is & blest
> Who in the wickeds counsals doth not wak,
> Nor zit in sinners wayis doth stay and rest,
> Nor sittis in seatis of skornfull men in talk,
> But contrair fixis his delicht
> Into Jehouwas law
> And on his law, doth day and nicht
> To think is neuer slow.
> He salbe lyk a plesant plantit tree
> Vpon a reuer syde incressing tal,
> That yieldis his fruit in saison dew, we see,
> Whose plesant leif doth neuer fade nor fal.
> Now this is surely for to say
> That quhat he takis in hand,

It sal withoutin doute alway
Most prosperously stand.
Bot wickit men ar nowayis of that band;
Bot of the caffe quhich be the wind is tost;
Thairfor they sal not in the iugement stand.
Nor yet among the iust be sinneris lost.
For gret Jehoua cleirly knowis
The iust mens way vpricht,
Be sure the wickeds way that throwis
Sal perish be his micht.

In Scottish dialect, written in King James'
own handwriting; 1603-1625

2

YGGDRASIL IN YOUR OWN BACK YARD

Yesterday, when earth was young, Yggdrasil grew in everyone's yard. But in front, where it loomed unusually large: a terrifying tree, really, whose roots and branches bound heaven and earth and hell together. Three fates, called Norns, were perpetually employed with pitchers to water its roots in the underworld, those roots gnawed perpetually by small serpents; while a larger snake was perpetually crawling upward, trying to kill the squirrel which scurried all day up and down the tall trunk taking news of underground ugliness to an eagle perched in the treetop, who in turn scanned high heaven for any hint of help from Asgard, the abode of the gods . . .

All day and all night, Yggdrasil! Yggdrasil!

So despairing have men always felt about seeking security on earth that this thought of a Tree of Life somehow symbolized their search—*Yggdrasil* for the Scandinavians; *Irminsul* for the Saxons; *oak trees* for the Druids throughout ancient Gaul and Britain; *Bo tree* for the Buddhists; and for earlier more primitive peoples,

Yaksha, the native spirit seen trampling on a dwarf, with *Yakshi,* his wife, a dryad seen dancing around a tree—the tortured praying of her arms at one with the upstretched writhing of the branches.

When that little old first grandmother of our race walked recklessly across the garden one day and recklessly bit a forbidden apple, she started the children of men in a movement nobody has stopped: the apple always being bitten again; men always *at one* yet *at outs* with the Tree. The record of it can still be seen in prehistoric paintings on old caves in Montinac, France, with dates going back as far as 20,000 B.C.—showing strange horned animals against a background of strange awkward trees. Our Bible records the same definite precaution: Abraham at Mamre in Hebron, entertaining angels under an oak; Gideon under an oak in Ophrah when the angel spoke to him; Saul and his sons buried under an oak; Absalom catching his hair on the branches of an oak, and dying, suspended; Deborah dwelling under a palm tree; and Zechariah standing under the myrtle trees, saying: "O my Lord, who are these?" and the answer: "These are they whom the Lord hath to walk to and fro through the earth, and they answered the angel of the Lord that stood among the myrtle trees and said: We have walked to and fro through the earth, and behold all the earth sitteth still and is at rest."

The Psalmist gave his own thumbnail sketch of this rest: "He shall be like a tree planted by the rivers of water, that bringeth forth his fruit in his season; his leaf also shall not wither; and whatsoever he doeth shall prosper."

Obviously something divinely safe was stepping into the picture, reassuringly.

Ezekiel gave more or less the same figure, except for the tumultuous rise of the waters of life: first, *to his ankles*—but the man with the line in his hands brought him through; then, *waters up to his loins*—but the man brought him through. Then they became waters to swim in, a river that could not be passed over, and behold! at the bank of that river "very many trees on the one side and the other: all trees for meat, whose leaf shall not fade, neither shall the fruit thereof be consumed: it shall bring forth new fruit according to its months because their waters issued out of the sanctuary; and the fruit thereof shall be for meat, and the leaf thereof for medicine."

Medicine for what? for whom?

For all God's people. "And for the strangers that sojourn among you, which shall beget children among you; they shall be unto you as born in the country among the children of Israel; and it shall come to pass that in what tribe the stranger sojourneth, there shall ye give him his inheritance, saith the Lord God."

What bitter medicine for God's people! "What do you see?" our Lord asked the blind man, centuries later; he was only partly cured, so he said: "I see men as trees walking!"

Our Lord knew that the cure had not gone nearly far enough, so He touched the man's eyes again, and made him look up; and then he was restored, and saw every man clearly.

It is, therefore, in the larger hope of this touching, this looking up, and this seeing every man clearly, that the stories in this book tell us about trees and men—for if we could once see the trees clearly, and then could identify ourselves with each man walking, we might see our kinship . . . alien and all . . . and all in all.

For every race has seen more clearly than we do now that Nature is God's other hymnbook, where He sings in the recurring rhythms of sun and rain and tree and fruit and food. For all men. The ancient Jews devoted six whole days to their Feast of First Fruits: people wore green garlands and wreaths of flowers, they carried white willow baskets of pomegranates, dates and figs, they bound their sheaves with lilies, and even their oxen went garlanded with roses as the gay processional climbed the steep streets to the temple, led by a pipe-player and a banner-bearer. Seeing in the tree and its fruit both their life and their Creator.

The secret of their Persian neighbors was bound up with the desert, the garden, *the rug*—where, in any green-flowering oasis, the landscape with a Tree of Life became a symbol of Paradise. Even the folk tales taught a concern for this memory. Do you know the one about Omar and Achmed, the brothers who died and left wills? Omar requested that his money be spent for an obelisk in his memory, with his name engraved on each side in large letters. Achmed asked that far out in the desert an oasis be made, with a deep well and many palm trees to keep his memory green. Almost as if obeying the old Persian proverb: "When you are crossing the desert, plant trees, for you may be coming back the same way in your old age when you will be glad of the shade." But Achmed *saw more clearly*—other men, strangers, enemies, friends: These, too, would need that tree! It was the Tree of Life principle woven, not into a rug, but into life itself.

Much of the same idea was wrapped up in the bundle of superstitious Druid practices. If you managed to wade through Caesar in school with wit and profit, you may recall his attending their ancient order of religious sacrifices in Gaul. If any Druid found mistletoe on a sacred oak, it was ceremoniously cut off with a golden blade, caught carefully in a white sheet, and small sprigs were given out as charms to the worshipers. But whether in Gaul, Britain or Scandinavia, mistletoe the "all-heal" stood as a definite hint toward the life of friend and foe. In Scandinavia, even warriors meeting by chance under an oak bearing mistletoe, flung down their weapons to keep a truce of absolute friendship until the next day. In early Britain, mistletoe over any doorway meant that whoever passed beneath it would be accepted in the spirit of forgiveness and friendliness. "All-heal!"

A custom so rich in meaning that, in due time, each Christmas in York Minster, behold the *Christian* priest carrying a gleaming bough of mistletoe to lay on the high altar, thus proclaiming: "A public pardon and freedom to all sorts of inferior and even wicked people at the gates of this city and even to the end of the earth."

And he looked up; and saw every man clearly!

Robert Herrick caught up this symbol in a poem, a picturesque sermon, really, dated 1591:

> Lord I am like a mistletoe
> Which has no root and cannot grow
> Or prosper, but by that same tree
> It clings about: so I by Thee.
> Why need I then to fear at all
> So long as I about Thee crawl?
> But if that tree should fall and die,
> Tumble shall heaven, and so down will I.

In any such litany of men as trees walking there ought to sound
the metrical version of the first Psalm, set to the tune of "Tallis,"
from the Scottish Psalter:

> He shall be like a tree that grows
> Fast by a riverside,
> Which in its season yields its fruits,
> And green its leaves abide.

To which should be added the Negro Spiritual:

> Steal away, steal away,
> Steal away to Jesus,
> Steal away, steal away home,
> I ain't got long to stay here.
> Green trees are bending,
> Poor sinners stand a-trembling:
> The trumpet sounds within my soul,
> I ain't got long to stay here.

Also there would be Brother Lawrence in the very same spirit,
walking across a French meadow several centuries ago "seeing a
tree stripped of its leaves, and considering that in a little time
the leaves would be renewed and after that the flowers and fruits
appear, he received a high view of the Providence and power of
God which has never since been effaced from his soul. This view
had set him perfectly loose from the world, and kindled in Him
such a love for God that he could not tell whether it had increased
in about forty years that he had lived since."

Cast in the pattern of Ezekiel: York Minster: the Scottish
Psalter: the Negro Spiritual: and St. Mark's gospel: He looked
up! He was restored! He saw clearly! *A dead tree . . . leaves would
be renewed . . . received such a high view of Providence . . . set him
perfectly loose from the world . . . kindled such a love . . .*

A love that leaps oceans and awakens identical renewal and
kindling in China. For as an old Chinese proverb says: "The tree
that fills the arms grew from the tiniest sprout; the pagoda of nine
stories rises from a small heap of earth; the journey of a thousand
miles begins with one step."

The first step that Hu Yong Mi took in his thousand-mile walk was to tear up his own father's Bible into small pieces, wishing he had a knife to cut out the hated name of "Ya-su," "Jesus," which still stared up at him from the torn fragments. A very mad young man! A very dead tree in winter!

But eventually flowers and fruits. Eventually he received such "a high view of Providence" that he was "set perfectly loose" from the old Chinese world, and became a presiding Elder in the Methodist Church in Foochow; eventually becoming a preacher with an impossibly dirty parish. There were filthy ditches, piles of refuse outside; inside, pigs, cattle, fowl, sheep. With not a chair to sit on. (And his wife brought up in a Chinese home of wealth and rank.) Can there be leaves and flowers and fruits here, with stones and brickbats being thrown at Hu Yong Mi for daring to have a "kindling love of God" as he stood in that filth, preaching Christ?

The best answer is the unusually symbolic picture which an artist painted of him, years later—a large picture, five feet high and three feet wide. The central figure seems to be a tree, under which is a man reading from a book. Lower down, some rocks. But look again! The tree is a Cross. And in the rocks are the plain semblances of human faces, all more or less perfect, all turned to the Cross. The artist had no other design than to prove that Hu Yong Mi as he preached the Cross turned even rocks into human beings, eager for release from their earthbound bondage. The up-and-down shaft of the Cross therefore lifts earth up to heaven. The widespreading arms of it the one safe hiding-place for the children of men—more all-healing than mistletoe over the door, taller than Yggdrasil in the back yard, older than all the oaks in history. But a person seeing only men as trees walking, needs his eyes touched again, that he, too, may look up! and see everyone clearly.

Lovely little symbol on a long lapel,
Or dangling from a golden chain about the neck.
Or maybe bigger, bolder, burnished—on a stand.
Improper art, in more than three ways wrong.

Wrong size: the Cross is bigger than a well-fed man.
And heavy, more than one can carry all alone.
Wrong place: the Cross is rightly worn upon the back.
Wrong finish: the Cross is rough, with ugly splinters all along.

Dan West, in *The Christian Century*

Religion's all or nothing; it's no mere smile
Of contentment, sigh of aspiration, sir—
No quality of the finelier-tempered clay,
Like its whiteness or its lightness; rather stuff
Of the very stuff; life of life, and self of self.

Robert Browning

When the winter is severe
The pine trees in this ancient land
Stay green throughout the year.
Is it because the earth is warm and friendly?
No, it is because the pine tree has within itself
A life-restoring power.

Old Chinese poem

A wind arose among the pines; it shook
The clinging music from their boughs, and then
Low, sweet, faint sounds, like the farewell of ghosts,
Were heard: O, FOLLOW, FOLLOW, FOLLOW ME!

Percy Bysshe Shelley

3

A TREE GROWS IN WASHINGTON

Never mind about Parson Weems. It seems that he made up his cherry tree out of his own head—root, trunk, and branch—with a hatchet thrown in as a moral; not to mention George Washington and the lie.

But the cherry tree in this story is absolutely authentic, down to the last blossom on the last twig; and you can go to Washington any April to see for yourself, both the tree and the trees which Mr. Ukio Ozaki sent us from Japan a number of years ago.

The thing which is not so easy to see is the passion and the patriotism which have bloomed and died, and bloomed again. Then died again, thank goodness. A few years ago, aged ninety-one, Mr. Ozaki and his daughter came over from Japan to see how his trees were getting on. They still stood in that most matchless semicircle beside the little lake which reflects the Jefferson Memorial. But Mr. Ozaki must have smiled somewhat secretly over the story of that building.

For when the architects first began visualizing how this Memorial ought to look from across the lake, when reflected in the water, they decided to cut down the fringe of cherry trees, because they might obscure the view too much. But you may have read in the newspapers about those Washington matrons who dedicate themselves to preserving and protecting the past. They became so thoroughly scandalized by such an outrageous sacrilege as cutting down such beauty, that they actually went out and lashed themselves to the tree trunks with ropes and chains, in passionate protest against such a chopping down. Which only goes to show that ladies from high society can do anything on earth they set their minds to do. For the architects were absolutely awed. The woodchoppers were scared stiff. The city was charmed by the uproar. And of course the cherry trees themselves bloomed safely from April to April, year after year.

That is, until December 7, 1941. After which it suddenly became an enormous embarrassment to have one of the most spectacular sights in the nation's capital a row of Japanese trees. Daughters of those earlier matrons, who now had the city's welfare at heart, considered such trees an alien menace straight from the enemy. Important men met to talk over their fate; and the verdict quite naturally was: Chop them down! Chop them down at once!

Immediately this news was wired across the Pacific. Large black headlines topped all other news in Tokyo papers that day: "WASHINGTON, D.C. TO CUT DOWN JAPANESE CHERRY TREES."

A wave of complete consternation swept Japan—for to high and low alike any cherry tree was really a religious matter, and was never grown for the sake of the fruit but for the sake of the

message it brought every spring. Of something eternal stirring
into new life each April, after the deadness of winter. It was on
account of this perpetual promise of renewal that famous men
would leave Japan's important business offices, to walk out under
the pink blossoms; solemn statesmen would feel inspired to write
verses to hang on the branches; and even the Emperor himself
never failed to walk under the trees and write his poem also. For
when God spoke in this annual miracle of beauty, the whole nation
was touched.

And it seemed practically impossible, therefore, to credit this
shocking headline from Washington. Did Americans have no
spiritual sense at all? Why did their radios blare out the song,
"Only God Can Make a Tree," if they had no reverence toward this
first fragile blossom brave enough to burst forth the moment the
weather warmed slightly? Was any tree Japanese, or American?
Was it not *God*? Even though Mr. Ukio Ozaki, "Father of Parliaments," was now in disgrace in Japan due to his outspoken disapproval of Japanese warlords and what they began at Pearl
Harbor, such was his age and his integrity that the military authorities let him live in retirement; isolated on his farm, unmo-
lested, and even forgotten, except as this news of his Washington
gift stirred the whole country from end to end. Was the Western
world losing its understanding, that innocent trees must be sacri-
ficed to such pseudo-patriotism?

Meanwhile, from a less religious motive, Washington itself was
forced into reconsidering its plan to chop, and chop quickly.
Hotel managers protested the whole idea vigorously—remembering how brisk business became when news went out that the trees
would be at their best during such and such a week. Restaurant-
keepers also realized what they could lose if thousands upon
thousands of hungry tourists did not drive up to their curbs on
the way to see those pink blossoms. Store managers said it was
their only sensible season to sell certain souvenirs. Garagemen
groaned over not gaining orders to pour gas into tourist tanks. In
fact, everybody looked to the Park Department to save those
Japanese trees, if some nationally creditable scheme could be
found.

It proved the simplest thing in the world. For a word did it! Why not call them *Korean* cherry trees? Why not, indeed! Come on, Tourists, come and see the exquisite Korean trees now blooming in your nation's capital.

So the trees went on blooming. The tourists kept on coming. The hungry kept on eating. The hotel guests kept on sleeping. April after April until the war was over.

Then in 1949 Mr. Ozaki came to Washington in person. City newspapers mentioned his many honors—aged ninety-one; Father of Parliaments; Mayor of Tokyo; slender and quiet, almost as fragile as one of his cherry blossoms. He bowed gently and said it was a pleasure to find his trees so flourishing after so long a time in our soil. No doubt he thought a few deep thoughts, politely; fortunately they were in Japanese, so none of us had our peace of mind too troubled. But his thoughts must have run along channels of goodwill and forgiveness, and renewal of ties between countries; for when he reached New York, and saw the site of the new United Nations building, he said with his usual simplicity: "And now you must please permit me to send some cherry trees to plant around these buildings, also!"

His daughter was with him and nodded her head, to show that she planned to remind him.

So we can afford to drop Parson Weems from our history— hatchet and all. But might it not be more wholesome to devote a page to cherry trees—"Japanese" again: with their message to tourists that men may come and men may go, but spring comes on forever, in newness of life, with beauty its natural blessing? Then, if only we had a law that on that day all Senators must walk under the cherry boughs and write poems on international goodwill; or even be urged to quote the last two lines of Joyce Kilmer's "Trees" ... if necessary!

❧

JAPANESE PROVERBS

Among flowers, the cherry blossom; among men, the Samurai.

It's the biggest cherry tree that attracts the wind.

It is foolish to try to graft a bamboo shoot on a cherry tree.
The wind and the cherry tree can never be good friends.

The reputation of a thousand years may be determined by the
conduct of one hour.

4

HE WOULD STILL PLANT

HIS APPLE TREE

(A CYCLE OF TWENTY SEPARATE STORIES: LIKE BRANCHES
OF THE TREE OF LIFE: BUILT AROUND ROMANS 8:35-39)

Sooner or later, every church member ought to try his hand at
putting down on paper what Christ means to him. Some may go
at it in roundabout fashion—as Martin Luther did, when every
authority in Germany was up in arms to silence him, yet he managed to write calmly: *"Even if I knew that tomorrow the world*
would go to pieces, I would still plant my apple tree!"
In desperate danger—to dare! In calamitous circumstances—to
care! In sudden shocks—to share! Ring by ring, to picture his tree
growing up. Apple by apple, to visualize its fruit feeding tomorrow's families. This sort of faith is tremendous; and in our own
day, when the world went to pieces for five years—from 1940 to
1945—it was exhilarating to hear of other men in other places still
planting apple trees. Some of them are set down herewith in
writing; nobody is especially beautiful, except Frau Forell—whose
face still has the madonna quality of one who has talked with angels
and touched divinity, and has therefore held that wonder the rest
of her life, written on her forehead with peace, and deep in her
eyes with compassion. But the others have done fabulous things
with such beautiful swiftness that they seem like footnotes on
Paul's letter to the Romans, and are so presented; ring by ring,
branch by branch, in this modern Tree of Life planting.

WHAT SHALL SEPARATE US FROM THE LOVE OF CHRIST?
SHALL TRIBULATION?

"No!" Martin Niemöller would have said. And proved it by
planting his tree in the only fashion possible for a minister whom
the Nazis were keeping in solitary confinement, in a concentration
camp for eight years. Separated from a congregation, maybe. But
in no way separated from the love of Christ. See him daily moving
his table under the high windows of his cell. See him placing his
chair on that table. See him climbing up on this chair to stand
on tiptoe, in order to get as close as possible to the grating of the
window above his head. See him waiting for the moment when
the strange sound of scuffling would begin rising from the courtyard far below—that crunching of feet on gravel which told him
that now the other prisoners were out for their daily airing. So
slow and so silent that he could sense their hopelessness from the
drag of their footsteps as they walked round and round in a circle.
Totally unconscious that they had been adopted as ground for a
future orchard. Totally unaware that seeds were being planted at
that very moment, as Pastor Niemöller stood on tiptoe and began
to whisper stirring passages from the Bible.

Day after day he waited for this brief interval, filling in the
time by a search for sentences steadying and inescapable: also
practicing the art of learning how to whisper powerfully enough
to penetrate the distance between his high window and those unseen scuffling passers-by, down below. Never, of course, to speak
loud enough to attract the guards; but somehow to discover how
to throw his voice in some low persistent fashion to catch the ears
of those discouraged men down there. Although there seemed no
earthly way for him to find out if anybody heard him or not, the
single fact that the scuffling sounds became less noisy on the
gravel was all to the good—might it not mean that the prisoners
were lifting their feet more lightly, in order to hear?

Through months of uncertainty he offered this mystical ministry,
always in prayer that God would use even such an absentee instru-
ment as a disembodied voice to awaken hope in the helpless, faith
in the faithless, love in the loveless. You are not surprised that on

his release at the end of the war, Dorothy Thompson reported on the striking incandescence of his face—tribulation having drawn him closer than ever to the Presence.

What Shall Separate Us From the Love of Christ? Shall Distress?

"No!" would have been the answer of certain wounded soldiers, on one of our hospital ships headed for home, during the war years. For although their bodies were badly broken, and their futures all uncertain, their own distress was made more endurable by the lavish care which the Red Cross gave—showering them with candies, cakes, cigarettes; far more than they could possibly use.

Out of somebody's sense that it is only common decency to share such abundance, the sick soldiers began pooling great piles of these presents to be sent below decks to the German prisoners of war in the hold of this same ship. Enemies, of course. Possibly the very men who had brought them to this present fix, by enemy action in surprise attacks with guns or bombs or firing squads. Nonetheless, here they were, themselves, broken in body, but headed for all the comforts of home and the consolation of loved ones, while the other poor guys down below were headed for discomfort and prolonged absences; and although mid-ocean may seem an odd place to plant an apple tree, how better could one describe a pile of presents put before prisoners? The Germans were absolutely overwhelmed by this sudden abundance of luxuries they had not seen in years. With each new mouthful, they wished they had something suitable to send back to those generous fellows up above. But what has a prisoner except the clothes he wears?

Then one of the Germans said: "Maybe we could sing something!"

But what could they sing in German that Americans could surely understand?

In the end, their choice was perfect. For up from the water's edge, out there in the middle of the Atlantic Ocean, rose the rich volume of German voices singing the old familiar "Crusader's Hymn," which could tell their victors up above everything they wanted them to know—"Fairest Lord Jesus," the Americans thought they sang; but the German words are lovelier still:

> Beautiful Saviour, ruler of all nature . . .
> Truly I'd love Thee
> Truly I'd serve Thee,
> Thou my soul's comfort, joy and crown.

WHAT SHALL SEPARATE US FROM THE LOVE OF CHRIST? SHALL FAMINE?

"No!" Dr. Henry Bovenkirk could say. For he only needs to close his eyes to see six of the world's most wonderful cupcakes, secretly brought into his prison cell one day by an unknown Japanese woman. Somehow she had managed to enter the gates of his concentration camp.

"But how on earth did you ever get in?" were his first words as she stood in front of him.

"I pretended I could not read the sign: NO ADMITTANCE!"

"But that is a desperately dangerous thing to have done!" Dr. Bovenkirk warned her. "And why did you ever risk it, when I think I must be a total stranger to you, since I have never been in this city before?"

"But that is just why!" the woman exclaimed. "I heard there was a Christian missionary interned here. I heard of the horrible way they kept examining you day after day, night after night, with torture. And I feared you might be starving too."

"Yes!" he agreed, and his mouth began to water as he looked at the first appealing food he had seen in many months. "But where did you ever get the flour? I have heard that it is rationed now, and expensive."

"Yes! But I saved up all my ration for these six cakes," she said quietly. "I only wish they were bigger."

Hungry as he was, he knew that before he ate he must help her to escape; for the risks she had run were alarming in a building surrounded by armed guards and firing squads, every entrance

watched both night and day. He led her down the corridor in the
vain hope of finding an easy exit; but they were both caught, and
the woman was soon confessing to the commandant that, because
she could not read, she had ignorantly walked in . . . the door had
been open . . . she was innocent . . .

To his horror, Dr. Bovenkirk saw her being dragged away savagely; while he himself was kicked back toward his own cell,
he heard her piercing screams from whatever punishment she
was receiving; and he began wondering if he could endure tasting
the delicacies she had provided at such a cost. But this need not
have worried him. For by the time he reached his cell, somebody
had stolen the cupcakes, and he never saw them again.

And yet to this day, all he needs to do is to close his eyes in
order to see them plainly. His mind gratefully reproducing a whole
row of scenes: the woman's compassionate concern that any
Christian of another race should be made to suffer unjustly in her
own town—her immediate plan to save up each small ration of
flour and sugar, week after week, secretly, perhaps even with her
own family around her—her stubborn determination to dare enter
a deathtrap nonchalantly, even if it was the last thing she did on
earth—her burning desire that at least one American should know
how keenly one Japanese felt about this ghastly war—

Little by little, the memory of six cupcakes became elements in
his "Eucharist": his "Thank you," uttered once more for a broken
body and the blood of sacrifice, in a communion of all true
believers.

What Shall Separate Us From the Love of Christ? Shall Nakedness?

"No!" Madelaine Forell would have said. For on the day when
the French police knocked at her door to take her to the concentration camp at Gurs, she had presence of mind to take along all her
dresses, all her aprons, and lots and lots of aspirin. For experience
told her that there would be women there brought to prison at midnight, perhaps, with nothing but the clothes they were wearing.
Frau Forell guessed what a comfort it would be if they could wear
a dress of hers while washing their own. As it turned out, sixty

women were crowded into one room where Frau Forell was also interned; and in no time at all she had shared the dresses and aprons, for nakedness was a natural terror in that miserable room— where the only water for bathing was from a tap located outside the door in a courtyard, where two soldiers stood on guard both night and day.

Yet there was another nakedness far worse, which Madelaine Forell found that she could clothe in even more permanent garments.

As in the case of a woman who had lost her mind ever since the frantic moment of her arrest in the north of France, one day when she was marketing. She had begged the policeman to let her go home first: "My little girl is in the house alone! You really *must* let me go back to get her!"

But the policeman had hurried her off to the train going south to Gurs, and shook her in violent annoyance at her protests: "Come along now, never mind about the child—you come with me!" And come she did: a day's journey south to Gurs.

But every morning when the sixty women were permitted to leave prison for an outing in the courtyard, she rushed over to the barbed wire fence facing north. Clinging there in despair, she would cry in constant heartbreak: "Where are you, my darling? Where are you, my darling: Where are you? Where are you? Where are you?" until all the prisoners grew restless and irritated at her grief. All but Frau Forell, who had given away her dresses; and now had something left for a soul stripped of all sanity.

For every day during their period for "play," she would put her arms around this panic-stricken creature, and begin weaving an almost tangible covering of love: "Can't you feel my arms around you, as the love of God is around you? I know just how it is with you—for I may never see Frédéric, my husband, again, since he is interned elsewhere in France! I may never see my younger son again, for he is interned in Australia! I may never see my aged parents, somewhere in Germany! I have had to give them into God's keeping. For He loves them more than I love them. He loves your little girl also, more than you love her. She is safe with Him now. His arms are around you, as my arms are around you. Can't you feel our love around you?" Over and over. Over and over.

Not a word did this woman answer. But at least, while Frau Forell was talking, she never called frantically, or clung to the barbed wire; and for this the other prisoners were grateful; especially as Frau Forell devoted all of these hours out-of-doors to the same urgent sentences said with such quiet gentleness: "Can't you feel my arms around you, as God's arms are around you? Can't you feel our love?" But still the woman never answered; her face never grew less desperate; her body never grew less tense. But stitch by stitch Madelaine Forell kept making the same patient pattern; months passed; until one morning when she said, as usual: "Can't you feel my arms around you, as God's love is around you?" the woman suddenly turned and said in a natural voice: "Huh? What did you say just then?"

And a Lutheran pastor's wife discovered that she had somehow planted Martin Luther's tree again: "beauty for ashes, the oil of joy for mourning, the garment of praise for the spirit of heaviness; that they might be called *trees of righteousness, the planting of the Lord,* that he might be glorified" (Isaiah 61:3).

Even to this day, in their New York parish, The Church of the Newcomers, the Forells still hold regular club meetings for the Ladies of Gurs; and out of this sisterhood of suffering further miracles are wrought for newcomers in need of being clothed, as Gideon once was, by the Spirit of the Lord.

What Shall Separate Us From the Love of Christ? Shall Peril?

"No!" the Norwegian mothers would laugh, reminiscently. For even during those dangerous days when the Nazis occupied Norway, and Quisling had tried to get rid of all Jews as Hitler required, even then there was a great game they urged their children into playing.

It went like this: the moment the curfew would sound, the moment every Norwegian was required to get off the streets, that was the very moment when the Lutheran mothers urged their children *back* on the streets, by calling through their homes: "Children! Children! The curfew has sounded!"

There would be a merry scramble toward kitchens. A big wet-ting of rags or sponges. Then a swift scampering down the street under cover of darkness, until they came to certain stores where the Nazis had printed in white chalk: THIS IS A JEWISH STORE! IT IS FORBIDDEN TO TRADE HERE!

The difficult game was to swoop past without stopping and yet somehow, in one sweeping gesture, to wash off the entire sign. No lingering! No fumbling! No fussing! No admiring of your success! Just one huge wet swish, and away you speeded. Boys were better than girls—they said it beat hockey for dash and derring-do. But girls got the hang of it, as winter passed, and would dart home to announce, triumphantly: "I did it again, little mother! I wiped off every single word!"

"Good!" said the Lutheran mother. "Very good!" But the real goodness was not in the accuracy, but in making it legal for one more Jewish store to stay open for business one more morning, in order that one more Jewish neighbor might earn enough to feed his family one more day; until the police would notice the absence of his sign, and reprint their legal warning.

But night followed day in Norway. And as soon as the curfew would sound, thousands of courageous Christian mothers would send thousands of courageous children out into the night to re-peat their risky errand. Entrusting them to the care of a just God, who must want His Chosen People fed! And always with the prayer in their hearts that the policemen, who might be parents themselves, would smile indulgently at the sight of so many small Norwegians dashing home in a hurry.

For God works in a mysterious way His wonders to perform. And this was simply the wonder of a Lutheran apple tree, mysteri-ously planted; and mysteriously watered; and mysteriously blessed.

WHAT SHALL SEPARATE US FROM THE LOVE OF CHRIST? SHALL SWORD?

"No!" Bishop Berggrav would vow. Especially after that dramatic day when the Primate of the Lutheran Church in Norway dared to walk boldly into Quisling's office to protest Quisling's daring to crowd five thousand schoolteachers aboard an ancient ship with a capacity for only one thousand passengers. Already it had sunk to the water line, and Bishop Berggrav dreaded to think of this voyage in the dead of winter, through rough seas, to a frozen concentration camp up near the Arctic Circle. All because these brave women had refused to teach the new Nazi textbooks, which spoke slightingly of religion, and urged children to treat Jews with disdain.

Bishop Berggrav faced Quisling fearlessly and let loose a vigorous vocabulary on him—unjust! disgraceful! barbarous! violating every decent code on God's earth!

Quisling rose at his desk, purple with rage at such language, and shouted in anger: "I could have you beheaded for talking to me this way!"

"Well, here I am!" Berggrav answered quietly.

But Quisling did not want to make this Bishop even more be-loved, as a martyr; so he interned him in a lonely cabin north of Oslo, with twelve strong Nazi guards to watch him day and night —swords drawn, guns pointing, in case he sought to escape.

But it was as if the Bishop lived in everyone's home. In isolation he was more present than ever. Word went the rounds that he was employing these lonely hours to translate the Bible into modern Norwegian. Word also went around that such was his charm that the German Storm Troopers had to be changed constantly, lest they befriend him too greatly. Even as it was, when they were sent down to Germany to rest, he would give them letters to mail; so that this saint-in-exile kept in lively contact with other churchmen: all through the medium of his own guards. In the midst of constant peril, planting the Tree of Life!

As It Is Written: for Thy Sake We Are Persecuted All The Day Long; We Are Accounted As Sheep for The Slaughter

At this point, midway of Paul's pointed questions to the Romans, it may be well to stop long enough to note that the persecution of a modern churchman differs little from the persecution of an Early

Church Christian. This graphic letter, dated A.D. 257, is from another Bishop, Cyprian of Carthage, who could write of his coming martyrdom:

O feet most blessedly bound with irons, not to be loosed by the iron-smith, but by the Lord! O feet most blessedly bound, guiding me along the way of Salvation to Paradise! O feet which are bound to the world for the present time, only to be made free by the Lord! O feet which linger awhile among the fetters and the prison-bars, only to run more quickly to Christ along a blessed road! Let envy, malice or cruelty hold you here in chains as long as they will, yet from the earth and from these sufferings you shall speedily enter the Kingdom of Heaven.

The body is not comforted in mines with soft chairs and cushions, yet it is comforted with the peace and solace of Christ. The body weary with labor lies prostrate at last, but there is no evil in lying down with Christ. Your unbathed limbs are foul and discolored with filth, yet within they are spiritually cleansed. The bread is scarce, but men live not by bread: they live by the word of God. Shivering you look for clothing: but he who puts on Christ is abundantly clothed and adorned.

NAY, IN ALL THESE THINGS WE ARE MORE THAN CONQUERORS THROUGH HIM THAT LOVED US. FOR I AM PERSUADED THAT NEITHER DEATH—

Death cannot separate a man from the love of God! Take the case of the German preacher sent to prison for his too-frank exposure of Nazi errors. The judge happened to be a former neighbor, and therefore inclined to be as lenient as possible: "My dear fellow," the judge implored him, "if you will only promise to stop preaching, I can not only save you now, but prepare a paper to guarantee your safety throughout the war."

"No," said the preacher. "No, I must preach!"

"Don't be so stubborn. I will give you three days to think this over, and let you come to your senses."

Back in his cell, with only three days left on earth, the preacher begrudged his solitary confinement when there were so many last testimonies he longed to give. Then he noticed that the walls of his cell were wooden, that there was a grating on the door, and that if he talked loudly enough he could catch the attention of the other prisoners and lighten their own loneliness with his messages.

So he used his three days and three nights, preaching as he had never preached before; pouring into every sentence all the passion of his Christian love.

When he was brought before the judge on his last morning, and the question was put: "Well, will you promise never to preach again?" he answered firmly: "No, I must preach!"

The judge waved his hand at the firing squad: "Take this man out, and shoot him."

As the shots sounded through the thin walls of the prison, men in confinement bowed their heads in deep pity, each one with a sharp remembrance of some part of the passionate appeals of the previous days. And this, too, was Martin Luther's apple tree, planted once more in a deathless dream of fruit tomorrow.

NOR LIFE—

There are nine Jews living today who are persuaded that "life" could not separate a Waldensian pastor in Italy from his love of God! Having fled here and there for safety in this town, with the police looking for them, they knocked at the Waldensian pastor's door in utter despair.

"But my house is too small!" cried the poor man, pointing at the small humble rooms, the few pieces of furniture, all utterly inadequate to hide even a child, if the police should start searching. But the pastor's mind had gone leaping over to his church—*how about pews?* But of course it would be useless to hide a Jew under a pew: in one moment they could be discovered. And then the one possible spot dawned on him: of course—*the organ!*

"Come!" he whispered. And in single file they hurried silently into the sanctury, one by one settling uncomfortably behind the tall pipes, or crouching low in the works. When all nine were safely concealed, he strolled nonchalantly home to await the police.

When they finally came, they probed and poked and pushed into every corner of the little chapel; they looked under all the pews; they shook the pulpit; they inspected the steeple; they ransacked the basement. Satisfied with their own thoroughness, they thundered off into the night. But, the pastor warned the Jews not to move, for it would be just like the police to return for a surprise search.

All night they stayed cramped in their strangely straight positions; all the next day, as well. Friendly Waldensian parishioners secretly supplied their pastor with bundles of food. And that night, Waldensian men guided the Jews on their dangerous underground journey up into Switzerland.

It is, perhaps, only human to wonder about the works! Could an organ possibly make quite such a joyful noise unto the Lord the following Sunday?

Nothing could ever persuade the pastor that some remarkable, moving new note had not actually been added! Although the likelihood is that the new note vibrated in the congregation the moment they saw their organ, or tried singing such a hymn as "Jesus Lover of My Soul":

> Hide me, O my Saviour, hide,
> Till the storm of life is past,
> Safe into the haven guide
> O receive my soul at last.
> Other refuge have I none,
> Hangs my helpless soul on Thee,
> Leave, ah leave me not alone,
> Still support and comfort me.
> All my trust on Thee is stayed,
> All my help from Thee I bring,
> Cover my defenseless head
> With the shadow of Thy wing.

If this were Martin Luther's tree, planted when their world was going to pieces, then no wonder they heard the leaves clapping their hands, exactly as Isaiah said.

NOR ANGELS—

In his book, *We Thought We Heard the Angels Singing,* James Whitaker writes about his endless days lost on a raft in mid-Pacific;

and says that more than almost anything else in the world he longed to get at a telephone, so that he could call up the brother with whom he had quarreled badly the last time they met.

For now, in the face of all eternity, on this endless expanse of water, with no help in sight, their quarrel suddenly seemed too silly for words. An ego pinched? So what! A dirty dig? Forget it! Entirely too much whitewash? Lay it on thick, brother, lay it on thick—I've done the same thing in your place!

How shocking it is that more of us cannot seem to find God— without a raft! Had you ever thought what a mortifying movie could be made at any Sunday service in church, just before the offering, if it were required of all members to live up to this drastic commandment: "If thou bring thy gift to the altar, and there remember that thy brother hath aught against thee, leave thy gift at the altar, and first go thou and be reconciled with thy brother; and then come and offer thy gift"? At least half the congregation would be in exit, sheepishly stealing down side aisles to telephone home: "Dreadfully sorry! Forget it, can you? I didn't mean a word of it! Do please forgive me!"

NOR PRINCIPALITIES—

In all Athens nobody was taller than Archbishop Damaskinos. Well over six feet; to which were added the extra inches of his high headgear. Even his long, flowing beard somehow emphasized his stature, so that he was easily the most unforgettable figure in Greece, impressing everybody with the majesty of his appearance and the importance of his position. Except, of course, the Enemy then ruling the country.

Everything these officers did was grim and brutal. And one day when a German had been killed in the streets, the Nazi commandant issued an order that seventeen Greeks should be shot in reprisal.

On receiving the news, Archbishop Damaskinos strode into the Commandant's office: "You can't kill those men!" he cried with the voice of authority. "All seventeen of them are not only innocent, but they are the fathers of families and will be desperately needed at home in the days ahead of us!"

The Commandant looked the Archbishop up and down—from the top of his high black turban, down the black beard, down the immense length of his long black robe to his feet; then he answered sarcastically: "But I have orders to kill seventeen Greeks! And I don't suppose you can give me the names of seventeen other Greeks willing to die in their places, can you?"

"Certainly I can!" cried the Archbishop. "I will make you a list, at once." While the Archbishop was busy writing, the Commandant waited in utter surprise. But his surprise deepened when he read the name of Archbishop Damaskinos himself at the top of the list of men willing to die, and noted that the other sixteen vicarious names were all bishops!

Principalities rarely want to make martyrs out of men who are already famous figures; so the order was countermanded. But from that moment the Archbishop walked the streets of Athens wearing a common hangman's rope as a girdle, to show the principalities that he was still ready to die for his people. Eventually the Nazi shut him up in his own residence where no one could see him. But his loyal people were more conscious than ever of all that he meant to them. It was natural, therefore, when the war was over, and the nation stood in need of a premier who would be absolutely dependable and upright, that the only name foremost in everyone's mind was Archbishop Damaskinos. Someone to whom they would dare trust their lives, since he had been ready to lay down his own life for theirs.

Nor Powers—

It is one thing to be a high church dignitary, used to matching authority with authority, boldness with boldness. But it is another thing entirely to hear of this simple peddler arrested in Yugoslavia for daring to distribute leaflets on the street. A practice strictly forbidden by law.

However, when the leaflets were found to be blank paper, the Powers-That-Be grew doubly suspicious, sure that this find was a great prize. They tested the blank paper with every known test to bring out the secret writing. But when neither special acids nor any kind of heat made hidden words appear, then the authorities began torturing the peddler, to make him confess what such papers might mean. His only reply was: "The people who got them will know what they mean." And this he kept stubbornly repeating no matter what screws they turned nor what bones they twisted out of joint.

For this had been his way of planting a Tree of Life in Yugoslavia, when their world had gone to pieces—and only a blank sheet of paper could tell something special on the day when a blank piece of paper was expected.

Nor Things Present—

No one thing is ever more present than a fence. There it stands, announcing to the world that something inside is being shut in; and something outside, shut out. And if that fence is around a Catholic cemetery, it means that all the earth inside is consecrated ground, only for those who have died in the faith. It was that way in Poland also, of course.

But during the war years a Quaker came to town. A man so gentle that although he had never been in Poland before and spoke no word of Polish at first, yet everybody knew exactly what he meant—and he knew that when they were too thin, they were too hungry; and if their feet were bare, they needed shoes. It was as simple as that, at first. They felt they had been born knowing him. And even after he learned plenty of Polish, he never scolded anybody who came back to his soup kitchen for more soup. Neither did he ever play favorites, and save out the best suits and coats for special friends. He never seemed to notice whether people were Polish or Jewish or Russian or German. So everybody told him everything in every one of these languages, all day long. For here he was: as present as the Golden Rule in action; as available as Come-Ye-Blessed-of-My-Father in the last judgment, who also had lavished love on the hungry, the naked, the prisoner.

So that his death was a total calamity. From overwork? From malnutrition? From a constant drain on his sympathies? Nobody knew, for sure. But when they began doing the last tender things which can be done for someone so beloved, the saddest calamity of all was the moment when it dawned on everyone that a Quaker is not a Catholic! They spoke earnestly to the priest: was it not possible, just this once, to lay such a saintly person in consecrated ground, inside the cemetery?

But the priest had to shake his head; for the rule of the Church was the rule of the Church.

Disconsolate, the people buried the body of their friend as close to the forbidden fenceline as possible. But they went home with heavy hearts.

After darkness had fallen that night, however, the priest himself went out, and moved the fenceline over far enough to include the new grave. For the rule of the Church is explicit enough about consecrated earth, and who may lie in it; but nothing whatever is printed in black and white about fencelines. One wonders about the priest's name in Polish—for it ought to have been Malachi, since he too knew that "They shall be mine, saith the Lord of hosts, in that day when I make up my jewels; and I will spare them as a man spareth his own son that serveth him."

Nor Things to Come—

If all the things that happened to all the people repatriated on the *S.S. Gripsholm* could be written in a book, it might well be chapter twenty-nine in the Acts of the Apostles. But it is my hope that at least one asterisk may twinkle at the bottom of one page to tell in a footnote what happened to three Japanese missionaries who did a glorious job on an outrageous old tub of a boat just before they were transferred up into the spotless shipshape liner.

This vile old tub had just brought those about to be repatriated from Japan to Goa, a port in Portuguese East India, where the *Gripsholm* awaited them. These three missionaries stood on deck, satchels in hand, staring with delight at the incredibly scrubbed sides of the *Gripsholm*—those beautiful blue sides, with those pale yellow stripes, set crosswise. Then they lifted their eyes to the deckline and saw a row of Japanese faces staring down.

"Diplomats?" the women asked one another. "The embassy

from Washington, perhaps? Is our country repatriating Japanese in exchange for our return?"

Immediately a simultaneous shock struck all three ladies. They looked down in disgust at the disgraceful state of the deck where they stood. For many a trip, rough or smooth, nobody had bothered to wash up the revolting remainders of old food, old paper, old seasickness. It lay there crusted, layer on layer.

Without a word to one another, they wheeled rightabout-face simultaneously, rushed inside and asked the shiftless sailors for buckets, scrubbing brushes and water. Then with the precision of a regiment, they marched back to the deck, fell on their knees and started to scrape, to scour, to scrub. It was in this astonishing position, so much like prayer, that certain newspaper writers caught them at their curious labor. These men had been sent half a world away from home to write up any unusual drama of disembarking and re-embarking which this repatriation business might include. But not one of them was prepared for this upsetting sight—

"Ladies!" they gasped in a shocked chorus. "What on earth do you think you are doing?"

The three missionaries, still on their knees, replied in an equally shocked chorus: "We think those Japanese gentlemen up there may be our diplomats. In any case, tomorrow and tomorrow we are going to need their friendship badly. So we decided to make at least our corner of this dirty deck more decent for them to stand on."

"Japanese are so scrupulously clean!" one woman added, in defense of her fanatic scrubbing.

"Immaculate is a better word!" the second woman said, continuing to scour.

"Dainty!" said the third, scraping away for dear life.

How those newspapermen in the East wrote it up for their readers in the West! You must have read about it, yourself. Probably thinking at the time that "Things to Come" would certainly be better if only more of this kind of individual responsibility could be felt. (But nobody gave a single thought to Martin Luther or to the Tree of Life. Although it can start to grow on a deck. Especially if the Japanese transferred the sapling to their gardens. They have a way with trees!)

NOR HEIGHT—

Height is dizzy enough. But add the Pacific Ocean, and an enemy or two, and height becomes disaster.

When his plane cracked up and went into a tailspin, the young airman jumped at the proper moment, did the proper releasing of his parachute, counted minutes, calculated distances, exactly as he had—in training. But there, a dozen other fellows had been practicing identical dives, close by. It was quite different with only the blue Pacific spread out at his feet, and only the blue sky everywhere else. Under the swift sinking and swerving of his parachute he was surprised to hear himself shouting the text of his father's favorite sermon: "The eternal God is my refuge; and underneath are the everlasting arms." He had not thought of the words in years, but they gave him courage to look down. He saw land—a small island, directly below. Whether this was good or bad would depend on the occupants, and his own state after landing. When near enough to see men in Japanese uniforms, marching, he felt helpless enough to need his text again, and shouted once more as he landed: "The eternal God is my refuge; and underneath are the everlasting arms." To his still greater alarm, he found that he had fallen on his back, tangled up in parachute ropes, directly in the path of the marching soldiers. He could, therefore, hardly credit his ears when he heard a Japanese voice calling: "For in Him we live and move and have our being. Right! Right! Right! Right!"

The young Japanese officer thus ordering his outfit into a wide enough detour to give the American time to get back his breath, disentangle himself, and—as it happened—find his way to a detachment of his own army also on the island. One man, at least, who knows for a fact that height could not separate him from the love of God, when the love of Jesus Christ had educated the enemy also.

NOR DEPTH—

During the war Captain Reginald Wheeler's work in the army was to meet troopships returning from Europe, and to gather the details of the soldiers' personal experiences, which more general battle records could never catch. One such personal report, given on a hospital ship, by a soldier suffering seriously from third degree burns, somehow gathers up all these preceding stories into a triumphant summary.

This soldier told Captain Wheeler that he had jumped overboard from a ship which had been bombed and was burning. He fell into a sea of oil which had caught fire. This meant that, at every stroke, he swam into still more burning oil, until his body was in absolute agony. Knowing that his only safety lay in swimming his way out of this blazing hell, he had grit enough to make every stroke to the rhythm of some half-remembered verses which had been stored up in some dim past, from Sunday-school memory work. Phrase by phrase, verse by verse, thought by thought, he managed to restore the entire sequence—

What shall separate us from the love of Christ?	(Stroke 1)
Shall tribulation?	(Stroke 2)
Or distress?	(Stroke 3)
Or famine?	(Stroke 4)
Or nakedness?	(Stroke 5)
Or peril?	(Stroke 6)
Or sword?	(Stroke 7)
As it is written	(Stroke 8)
We are persecuted	(Stroke 9)
all the day long	(Stroke 10)
we are accounted	(Stroke 11)
as sheep for the slaughter	(Stroke 12)
Nay, in all these things	(Stroke 13)
we are more	(Stroke 14)
than conquerors	(Stroke 15)
through Him	(Stroke 16)
that loved us	(Stroke 17)
For I am persuaded	(Stroke 18)
that neither death	(Stroke 19)
nor life	(Stroke 20)
nor angels	(Stroke 21)
nor principalities	(Stroke 22)
nor powers	(Stroke 23)
nor things present	(Stroke 24)

nor things to come	(Stroke 25)
nor height	(Stroke 26)
nor depth	(Stroke 27)
nor any other creature	(Stroke 28)
shall be able	(Stroke 29)
to separate us	(Stroke 30)
from the love of God	(Stroke 31)
which is in	(Stroke 32)
Christ Jesus our Lord	(Stroke 33)

And lo! the score came out even! the last phrase of Stroke 33 bringing him into clear sea, with no burning oil. He lay on his back floating, until he was picked up, a mass of burns, over which the doctors had been in despair.

But as he thought back over his experience, he realized that he never could have "made it" if half his mind had not occupied itself in the intense search for that long string of half-forgotten phrases: almost like a student in some final examination on which everything depends. Today we call his method mental therapy; but the saints had a choicer phrase: they "endured as seeing Him who is invisible." In order not to omit Stroke 28, a quotation from Tertullian adds the Early Christian's endurance:

NOR ANY OTHER CREATURE—

So we spread ourselves before God, while the hooks pierce us, and the fires blaze on us, and the swords slit our throats, and the beasts leap on us. Even the posture of the Christian at prayer shows his readiness for every manner of torture. Here lies the crime: Where God's truth is, there is devotion.

Tertullian, A.D. 230

We are born believing. A man bears belief as a tree bears apples.

Ralph Waldo Emerson

Good works do not make a man good; the fruits do not bear the tree but the tree the fruits.

Martin Luther

5

TWO PETALS FROM THE WILD-ROSE TREE

The letter made her mark down the date on her calendar: "Wouldn't you love to be able to say about yourself what St. Paul wrote of his going through life *diffusing the perfume of His presence everywhere through me, a perfume vital for life?* (Moffatt translation.) It has been said that when the Bulgarian workers go home at night from perfume factories, no whistle needs to tell their town that their day's work is over—for a penetrating loveliness suddenly spreads from street to rooftops wherever they walk! Believing with all our hearts that something as matchless as this needs to be recaptured in all our lives and cling to our very clothes, the members of our society plan to hold a 'Quicken Day' from ten to twelve on Tuesday. We want to learn in an absolutely fresh fashion how to use our Five Senses—for we are unto God a sweet savor of Christ (2 Corinthians 2:15). Therefore we plan to begin this unusual quickening by dipping our fingertips in actual fragrance at the door as we enter! Mrs. U. and Mrs. V. have agreed to greet us for this exhilarating renewal and rejoicing together. Then, at high noon as the clock strikes, we will receive 'two petals from a wild-rose tree'! Which will probably be your favorite moment in this strangely moving morning. You realize perfectly well that No! we have never done *anything* at all like it before. And Yes! we do indeed hope that you may feel the need for such a morning of Recollection."

It was a proper tonic to be met in the vestibule by the two charming young matrons who rarely "darkened the church doors," now lighting them—both in choir gowns; Mrs. U. holding a deep silver bowl full of perfume, into which each woman entering dipped all ten fingers, Mrs. U. saying with quiet reverence: "After you are seated, you will notice that everybody is praying with hands clasped like those in the Albrecht Dürer picture on our worship center; our bowl of perfume will be placed there, a little later. Mrs. V. will give you a sealed envelope before you go in."

These unusually long legal envelopes were printed lengthwise on both sides, the front side reading:

THE DOOR BEING SHUT, JESUS HIMSELF STOOD IN THEIR MIDST AND
SAID: "RECEIVE YE THE HOLY SPIRIT."

(*"All my stock of Christ is a little hunger for Him."* St. Teresa.)

A. CALL TO RECOLLECTION: Let my prayer be set before Thee as incense; and the lifting up of my hands as the evening sacrifice. (Psalm 141:2)

B. HYMN ("Duke Street"): To Him shall endless prayer be made,
And endless praises crown His head;
His name like sweet perfume shall rise
With every morning sacrifice.

C. MOTTO FOR OUR MORNING OF RECOLLECTION: And the Whole House Was Filled with the Fragrance of the Perfume. (John 12:1-8; Goodspeed translation.)

D. HYMN ("St. Anne"): Come, Holy Spirit, Heavenly Dove!
With All Thy quickening powers;
Kindle a flame of sacred love
In these cold hearts of ours.

E. THY QUICKENING POWERS: At the foot of each envelope had been written a *different* Bible verse about "quicken," such as Psalm 71:20; Psalm 119:25, 37, 40, 50, 88, 93, 107, 149, 154, 156, 159; Psalm 143:11; John 5:21; John 6:63; Romans 8:11; Ephesians 2:1, 5-6; Colossians 2:13; Luke 14:21; Revelation 2:5, 16; 3:11; 22:7, 12, 20.

Inside each envelope had been sealed: (1) nine small plain white rectangles of paper, (2) one similar blue rectangle, (3) two rose-colored crepe paper rose petals, about an inch in diameter, which had been perfumed.

The procedure then was as follows:

1—Call to Recollection: (A) read in unison.
2—Hymn: (B) as on envelope.
3—Sentence prayers: that the outreach of our influence may be fragrant:
4—Prolonged Period of Recollection: "Thy Quickening Powers."
   (1) in our homes;

(2) toward all our neighbors;

(3) among all our fellow workers;

(4) inside our church.

(5) Between each of these groupings of prayers Hymn (B) was repeated, so that it took nearly half an hour.

The Leader then said that people seem to feel a resistance toward the quickening of the Holy Spirit, really such as Peter felt on the housetop in Acts 10:9-20. This was read very graphically with special emphasis on the alarming verse: *"I have sent them!"* For at this point the worshipers were asked to open their envelopes and remove the ten rectangular pieces of paper, letting them represent ten actual persons whom the Spirit was sending to quicken everybody in the room! The members were asked to hold the blue slip of paper in their hands, first, as (1) they recalled somebody especially hard to love—and yet our Lord asked us very specially to "pray for those who despitefully use you" (Luke 6:27, 28). In a period of Silent Recollection each blue slip was held in fragrant hands of prayer; then simultaneously, a quiet prayer for forgiveness was murmured. This was a moving experience, too low for anyone else to hear; and a practice much used on mission fields where many dialects make public prayer unintelligible. (*A Christian is someone to whom God has entrusted all his fellow men.*)

(2) Next, a white slip of paper was held as the group each recalled someone *they* had wounded. Matthew 5:23-24 was read, and both the silent Period of Recollection and the quietly-murmured prayer followed, as with each of the next slips of paper.

(3) This third slip was to represent someone toward whom frequent jealousy had been felt; in the silent period the request was to acknowledge to our Heavenly Father exactly why this other person seemed so unacceptable.

(4) Prayer for someone in trouble: who had been neglected.

(5) Someone poor, out of work, unpopular; rejected by others because of race or color or creed. (6) Those to whom letters are owed: to whom this silence may cause pain or anxiety, and a total lack of joy—Recollection. Prayer of promise.

(7) Recollection of persons, known well, but with whom Chris-

tian matters have never been mentioned. Since God has "sent" them, how worship Him with all Five Senses without this exhilaration proving infectious to them? Quiet prayer for guidance followed. (8) Recollection of those who detest the church and Christians—why? how best can they be influenced, naturally and deeply? (A mission study book a few years ago said that "it takes twenty-five adults to interest one person in a change of heart toward Christianity today"—why?) (9) Children running wild. Recollection of influences in each person's past. Realistic ideas a child may now have of importance of religion in life after watching certain church members—why? Prayer. (10) Aged and lonely persons: what simple tenderness they hunger for: who has the answer?

The Leader then said an unusual thing: "Our two ushers are now bringing down the aisle an open sheet; please put in it all those slips of paper representing actual persons about whom the Spirit has said: 'I have sent them.' " The sheet then was carried slowly down the aisle, waiting at each pew as women thoughtfully laid their papers in it. The leader then emptied these slips of paper, by hand, into a large, deep cooking kettle, which had incense in it. Then she lighted a match and set fire to all the names, safely on the bottom of the kettle; immediately the piano began to play the tune "St. Anne" very softly, as the incense started to spread through the room; with the leader speaking above the music: There was a woman who could have saved a city—a city called Sodom—if only she had been quickened enough to save ten souls! But she let things slide. It was not convenient that day. It was too embarrassing to speak up. And, socially, it was not quite the proper thing to do. So she went right on with her private dislikes—her public disdain—her busy career, until God Himself saw that it had gone too far; the city was lost; and the woman was lost—although she could have saved it! But it need not happen here. It need not happen to us. Let us sing as a prayer the hymn on our programs (D) "Come Holy Spirit."

This was followed by the reading of the various verses in Section E, each woman reading in turn. And then, as noon approached, everyone was asked to turn to the other side of their envelopes where three items were printed—a poem, a quotation, and a hymn; and to stand in order to read the poem in unison:

> My mind lets go a thousand things,
> Like dates of wars and deaths of kings,
> And yet recalls the very hour—
> 'Twas noon by yonder village tower,
> And on the last blue noon in May—
> The wind came briskly up this way,
> Crisping the brook beside the road;
> Then, pausing here, set down its load
> Of pine-scents, and shook listlessly
> Two petals from the wild-rose tree.
>
> THOMAS BAILEY ALDRICH

The Leader then asked every woman to remove from her envelope the two scented rose petals, and to hold them in her hand while she read aloud from the envelope the brief quotation which was like a clue to the whole morning:

> The path of a good woman is indeed strewn with flowers; but they will rise *behind* her footsteps, not before them!
>
> JOHN RUSKIN

For it was suggested that as the audience filed out, each woman should symbolically scatter her two rose petals behind her, letting them flutter to the floor as she went down the aisle toward the door, singing with everybody else (to the tune of "Duke Street") the following verse, repeated over and over until all had reached the vestibule:

> Ye Christian heralds, go proclaim,
> Salvation through Emmanuel's name;
> To distant climes the tidings bear,
> And plant the Rose of Sharon there.

The two young ushers then held up their hands for silence and pronounced the benediction, Mrs. V. saying: *"Let my prayer be set before Thee as incense, and the lifting of my hands as the evening sacrifice"; Mrs. U. adding: "And the Whole House Was Filled with the Fragrance of the Perfume."*

Needless to say, people left the church in utter silence, for the whole experience had been like a footnote on Revelation 5:8: "And golden vials full of odors, which are the prayers of the saints."

Eyes shut to the landscape where we are
Open elsewhere
When the soul yields to prayer.
The soul deep in prayer
As a hyacinth
Stretched forth its pillar of bloom
Feelers of fragrance unseen
To the edge of the room.
So, held still and serene
Of its outpouring gift unaware,
With radiance redeeming the gloom,
With sweetness assaulting the air,
Is the soul deep in prayer.

                                        Evelyn Underhill

A blind person, asked what forgiveness is, said it was like the perfume of the hyacinth when stepped on by mistake.

                                        Indian saying

6

CONSIDER THE CATERPILLAR

Most people do not like to consider the caterpillar, closely. Although it is fully as biblical a thing to do as to "go to the ant, thou sluggard" or "consider the lily, Solomon in all his glory", *et cetera, et cetera.* The difference being that the conduct of certain caterpillars is uncomfortably like certain churchgoers, and indeed like many Bible characters also.

Consider the processionary caterpillar, for instance. When Jean Henri Fabre considered them, he discovered that they had a terrifying tendency to go around in circles following a leader: each caterpillar's front end against the rear of the caterpillar ahead. One day the great French scientist experimented with them to see how far they were willing to carry this curious custom; and they were willing to carry it very far indeed!

Knowing that their only necessary food was pine needles from their natural habitat, the pine trees, he filled up a flowerpot to the brim with fresh needles; and then arranged his caterpillars in a circle around the rim of this same pot, their front ends against the backs of the caterpillars ahead; their food readily accessible within a mere fraction of an inch.

Immediately they started their tireless procession, going around and around and around without once stopping, day or night, even for food. He was fascinated to find that they kept up this monotonous marathon one day; two days; three; four; five; and even six. But on the seventh day they all died—from sheer exhaustion, and from lack of food, of course: although their necessary nourishment was only a hairbreadth away; a mere turning of the head, and they could have lived. But they were frantically intent on this reckless ritual of revolving.

Pine trees are still full of them.

And pews, also!

Even in the days when Jesus was here among men. Consider a certain crooked woman in the thirteenth chapter of Luke: her life of necessity narrowed down for eighteen years into a patient pattern of small processionals. The gospel tells us that she was so bent over that she could in no wise help herself. In this stooped-over state, think of all the weary round trips she must have had to learn by heart, inching her way in a circle from her home to the market place and back again—since even a crooked woman needs to eat. Inching her way in a circle from her home to the well, and back again—since even a crooked creature has to drink and bathe. Inching her way from her home to her friend's home, and back again—since even a crooked woman needs companionship. And then, when the Sabbath day dawned, she would begin inching the slow monotonous circle to the synagogue and back again—since even a crooked woman might as well worship God—the route had grown familiar: first passing this large boulder; then that sycamore tree; next, this flat ledge of rock; then that clump of scarlet lilies; and there she was, at the synagogue.

No matter where she went, always the same set of sandals to see; just as on this particular Sabbath, when Jesus was there, even His sandals seemed no more surprising than any of the others, until the superb thing happened: *He saw her!* And way up above her bent back she heard His beautiful voice saying: "Woman, stand up straight! Straighter than that!" Compelling enough to make her hunger and thirst to see that face; and in the desperate struggle to obey His command, she felt herself suddenly loosed from her infirmity—and straightening.

St. Luke tells us how indignant the ruler of the synagogue became: such healing was completely out of order. He reminded Jesus that six days were for work; let people come for healing then; but never on the Sabbath.

Our Lord's reply was devastating: "Thou hypocrite! Don't you water your ox and your ass on the Sabbath day? And ought not this poor woman, bound these eighteen years, to be loosed from these bonds?"

There follows the only place in the New Testament where it is recorded: "All His adversaries were ashamed; and all the people rejoiced for the glorious things done by Him."

Ours is a crooked and perverse generation, also. Group-conscious. We spend our days going in circles. To work and home again. To market and home again. To church and home again. Just like the person ahead of us. With no expectation of change. And indeed, little desire to step out of line and be different. But suppose that next Sunday the startling sentence could sound at the end of each pew: "Stand up straight! Oh, straighter than that!" Think what a shocking series of straightenings could be seen . . . people struggling to rise out of their warped low selves, out of sullenness of spirit, out of petty pretenses of piety, into a new uprightness of heart.

Such as those Two Men who go up to the temple to pray every

Sunday in every church in every city. One of whom is too satisfied to want to be changed; he even boasts in his prayer about going in circles the past week from his counting house (where he took out his tenth!) past his dining-room door (where twice he refused to go in; fasting as a good man should!) with little comprehension of the crookedness his very virtues are producing: "Lord, see how straight I am! See that publican there, all bowed over! But as for me, You must have noticed me, how I give tithes of all that I possess! I fast twice in the week! I! I! I!"

Also in every congregation sits some Elder Son, coming to church after a week of going in circles from house to field and back again, dependable as clockwork; round and round, day in day out; rain or shine; until that bitter evening when he nears home and hears his father giving a party for his prodigal brother; and bursts forth in anger, refusing to go one inch farther: "Lo, all these many years do I serve thee, neither transgressed I at any time; and yet thou never gavest me a dinner party so that I might make merry with my friends. I! I! I!" You may recall the sequel: how his father had to come outdoors and implore this crooked fellow to stand up straight; straighter than that.

Then, of course, in every church sits Martha who has spent the week going in circles from kitchen stove to market place and back again; from kitchen to pantry to dining room, and back again; grumbling every inch of the way: this food! this dish! this meal! this sister! this guest! Working my head off! I! I! I! Until she bursts forth in anger to the guest: "Tell my sister . . ." and the Master tells her to stand straighter, straighter than that! for only one thing is needful, and Mary had chosen it, and would never lose it!

One thing needful?

The processionary pine caterpillars circled it for seven days. But starved to death rather than swerve a hairbreadth to choose that good thing.

The Pharisee circled it. But starved his soul by forever following his own ego round and round, passing by the real blessing.

The Elder Son circled this same feast; starving, not choosing to share it with a brother who had made a bad mistake.

And Martha circled it; refusing to stop long enough to sample our Lord's recipe for One Needful Thing. But there seems less excuse for someone who has considered the caterpillar not to sit quietly with the Master, long enough to taste and see that the Lord is good.

❦

M. O Lord, Thou hast searched me and known me. Thou knowest my down sitting and mine uprising.

P *How earth-bound, work-bound, habit-bound I am . . . How small the cycle of my days: from home to work, from home to market place, from home to church . . . Set my feet in a large room.*

M/P Thou understandest my thought afar off—

How intent my thoughts are on trivial duties . . . this task! this housework! this meal! this hurt! this annoyance! this monotony! this purchase! this praise!

M Thou compasseth my path and my lying down, and art acquainted with all my ways—

P *all my ways with my family . . . with my friends . . . with my fellow workers . . . with shopkeepers and the general public . . . should they not receive more loving-kindness from one who seeks Thy presence in this church?*

M For there is not a word in my tongue, but lo, O Lord, Thou knowest it altogether—

P *my too quick anger . . . my too slow apology . . . my foolish boasting . . . my petty gossip . . . my grudging gratitude . . . my lackluster praise of Thee.*

M Thou has beset me behind and before, and laid Thine hand upon me—

P *at my desk, there are letters to write for Thee . . . at my telephone, there are invitations to Thy House . . . at my dinner table, there is conversation I could start to make Thy beauty and Thy power irresistible.*

M Such knowledge is too wonderful for me, I cannot attain unto it . . . where shall I go from Thy spirit? or whither shall I flee from Thy presence?

P *Send me from this place filled with Thy joy . . . since it is in Thee I live and move and have my being.*

7

THERE WERE ALSO OTHER LITTLE SHIPS

It may be somewhat dangerous for a man to love Isaac Watts all his life. But at least it helps the choir on the day of the funeral to choose the very verse which shaped that man's decisions—although the soprano and contralto barely managed to sing without tears:

> Must I be carried to the skies
> On flowery beds of ease,
> While others fight to win the prize,
> And sail through bloody seas?

A verse which made his minister mention those bloody seas and his parishioner's small ship as sacredly as if it had been built in the carpenter shop at Nazareth; for to himself he said that although this parishioner dropped all his aitches, at least he had never dropped his anchor until his dangerous voyage was successfully completed. Piece by piece he had gathered up that story on his pastoral calls, and saw this poor wreck of a fellow lying there in perfect peace, rehearsing the drama of his great adventure . . .

So you come to h'inquire 'ow H'I 'appen to 'ave crossed the H'English Channel h'in h'a boat H'I h'ad'nt never 'andled before in me whole life? Well sir, my pop 'e willed me that boat, 'e did, h'in 'is last will h'and testament; my pop 'aving been h'a tugboat captain h'all 'is born days. Funny to mind 'it now, but says H'I: "H'a *boat?*" says H'I, "h'and me h'a blooming plumber!" The missus, her didn't take to the boat, nuther, me being h'a plumber, h'as you might say, man 'and boy.

But then come that bad bit h'of news h'over the B.B.C.—'alf h'a million H'English soldiers h'on the beaches h'at Dunkirk, being blasted h'into Kingdom Come by them blooming Nazis! H'and me with h'a tugboat to go h'and fetch them 'ome!

Missus she took h'on something fierce: " 'Arry," she says, "you're no 'ero," says she, "h'and h'its no sort h'of h'a night to go crossing that there H'English Channel when you h'aint never so much h'as touched your pop's boat," says she. To tell the gospel truth, domi-nie, H'I 'ad'nt known the missus was so took with me! Blimey, h'if she didn't wring 'er 'ands, h'and cry h'into 'er blooming 'and-kerchief h'as h'if 'er 'eart would break. H'and us married nigh h'onto forty-two years. Takes h'a 'eap of danger to pry tears h'out h'of 'er; but when she cried she cried, h'and took h'on something fierce: " 'Arry, h'it's fool 'ardy," says she. "You never drove no tug-boat h'in your life."

"But now H'I got me this 'ere boat, mama," says H'I. "Seems like God was giving me 'ints! Seems like my pop must 'ave guessed Dunkirk was coming."

" 'Arry," says she, "that there H'English Channel h'aint no lady's bathtub! That North Sea h'aint no pipe-h'and-drain!"

"H'Emily," says I, "H'England h'expects h'every man to do 'is duty! H'aint you forgetting the H'Invincible H'Armada, year 1588? Them blooming Spaniards had 129 ships, h'and we H'English, we 'ad h'only h'eighty, h'and no soldiers to speak h'of. But what 'ap-pened, H'Emily? Why, God 'E sent a blooming wind, 'E did! H'and what 'E did three hundred years h'ago, 'E can do h'again, h'in 'Is h'own way, me love," says H'I. "God h'aint scared h'of them Nazis, H'Emily!" says I; h'and H'I sings 'er me favorite 'ymn: "Must H'I be carried to the skies, h'on flowery beds h'of h'ease?"

"Don't 'Arry!" she begs me. "Don't *sing!*" But H'I 'ums that blooming tune down to pop's tugboat, H'I did! H'I fills 'er h'up with this h'and that; h'and blimey, h'if H'I h'aint h'off h'across that H'English Channel with h'a lot h'of h'other little boats, me h'and H'Isaac Watts! 'E knew what 'e was writing h'about, 'e did, for them seas was sure "bloody"!

H'all 'ell broke loose h'on them beaches h'at Dunkirk! Nazi bombers dropping bombs; striking the sand; 'itting the wounded;

sinking ships; ripping men to pieces before h'a fellow's h'eyes. H'and, blimey, h'if then that Jerry 'e don't bomb 'Arry 'Olmes— this 'ere leg, h'and this 'ere 'ip; just when H'I got me tugboat filled up with them soldiers—Zip! me leg! Zip! me 'ip!

Then this 'ere batch h'of soldiers took h'over: "Lie down, pop," they says; "take h'a nap, pop," they says; "we'll sail this 'ere bath-tub back to Dover!"

"*Bathtub?*" says H'I, " 'ow come you knew H'I was h'a blooming plumber?" says H'I.

But you know what? 'alf them fellows with ships was cabbies h'and bus drivers h'and grocers; but there was 1000 h'of them boats; h'and blimey, h'if we didn't rescue 335,000 men, safe h'and sound! 'ow did we do h'it, sir? We did h'it, because why, God 'E made the Channel calm, 'E did! Because why, God 'E sent two days h'of 'eavy fog, 'E did!

So now H'I lies 'ere h'on this 'ere flowery bed h'of h'ease, h'and me h'and H'Isaac Watts we talks man to man.

"H'am H'I h'a soldier h'of the cross?" says H'I.

"No, 'Arry, you h'aint!" says 'e; h'and h'explains to me that h'if H'I 'ad h'ever cared sooner about rescuing people h'in trouble, right h'in me h'own town, *that* would be h'another Dunkirk for me to be prouder of. The missus she said the H'English Channel h'aint no bathtub! The North Sea h'aint no pipe-nor-drain. Well, sir, that made me miserable, it did! So H'I got the missus to write letters to h'every blooming customer H'I h'ever fixed plumbing for. H'I said 'ow H'I 'ad been mortal wounded h'at Dunkirk, but before going to 'eaven there was something special H'I h'ached to say to them, h'if they could please make h'it convenient to call by. H'any day. H'any 'our.

So they do come. The whole blooming lot comes, first h'and last. So H'I apologizes h'if h'any pipe h'aint been done good, so h'it lasted! H'or any drain h'aint cleaned right. H'I said 'ow much h'it would please me to come to h'all their places h'and make things ship-shape before facing me God; but 'ere H'I be, tied to this 'ere flowery bed h'of h'ease. H'I said: Zaccheus, 'e wanted to give back sixtyfold, wasn't it? But me, H'I begged their pardons, h'and h'ex-plained h'it was h'a 'orrible thing to be called h'a blooming 'ero for sailing h'a tugboat to Dunkirk h'and back, h'if H'I 'adn't managed to get h'across their bathtubs h'and back, just h'as safe!

They was h'all very h'agreeable with me. Plenty said: "Yes, Mr. 'Olmes, that tub never *did* h'empty, proper-like. But H'I sure couldn't 'old h'it h'against you now, 'ero h'and h'all."

So then H'I says: "No, sir! No, sir! Don't think h'of me h'as no 'ero—for why did H'I go to Dunkirk? Because me pop left me 'is tugboat, that's why; h'and h'a fellow 'ad h'ought to use what h'es got! But what 'Arry 'Olmes 'as really got h'is 'is plumber's tools! But 'e don't treat them 'ero-like—'e don't point to no bathtub with no pride h'and say: "H'I swum that there tub on June 1, 1940, H'I did!" Tools 'ad h'ought to be 'eroic, like they come h'out h'of the carpenter's shop. But since H'I can't never leave this blooming bed, maybe you h'and me h'and God could fix h'up h'a bargain— you promising God h'a whole day h'every month h'in my memory when you gives God h'and H'England the neatest nicest job you h'ever done. H'every blooming thing h'all day long just perfect-like. Nothing could make me die more 'appy than feeling folks was playing square with tools like H'I was playing square with that there blooming tugboat—because why H'I *'ad* 'er, h'and 'ad h'ought to use her, proper. Could you shake h'on h'it? So they shakes me 'and, dominie! That's why H'I can lie here, peaceful-like, thinking h'of h'all them little fellows giving h'extra-fine service, to make h'up for 'Arry 'Olmes's mistakes . . .

And that, of course, was why the funeral was so wonderful, even if the soprano and contralto nearly broke down when they sang Harry Holmes's favorite hymn; for the congregation of his former customers sat there, lost in recollection of their slipshod pasts and their future resolutions—promised to their plumber.

The minister needed to say very little. It had all been said. So he read from the fourth chapter of Mark:

And the same day, when the even was come, He said unto them: "Let us pass over unto the other side." And when they had sent away the multitude, they took Him even as He was into the ship. And there were also with Him other little ships. And there arose a great storm of wind, and the waves beat into that ship so that it was now full. And He was in the hinder part of the ship, asleep on a pillow; and they woke Him and said: "Master, carest Thou not that we perish?" And He arose, and rebuked the wind, and said unto the sea: "Peace be still." And the wind ceased, and there was a great calm. And He said unto them: "Why are ye so fearful? how is it that ye have so little faith?" And they feared exceedingly, and said to one another: "What manner of man is this, that even the wind and the sea obey Him?"

As to Harry Holmes himself, the minister said how often he had been reminded of Robert Louis Stevenson all of whose family had built lighthouses. So when he remembered the lives other Stevensons had saved, he grew disgusted with his own easy life with prose and poetry—

> This thou hast done, and I—can I be base?
> I must arise, O Father, and to port
> Some lost complaining seaman pilot home.

GREEK LINES UPON A DROWNED SAILOR

A ship-wrecked sailor, buried on this coast,
Bids you set sail,
Full many a gallant bark,
When he was lost,
Weathered the gale.

Come, my friends,
'Tis not too late to seek a newer world.
Push off, and sitting well in order, smite
The sounding furrows; for my purpose holds
To sail beyond the sunset, until I die.
Though much is taken, much abides; and though
We are not now that strength which in old days
Moved heaven and earth; that which we are, we are;
One equal temple of heroic hearts made weak by
Time and fate, but strong in will
To strike, to seek, to find and not to yield.

Alfred Tennyson

8

BETTER THAN A FINGER IN THE DIKE

The man from Harlem, New York, was a teacher. So he figured that the least he could do for his profession was to go to Haarlem, Holland, in order to report having been in the home of the famous Dutch boy who put his finger in the dike. For he was always in search of heroes, and he hoped that this visit might be the thrill of a lifetime—heroes being scarce on both sides of the Atlantic; and already he was rehearsing the story of his trip.

"I shall begin by telling them that nobody asked that little fellow to do it. He just saw that hole, with the whole North Sea threatening to roar through, the way only the North Sea can roar; so, as calm as you please, he stepped right over to that hole. And in case you are wondering what one boy has, to stop a heap of angry waves, why, he has his finger, hasn't he? So, he put it in that hole. And the day I called in Haarlem at his house, a hundred years later, there was Holland as safe and as dry as this schoolroom floor, all on account of one boy's knowing that it all depended on him."

You can see for yourself that this was a sensible enough rehearsal. But all his plans were completely upset after a Dutch lady on the bus ride to Haarlem smiled at him and said in careful English: "You been American? Ja?"

Now, of course, it did not take too much common sense to notice how black he was. So he smiled in his beautiful broad fashion and said: "Yes ma'am, I'm an American from Harlem, New York, and before I leave Holland, I thought I had better see the house of the boy who put his finger in the dike. For ever since I was a little kid, down South, I liked knowing that one kid can save a whole country."

The lady suddenly raised both her eyebrows and both her hands in horror, and said: "But!"

"But what?" asked the man from Harlem, New York.

"But there never has been such leetle boy! Somebody just made him up, once."

"Now wait a minute! Wait a minute!" he begged softly, searching through his guidebook; then laid a large black finger triumphantly on this suggested side trip to the house of the boy who . . .

"Ja! Ja!" nodded the Dutch lady, pushing his finger from the guidebook. "Ist like this—all time ist coming American tourist, asking: 'Where ist leetle house of these leetle boy? Where ist leetle bett he sleeping in?' But we got nothings for showing. No house! No bett! Nothings! But all these tourist not liking that. So we been very poor, after these bad war; and we say to ourself: 'Why not find nice leetle old Dutch house in Haarlem? Why not find nice leetle old Dutch bett for leetle boy sleeping in?' So we find him. And all the tourist they like paying to go in, see! O.K.! O.K.! But what all these tourist should ask ist: 'Where ist dike leetle boy put finger in?' For these dike ist maybe eight foot thick. Ja! Ist *some* finger these leetle boy got! Ja!"

"Ja!" sighed the man from Harlem, New York, in the first Dutch word he had ever spoken. "Some finger! But it says right here in my guidebook to be sure to see the statue put up to this little Peter; it says that Queen Juliana came, herself, and that the seven-year-old Princess Margriet dedicated it! And it says that under the bronze statue of Peter is the inscription in Dutch and English: *Dedicated to our youth, to honor the boy who symbolizes the perpetual struggle of Holland against the water!*"

"Ja!" laughed the lady from Haarlem, Holland. "Ist goot for teaching Dutch kids they should save Holland from enemy, if water ist enemy; from Nazis, if Nazis ist enemy. But it never really happen, that Peter! So now I could telling you much gooter story than finger in dike. You could finding Dick Willemzoon in real history book; you go look him up in Mr. Motley's *Rise of the Dutch Republic*. For Dick ist real boy. Three hundred years ago some people not let Dutch be Protestant; not reading Bible; not going church. Ist dangerous! Ist forbidden! But these Dick Willemzoon ist found reading Bible. Ist seen going to church. Ist bad. So they catching him, and arresting him, and condemning him to dying. Ist difficult. Ja?"

"Ja!" said the man from Harlem, New York, starting to write this down in the front of his guidebook.

"But he try escaping over ice in canal in winter. These ist not goot idea. These ice ist thin. It cracking. So Dick, he lying down on his stomach; and, like swimming, he crawl that way real careful till reaching other bank, safe. Goot?"

"Goot!" echoed the man from Harlem, New York, using his second Dutch word with delight. "I'm glad he escaped."

"Nay! nay!" sighed the lady. "Dick *could* escaping; but he chose not escaping! Ist these way: comen big soldier over these ice for arresting Dick. But these big soldier ist too big. These thin ice ist too thin. It cracking. In he fallen. Down he sinken. Up he comen. 'Helpen! Helpen!' he callen. Now what shoulden leetle Protestant boy doing? He ist standing by canal, he ist seeing soldier sinking. So Gott ist saying: 'Better you go saving him, quick!' Once more leetle Dick Willemzoon ist getting down on his stomach, ist swimming over these thin ice to place where soldier ist sinking. He ist pulling him out, safe. He ist showing him how he could crawling over these ice, like swimming. They ist reaching shore, all safe. These ist goot story? Ja?"

"Ja!" said the man from Harlem, New York. "Goot!"

The lady sighed: "But now ist not so goot. For these soldier ist arresting Dick Willemzoon. Ja! Ist putting him in prison, all over, once more. Judge ist saying: 'These boy ist bad. Must die.' So they maken big bonfire in Holland, three hundred years ago. Ja! Ist bad day, these one. Nobody watching can have dry eye. Nobody watching these goot boy burning can sleeping that night in their betts. Their heart ist breaking. Ist not goot business killing boy for saving enemy, all on account he loving Gott more than his own safety, and ist obeying Bible. So you know what? All these Dutch people alive then, they making these big vow: 'These ist last martyr Holland should ever have—*ever!*' And it ist true. No more martyr. Ever! So we been proud over Dick Willemzoon. We got free Bible, free what you calling 'Religious Liberty,' free church.

You think maybe these story of boy who give his body to Gott ist maybe better for kids in Harlem than just story of one leetle finger in one big dike? Ja!"

"Ja!" agreed the Negro from Harlem, New York.

God's service has sure walls.

Dutch proverb

Out from the heart of nature rolled
The burdens of the Bible old.
The litanies of nations came,
Like the volcano's tongue of flame,
Up from the burning core below—
The canticles of love and woe.

Ralph Waldo Emerson

9

LISTEN TO THE LINTELS

(SERMONS OVER ONE'S HEAD: FOR AN UNCOMMON
BOOK OF UN-COMMON PRAYER)

A person can learn a great deal by listening to lintels. A far more durable satisfaction than collecting shaving mugs, or silver spoons, or antique furniture one dares not sit on, or even first editions of rare books. Since all of these add up to a great deal of money in the end, and have to be watched lest they break or tarnish or get stolen. Whereas with a lintel, two thumbtacks will do, on a strip of gray paper with some such magical memorandum as a poor school-teacher in Europe once put over his doorway:

DANTE, MOLIÈRE, & GOETHE
LIVE IN THIS HOUSE

Instantly he stood straighter in the presence of such celebrated company, for had he not achieved the practical impossibility of bringing together under his roof three writers from three different centuries and three different countries? So what if his own visible means of support were at the vanishing point, the invisible Dante still spoke to him with "the voice of ten silent centuries," reminding him that "Sorrow marries us to God!" Whereupon Goethe could match this out of his works, also: "Every time I had a sorrow I wrote a poem!" The schoolteacher could then refresh his memory by recalling that even as Goethe lay dying his last whisper was lively and lovely: "Light! More light!"

For if a lintel is any good at all it teases and tempts, exactly as the Psalmist said: "I will lift up mine eyes"; or, with a touch of liturgy, a lintel can say between Sundays: "Lift up your hearts!" and the owner of the lintel can respond: "We lift them to the Lord!" So that without benefit of clergy or ships or planes or traveler's checks or visas, a lintel can transport the most poverty-stricken mortal to the ends of the earth and back again in the twinkling of an eye; or even to church, with a sermon sure to be over his head . . . to haunt him between Sundays! For Henry Scougal may have been right, three centuries ago, when he said that "the vulgar that commonly sit under the pulpit are commonly as hard and dead as the seats they sit on, and need a mountain of fire to kindle them." These are strong words out of Scotland, by the mystic who later wrote *The Life of God in the Soul of Man;* but think what the lintel over John Knox's house on High Street said in its wooden way to his congregation in Edinburgh:

LUFE GOD ABUFE AL
AND YI NICHBOUR
AS YI SELF

Tall as he was and stern as he was, John Knox preaching in church of a Sunday "bade fair to ding the pulpit into blads"; but from Mondays through Saturdays his lintel on High Street could tell every passer-by precisely what sermon his tempestuous thinking was preaching! People would remember his terrible years, when the powers-that-be had forced him to serve as a galley slave on French ships, where his constant prayer had been: "Give me Scotland or I die!" And God had given him Scotland. So that it was Mary Queen of Scots who then said that she was more afraid of John Knox upon his knees than of all the armies of the Queen of England; and well she might be afraid when he took up his pen and thundered on paper "The Blast of the Trumpet against the Monstrous Regiment of Women"—"of necessity it is that this monstiferous empire of women (which among all enormities that this day do abound upon the face of the earth is most detestable and damnable) be openly and plainly declared to the world, to the end that some may repent and be saved."

All because Mary Tudor in England, being of Rome, had exiled him; and Mary of Guise, of France, had turned him into a galley slave. Yet nobody missed the point that his real aim was what the lintel suggested YI NICHBOUR AS YI SELF, when John Knox described the victory of the French at Leith, on May 7, 1560: "The French, proud of the victory, stripped naked all the slain, and laid their dead carcasses before the hot sun along their wall, where they suffered them to lie more days nor one: unto the which, when the Queen Regent looked, for mirth she hoppit, and said: 'Yonder are the fairest tapestry that ever I saw; I would that whole fields that is betwix this place and yon, were strewn with the same stuff.' "

Suppose that, between Sundays, some placid Protestant printed John Knox's lintel on a strip of gray paper, thumbtacking it over his own doorway, might he not be stirred into realizing that "at a great cost obtained I this freedom" of worship? Might he not pray that— less woodenly—he might listen next Sunday, if his own modern minister mentioned modern misdemeanors? Might he not delight to know that on John Knox's grave the headstone reads: "HERE LIES ONE WHO NEVER FEARED THE FACE OF MAN"? Might he not throw himself more ardently into letting his own preacher thunder tempestuously also, to the end that all Protestants might bring to pass John Knox's unfilled dream:

As we believe in one God, Father, Son and Holy Ghost; so do we most constantly believe that from the beginning there has been, and now is, and to the end of the world shall be, one Kirk; that is to say, one company and multitude of men chosen of God who rightly worship and embrace

him by true faith in Christ Jesus, who is the only head of the same Kirk,
which also is the body of Jesus Christ; which Kirk is Catholic, that is
universal, because it contains the elect of all ages, of all realms, of all
tongues, invisible, known only to God, commonly called the Kirk
Triumphant.

LET GLASGOW FLOURISH
BY THE PREACHING
OF THE WORD

The last lintel having leaped four hundred years backward in
time, to Edinburgh, this much more civic lintel goes back a thousand years before John Knox, to the days when Glasgow was
nothing but oak trees growing by the River Clyde—until another
preacher arrived in Scotland, destined to be called St. Mungo (this
name meaning "Dearest"). St. Mungo made a crude cell under an
oak tree, used a stone for a pillow, recited the Psalter standing out
in the River Clyde, and drew around him a few other cells, a few
other huts, a few other worshipers. All of which was the beginning
of Glasgow itself; St. Mungo's whole life story is told on the arms
of that city—his oak tree, a bird on its top branches, a bell hanging
midway to call people to worship, a salmon with a ring in its mouth.
But even better known is the motto he gave to appear on the city
lintel: "LET GLASGOW FLOURISH BY THE PREACHING OF THE WORD"—
for when St. Mungo's bell would ring the people would flock to be
instructed and to lift up their hearts. In the end they built a beautiful old Cathedral of St. Mungo, which is still standing; and to this
very day the motto on the lintel is still used; except that in the
course of time other lintels had had to be made, and other carvers
had complained to the city fathers that that was a pretty long motto
to fit on a piece of wood, wasn't it? Perhaps it could be shortened
without harm?

And, of course, it could be shortened; for it seemed sensible to
everybody just to have the lintel say: "LET GLASGOW FLOURISH!" So
that to this day and year, this is the shortened motto which the city
still uses; actually cutting away all the root of ancient oak trees in
order to be brisk and brief about their hopes.

But Glasgow is not the only city playing fast and loose with lintels! For Pittsburgh discovered rather recently that, somehow or other, ever since 1816 their town had carelessly dropped from the city motto two Latin words on William Pitt's original coat-of-arms: "BENIGNO NUMINEE"—meaning: "BY DIVINE PROVIDENCE." In 1950 the Pittsburgh civic council voted to restore the lost words. Now that it seems wise, even to those "who are commonly as hard and dead as the seats they sit on," to lift their eyes high and acknowledge that a city is neighbors and God, children and Divine Providence, business and the life of God in the soul of man. And at least Pittsburgh has a right to be proud that their Allegheny County Courthouse has always had the Ten Commandments printed on it. Even if those who collect lintels for inspiration prefer something rather more intimate and spiritual such as:

WUTAAPESITTUKSUNNAUWEHTUNKQUOH

For by living with this enormous word on his lintel, the owner ought to produce in himself immediate curiosity about the man who first wrote it in the first book ever to be printed on the North American continent, published by Harvard College. For one thing, it will soon be obvious that John Eliot certainly lived up to his own personal motto: "Prayer and pains through Jesus Christ can do anything"—or else, how on earth could he have taken the pains to learn how to get down in writing, for the first time, an Indian language so intricate that it took thirty letters to translate the five letter word "kneel," in Mark 10:17? For another thing will soon be obvious also, that Harvard College lived up to the carving over its own gates:

After God had carried us safe to New England, and wee had builded our houses, provided necessaries for our livelihood, rear'd convenient places for God's worship and settled the Civill Government; one of the next things wee longed for, and looked after, was to advance *Learning*, and perpetuate it to Posterity; dreading to leave an illiterate Ministry to the Churches, when our present ministers shall lie in the dust; etc.; the college being duly dedicated to the "education of English and Indian youth in knowledge and Godlynes."

At the 250th anniversary of Harvard there was a long torchlight procession of men from previous classes, all carrying original banners; but the freshman class, only a month old, carried at their head a motto announcing: "THIS UNIVERSITY HAS BEEN WAITING 250 YEARS FOR US!" Which produced immediate laughter wherever they passed; but one look at John Eliot's Indian word for "kneel" might well arouse a sense of atonement: the Indians have been waiting 250 years for white men to kneel in contrition, on their behalf!

Or suppose the owner of the long lintel could add to it a shorter Indian motto over the portal of the Historical Museum in Buffalo:

NEH-KO, GAR-DAH-YEN-DUK

for this would then say to him: "OTHER COUNCIL FIRES WERE HERE BEFORE OURS"; and he would be reminded of the Wyandotte Indian who listened to John Woolman and then said with reverence: "I like to feel where words come from!" For although he understood no word John Woolman spoke, the man's gentleness shone through. In a very different connection this beautiful Quaker saint once said that if we are faithful in following Christ, our lives will be an inviting language. The Indian has always called God *"Gitchie Manitou,"* the Unclaimed Spirit; and has been wise enough to beat out his silver bracelets so that they never quite meet around the human wrist—to leave a little space for the Spirit to enter. Often with a turquoise or two as a touch of blue sky, to remind the Indian on earth of the Spirit above him. Obviously, "WUTAAPESIT-TUKSUNNAUWEHTUNKQUOH" is a legitimate lintel for a Christian to live with whenever those who sit under the pulpit are commonly as hard and dead as the pews they sit on, and need a mountain of fire to kindle them . . . "Have ye received the Holy Spirit since ye were baptized?" the early apostles asked, and the answer was a blank stare: "We had not so much as heard that He had been given!"

Unclaimed. Therefore . . . kneel!

And having knelt, it might be wise to thumbtack next a lintel from a beautiful old home in Bruges where the main beam says:

MORE BEYOND

For this could be a sermon between Sundays with a marvelous everyday mystery for the most wooden worshiper to think through! Evelyn Underhill could give him her version:

> I come in little things,
> Saith the Lord:
> My starry wings
> I do forsake,
> Love's highway of humility to take.
> Meekly I fit my stature to your need.
> In beggar's part
> About your gates I shall not cease to plead
> As man, to speak with man—
> Till by such art
> I shall achieve My Immemorial Plan:
> Pass the low lintel of the human heart.

Or, into his Book of un-Common Prayer, the owner of the lintels might write Martin Luther's petition: "Enable us to rise above ourselves to Thee; and from Thee to go below ourselves in love and to remain always in Thee, and in love."

For while it is true that God comes in little things, it is also true that mankind lets little things separate him from God and his neighbor in the most wooden sort of way. The following lintel belongs in every collection, therefore:

THEY HAIF SAID

QUHAT SAY THEY?

LAT THAME SAY

This inscription is over the entrance to Marischal College in Aberdeen, Scotland; and George Bernard Shaw was so taken with it that he had it carved on his own mantelpiece. But it belongs in every household, over every door. The wisdom of Solomon might add a few extra sentences: "Hast thou heard a word against thy neighbor? Let it die within thee, trusting it will not burst thee" (Ecclesiasticus 19:10); or Thomas à Kempis might make his hint also, "That A Man Must Not Be Thrown Down Too Much If He Fail In Any Faults":

Why doth a little thing said or done against thee make thee sorry? It is no new thing; it is not the first, nor shall be the last, if thou live long. . . . Restrain thyself and let nothing unlovely pass thy mouth that might be to the small and the feeble an occasion of falling . . . . Be mighty in soul and gird thee and make thee ready to more sufferance. . . .Thou art a man and not God, thou art flesh and no angel.

In case there should be a real suffering of the flesh, let no owner of lintels be without a caduceus, that serpent-wreathed staff carved over the entrances of medical schools: sign and symbol of healing—a rod with two wings at the top, two snakes entwining it. For the memory is sacred, carrying the owner back to Moses, then to Paul, in a reassuring fashion. Or perhaps the words over the fire-place in a room at the Harvard Club are more reassuring still, for the room is set aside for the graduates of the Harvard Medical School, and the motto is an ancient one:

WE DRESS THE WOUND
GOD HEALS IT

Or, if packing to go for an operation, perhaps a lintel might be borrowed from New York:"ST. LUKE'S HOSPITAL IS A CHRISTIAN HOME ALL OF WHOSE GUESTS ARE ILL."

A wide variety of choices from the Book of un-Common Prayer could lend a new lining to the dark clouds; St. Teresa's would prove the most arresting: "My health is very bad, but God does so much through me that I laugh heartily at myself!" (How she would have found the conduct of "Humpty Dumpty" authentic, or the "Bishop's Shadow," blessing like Peter's, or Helen Keller's "Jubilate, Amen," or "Intolerable Compliment" mentioned in this book; for St. Teresa was one who said: "God deliver us from gloomy saints!" and these blessed ones all endured with engaging simplicity.)

Yet actually John Donne of early England, so often ill himself, spoke a more usual language: "Put all the miseries that man is subject to together, sickness is more than all. In poverty I lack but other things; in banishment I lack but other men. In sickness, I lack myself."

But for the looseleaf Book of un-Common Prayer the next few entries lie ready to help God heal—Meister Eckhart's suggestion that every pain be greeted with the words: "Welcome, my one dear trusted friend! I should hardly have expected thee nor have hoped to see thee. I bow to thee with all submissiveness."

St. Augustine, a thousand years earlier: "Watch Thou, dear Lord, with those who wake or watch, or weep tonight, and give Thine angels charge over those who sleep. Tend Thy sick ones, O Lord Christ. Rest Thy weary ones. Bless Thy dying ones. Soothe Thy suffering ones. Pity Thine afflicted ones. Shield Thy joyous ones. And all for Thy Love's sake. Amen."

No wonder he could write in his *Confessions* fifteen centuries ago: "It is not by feet or change of place, that men leave Thee or return to Thee . . . rather in lustful darkened affections is the true distance from Thy face."

The un-Common Prayer Book might well contain this charming comment by Bernard of Clairvaux for a restless midnight hour: "Do you wake? Well, He too is awake. If you arise in the night-time, if you anticipate to your utmost your earliest awaking, you will already find Him waking—you will never anticipate His own awakeness. In such an intercourse you will always be rash if you attribute any priority, any predominating share to yourself; for He loves both more than you love, and before you love at all."

This shows so perceptive a practice of the presence of God that nobody should be surprised over the fact that Bernard liked to startle himself into ever new awareness by writing out lintels, one of which probed deep into every plan he made:

BERNARD,
WHY ARE YOU HERE?

This is so totally uncomfortable and totally practical that it is no astonishment to wander through St. Patrick's Cathedral in New York and come across an inscription to St. Bernard which reads: "FAMOUS FOR HONEST SELF-EXAMINATION"! For this, too, would make a relentless lintel for more easygoing saints, more ready to sing Bernard's beautiful hymn than to face their own lack of practical application:

Jesus, Thou joy of loving hearts,
Thou fount of life, Thou light of men,
From the blest bliss that earth imparts
We turn unfilled to Thee again.

For here was a medieval saint mentioning water and light and earth with a spiritual application toward practical living; while six hundred years later, there would be an equally beautiful saint mentioning water and light and earth with a practical application toward spiritual living. For George Washington Carver put over the door of his laboratory at Tuskegee a sign suitable for every factory, office or tool shed:

GOD'S LITTLE WORKSHOP

Everybody prizes the story of the day he held a peanut in the palm of his hand, and asked God to tell him its secret, but found that God was suggesting that he should go back into his workshop and simply use the three laws God had already given him—temperature, pressure and compatibility—and put together the different parts hidden in the peanut. Dr. Carver took God at His word! And found a wealth of revelation no other scientist had ever discovered —proteins, carbohydrates, oils, pigments, cellulose; from which he made over three hundred products, from the peanut alone: rubber, shoe polishes, mock soups, dyes, stains, synthetic leathers, soaps, explosives, beverages and milk—milk which would go to the same Africa from which this slave boy had come: milk for African babies in need of it, in a country where cows cannot live. So that a slave boy who had once been exchanged for a race horse turned into one of the world's greatest scientists. And Dothan, Alabama, would hold a national festival in honor of Dr. Carver's peanut which had brought prosperity to the farmers of their state at a time when bankruptcy faced them as a result of the boll weevil; and Enterprise, Alabama, would put up a statue to the boll weevil whose havoc had ruined their fields but turned them, with gratitude, to the raising of peanuts; and a sixty-million-dollar business!

But their real debt was to "God's Little Workshop" and to God's little black saint who handled water and light and earth as sacred discoveries for the help of all mankind. For as Albert Einstein wrote on a Princeton College fireplace: "GOD IS A SCIENTIST, NOT A MAGICIAN"—and He is always in search of a man who will "LUFE GOD ABUFE AL AND YI NICHBOUR AS YI SELF."

Between Sundays such lintels should seem like stimulating

sermons over the owner's head, until the Lord's Day arrives again. How wonderful, then, if the entrances to his particular house of God could have lintels bearing inscriptions such as those over the three great doors into Milan Cathedral, which read (in translation):

ALL THAT WHICH PLEASES IS
BUT FOR A MOMENT

ALL THAT WHICH TROUBLES IS
BUT FOR A MOMENT

THAT ONLY IS IMPORTANT
WHICH IS ETERNAL

The third lintel appears under the great entrance to the main aisle. But lacking such chiseled reminders, the more usual sign saying: "ENTER REST PRAY" will serve as perfectly as this hint, copied from a little twelfth-century church on a hill in Boldre, England:

You enter this church not as a stranger, but as a guest of God. He is your Heavenly Father. Come, then, with joy in your heart and thanks on your lips into His presence, offering Him your love and service. Be grateful to the strong and loyal folk who in the name of Jesus Christ builded this place of worship, and to all who have beautified it and hallowed it with their prayers and praises. Beseech His blessing on those who love this home of faith as the inspiration of their labor, rejoicing in the power of the Holy Spirit. May this blessing rest on you, both on your going out and your coming in.

For there could be nothing wooden about such worship; nor anything common about such an uncommon stanza as this one carved in the Whispering Gallery of Gloucester Cathedral, in England:

Doubt not that God who sits on high Thy secret prayers can hear when a dead wall thus cunningly conveys soft whispers to the ear.

MARTIN LUTHER, ABOUT SERMONS:

We preachers when we talk of Jesus Christ are at best like infants, gooing and gurgling, using half words and quarter words. Don't judge us by our poor efforts.

RALPH WALDO EMERSON ABOUT HIS OWN SERMONS:

Fine things, pretty things, wise things—but no arrows, no axes, no nectar, no growling, no transpiercing, no loving, no enchantment.

CHARLES KINGSLEY WRITING TO YOUNG MEN IN HIS CHURCH

My dear young men: The human race may, for practical purposes, be divided into three parts—honest men who mean to do right and do it; fools who mean to do whichever of the two is pleasanter and these last may be divided into black fools who would rather do wrong than right, but dare not unless it is the fashion; white fools who would rather do right than wrong, but dare not unless it is the fashion.

10

DOXOLOGY FOR A DANGEROUS DOOR

*Lift up your heads, O ye gates,
and be ye lifted up, ye everlasting doors,
And the King of Glory shall come in.*
                                    PSALM 24:9

This is the story of the day when a certain Chinese door lifted everlastingly, in the year 1900, and the King of Glory came in. But at the moment nobody recognized the glory; least of all, Mary Morrow who did the lifting, in what she feared was a frail and feminine fashion. Although there was force enough to frighten a fierce mob, and scatter them in the imagination of their hearts. At least, pro tem.

It is always to be remembered about the year 1900 that all over China the Boxer Movement had taken hold of the nation, and mobs went rushing furiously down every street, thundering noisily at all doors to ask their single question of each family: "Is anybody here a Christian?" Whenever the answer was "*Yes*," a sharp choice was offered—either to stamp on a cross drawn in the dust of the street, or to die. And ten thousand Christians had died rather than deny their Lord.

Mary Morrow herself was young. Moreover, she had just come to China, still caught up by a vision of herself planting the Christian faith under picturesque roofs, to spellbound people, the moment she had mastered the new language. With never a notion of this peril and this panic which began seizing her now: now that the malicious mobs were going from street to street, from door to door.

"Suppose they come to our door next? Dear God, what on earth shall I do? Will I disgrace myself in the eyes of all these missionaries? They will hardly expect to see me cowering in a corner this way, clasping and unclasping my hands! O God, if only I could be braver than this! Yet here I am, shaking like a leaf—timid and useless and scared to death. Do hear my prayer! Do make me calmer! If only I could have the kind of courage Jesus Christ had! O dear God, dear God, I hear those horrible men banging on our compound door this very minute—What on earth shall I do? *What shall I do?*"

Whereupon the thing she did was such an unplanned astonishment that it is hard to tell whether she or the mob received the greater surprise when she found herself actually opening that door to step quietly outside, closing it behind her, and standing with her arms outflung as if she were a literal lock to safeguard those inside. With a white face, and an unearthly look in her eyes, she began calling in clear tones: "Listen to me, all of you! Listen! Can't you hear what poor Chinese I speak? I'm really no good here, yet.

So why don't you just kill me, and save all these splendid people indoors? For what have they ever done here but heal your sick and teach your children and love you, all day long? So tomorrow you will surely want them back again. But me, I am too new and too green to be of any earthly use to anybody. Just hear what wrong words I speak—aren't you ashamed of my stupidity for fumbling with your beautiful language? So kill me! Here I am, no good to anybody. Come, get to work with your clubs and swords! Come on! Quickly, quickly!"

It was so uncanny that the soldiers were shocked into silence. Their scalps prickled. Their blood ran cold. They lowered their clubs, foolishly. One by one they began backing away, almost on tiptoe, toward the street corner.

But Mary Morrow stood there, startled. Going? Were they going? She kept her arms outstretched stiffly across the compound door, a human padlock, still lost in the sharp suspense of the short scene.

Down at the street corner the Boxer captain came to his senses: "What's the matter with us? Are we men or aren't we men?"

"Men!" the Boxers shouted.

"Then go back and do men's work!" he ordered. In a shamefaced fashion they turned on their heels and went slowly back toward the mission compound. They tore Mary Morrow's arms from the door and broke her bones as if they were chopsticks. They flung her on the entrance steps and killed her savagely; then dashed indoors to slaughter all in the household.

And of course you can supply the sequel—the Women's Board back in America holding a memorial service, with all the members sighing sadly: "Dear little Miss Morrow, so young! And her stay in China so short; not even long enough to finish Language School. Really, hardly worth her passage money, or the cost of all that equipment!" For that is the way in which those who administer denominational funds are bound to talk about money given sacrificially by people in the pews back home.

The following year, the faithful secretary probably reviewed her Minutes, and reminded the Board: "We recall with deep sorrow that twelve months ago today our beloved Mary Morrow was killed by Boxers in China." The members shuddered slightly. Poor, poor Miss Mary. But as to a second anniversary, it is uncertain about the Board: for memories are bound to be short and agendas long; and of course a new secretary had all she could do to record present disasters. So that the long years undoubtedly passed—three; four; five; six; with Mary Morrow becoming a sacred but unmentioned memory; ten; fourteen; sixteen; eighteen; nineteen; so when the twentieth year dawned, who on earth would be remembering that unfortunate girl slaughtered long ago in China?

But of course, with God, a thousand years are as one day. So that twenty years were merely long enough to let the echo of one knocking at one compound door reverberate in the knocking at another mission compound door: *"Lift up your heads, O ye gates! And be ye lifted up, ye everlasting doors"!*

And, this time, nobody was at all afraid; but, from the oldest to the youngest, everybody greeted the well-known Chinese soldier: "Welcome, General Feng!" the missionary called, hospitably. "To what do we owe this great honor?"

General Feng sat down and said simply: "I came because I am a Christian, now; and I would like to join a church. But it is a long story. It goes back twenty years to the time when I was a young soldier from the hills. I joined a Boxer mob to wipe out all the Christians. We hated all Christians. Our foolish leaders told us it was Christians from overseas who were dividing up our nation, making new laws of their own; planning to push us out altogether —well, we believed them! So one day we came to the Presbyterian Mission door and banged away for dear life. We were thunderstruck when it opened, and out stepped a young woman. She closed the door behind her. I can see her yet—standing there with her arms spread wide as if she were sealing the door shut. Well, maybe she was! Maybe she was! For although she was a thin little creature she scared us all stiff; nobody budged! Her skirts blew in the wind, her hair blew also. We just watched her and watched her. Her eyes flashed as if she saw something far away. Her voice shot out like firecrackers: 'Kill me!' she ordered us, 'Kill me, instead of anybody else inside this house! Hear what horrible Chinese I talk—see how stupid I am! Come on, kill me and save these others.

Hurry up!' Maybe she really did talk abominable Chinese, but it was good enough to make us feel goose pimples all over us, and our hair stood up on end!"

"Yes," the missionary agreed, "I can see why! But please go on, General."

General Feng looked miserably at the floor: "Perhaps you know that once in a while soldiers go soft and sentimental. And that girl startled us out of our senses, for a while. But then, of course, we began to bluster boisterously to prove how big and brave we were. And this time we broke that young girl's body to pieces, with our own arms and our swords. But all my life, since then, she seems to have been painted on my eyelids, sir! Even now I can see that frail form lying there, broken and bleeding, silent at last. So I would keep saying to myself afterward: 'What made a quiet girl speak up so bravely?' For even I could see that she knew all the Chinese she needed to know to haunt me and haunt me. I still know every word she said! Finally, somebody told me that these Christians have a remarkable Book; perhaps that was what gave her such a backbone. So I bought a Bible. I keep reading it and reading it. I can find that girl's whole life, again and again. So now that I am a Christian, could you take me into your church?"

After he had been baptized into the Methodist Church, General Feng was known all over China as "the Christian General." He bought Bibles for his soldiers, and held Bible classes. Each year he subscribed for the little Christian magazine called *Happy Childhood* for his soldiers to read; and all over America his name became known to various World Day of Prayer observances—for part of each offering was always sent to underwrite that magazine—and church women delighted to hear that wherever his army went in China, the crops were safe— since his soldiers did not steal; and the women were safe—since his soldiers did not rape.

Year after year this story of the Presbyterian girl had its exciting ecumenical effect in Methodist circles, of course. Then suddenly the incredible news leaked out: General Feng had become a Communist, but still called himself a Christian. How could this be?

Eventually he crossed the Pacific; made speeches here and there; and Christians argued this and that about him ... some saying that he had changed only outwardly, because he had become heartsick over rottenness in high places on the side where he used to belong; because he had waited in vain for any progress in human justice and goodwill; because he hated the old "squeeze" system; and he hoped that the newer ideals held more honest concern for the poor . . . he hoped . . . he hoped . . .

And of course those who were violently disappointed in him for going over to the other side said violent things against him: how he had gone back on every Christian thing he had ever said or done or believed.

For myself the instant disappointment was: had he even gone back on Mary Morrow? After twenty years of being haunted by her beauty, and another twenty years of being blessed by her bravery, now *this?*

But then he died.

And that was the day when it seemed reasonable to take the only liberty with his story by adding a scene: for just how would it be if Mary Morrow should meet the General at those most everlastingly difficult doors, to enter which man must have clean hands and a pure heart, and not have lifted up his soul into vanity? How would it be if she should say to him: "But General, what on earth led you into this new notion of another Boxer Movement on an even bigger scale? Didn't you visualize that once again, at every Christian door, other Mary Morrows would be bludgeoned with other brutal blows until they, too, would bleed to death? O General, how could you? Or did you count on other soldiers, seeing such atrocities, having these scenes painted indelibly on their eyelids too, for another twenty years, until from such new martyrs should come new Christian generals? Or, what *did* you have in mind?"

And it would seem as if, like the man who came to the feast, but without a wedding garment, the General also might be speechless.

And Diomedes slew Axylus—a man beloved of all men. For he dwelt in a house by the side of the road and gave hospitality to all who passed by.

Homer, *The Iliad*

He who seeks revenge, digs two graves.

Chinese proverb

It is true that around every man a fatal circle is traced beyond which he cannot pass; but within the wide verge of that circle he is powerful and free. As it is with man, so with communities. The nations of our time cannot prevent the conditions of men from becoming equal, but it depends upon themselves whether the principal of equality is to lead them to servitude or freedom, to knowledge or barbarism, to prosperity or wretchedness.

Alexis de Tocqueville, 1838

11

"HIS GRACE INTO A LITTEL OX'S STALL"

He had been imprisoned alone in this dingy cell since December 8, 1941. Alone, except for a single secret possession—a rusty old screw, found in a dark corner of the floor. With this treasure he had been scratching one secret line on the wall every morning, to mark the arrival of a new day: thus making his own calendar by crossing off seven of the lines when a week was past. In this way he knew for a certainty when December 8 had finally managed to turn into December 25. He wished to goodness that he need not have awakened quite so early on this most dismal of dates. For where was his family? He had no idea. Dead or alive? He had no idea. In Japan or repatriated? He had no idea. Where was this prison located? He had no idea. When, if ever, would he get out? He had no idea. With a mind lower than low, and a heart sadder than sad, he stood there with the screw still in his hand, looking at the small scratch on the wall that told him today was Christmas.

"Christmas!" he cried, sunk between wretchedness and remembrance. "*Last year!*" he groaned. "Only last year we were saying:

'Why not have a little tree, this time?' " In his mind's eye he was seeing that bright touch of America glittering in their Japanese home. The memory hardly made him merrier. Yet he found himself taking his screw and drawing an immense tree. He was no artist, but what is a Christmas tree but a huge triangle? When it stood in outline on the wall of his cell, he scratched in its trunk, also; and noticed that it seemed to rest on a good-sized rectangular stone. He outlined the stone, also; and in a half-hearted mood of remembrance said to the oblong shape: "You are the box I gave my wife last Christmas. But what in the world did I give her?"

For you must have noticed that men are incredible creatures when it comes to things of this kind. So he had to think and think, and then continue thinking: "Whatever did I give Josephine last year?" With half his mind he was glad that all this searching ate up its share of the lonely day. But finally, of course, he remembered the thing; and triumphantly wrote the word lightly across the stone which represented his wife's box; but the real thought in his heart was the frank feeling that this hadn't been much of a present to give a woman whom he would give anything on earth to see this minute.

Since he had children also, he outlined two stones for their boxes; and began to grope into his past to recall, if possible, What? Oh what? Oh what? had he given to each of them? This proved a tedious process; but was such a rewarding way to spend a lonely morning, that after he had managed to reconstruct all these 1940 gifts, and written them in their outlined boxes, he was faced with the remainder of his forlorn day and with the remainder of the stones in his forlorn cell. He was wise enough to prolong the play by thinking: you could never afford it in real life, of course, but how about giving something today to each of the deacons in your church? And since the sky's the limit, this Christmas, what will you give them, anyhow?

One by one their faithful Japanese faces seemed to rise before him. He realized with deep pain that some of them might be suffering for their very faithfulness. And many would be in sudden need, now that war and taxes would eat up their earnings. Well, today was a day when he could afford to shower things on them! One by one, therefore, he outlined each block of stone thoughtfully, and wrote in with a lavish generosity the gift each of these beloved men richly deserved. Then, because there were plenty of stones as well as plenty of time, he decided that it would be completely proper—just this once—to give something surprisingly adequate to the wife of each deacon. How quiet and self-effacing they had been, through the years! How useful in his parish!

This proved a warmhearted occupation under such cold-blooded circumstances. So you have guessed that the trustees had their turn, next. Then their wives. Their children. This sent him back to the deacons' side to give something to *their* children. And then, of course, the Sunday school superintendent. All his teachers. All their pupils. All their parents. The janitor. His family. Each and every member of the church. He liked calling their faces to mind; and enjoyed donating these surprise packages to brighten their lacklustre lives.

By this time he ran out of people in his own membership. But he crossed the street to the Presbyterian pastor: was this dear fellow locked up somewhere, also? Then why not send him a turkey and all the fixings? And his wife, something superlative, also? When he ran out of Presbyterians, he began remembering Methodists, Lutherans, Baptists. When his memory of these was exhausted, he continued this Day of Recollection with policemen in town, storekeepers, bankers, barbers, tailors, jinriksha coolies; until finally every stone in his cell had been lightly outlined and lightly inscribed in this lively, loving fashion. All but the long narrow slab of stone set high above the doorway, streched as wide as the entrance itself, but too high to reach. In any case, who was left in his city to receive such a mammoth gift?

Suddenly he remembered the one man whom nobody ever saw. Or, if you were admitted to his presence, must kneel and kow-tow—forehead on the ground. But what had a mere missionary to give to the Emperor?

In no time at all, he knew.

Something far lovelier, far richer, far more majestic than the Emperor had ever owned. Once before, High God had sent His grace into a little stable no larger than this tiny cell to bless emperors . . .

The lintel proved too high to reach. But he dragged his cot to the doorway; and even when he stood on tiptoe, he barely managed to mark an "X" up there: "X" for Christmas and Christ.

Elated by this overwhelming desire to give Christ to the Emperor, he stood in the center of his cell, stricken to see how he had wasted Christmas in giving only temporary trifles—kimonos! quilts! a few pounds of rice, here! Of tea, there! Of candy! If his real wish could come true, was there any dearer treasure to share than the Saviour of the whole world?

In a spirit of deep intercession for the deepest needs of all these Japanese, he went from stone to stone, wetting his finger to erase the mere trinkets he had been content to give away; and almost like a medieval monk illuminating a sacred manuscript, he substituted in every stone the symbol "X." It took all morning; for he stood, holding each person in remembrance, as he made the mark on their stone.

When this labor of love was done, and all the faintly-scratched crosses began twinkling at him like eternal stars in this black night of his soul, suddenly a sharp sense of Presence stole over him: he need never lose this beloved community now! Week after week after week they could still surround him: a parish to pray for. He had no Bible to read the words of the Psalmist, but they had come true once again: "Thou hast not shut me up in the hands of the enemy. Thou hast set my feet in a large room."

Among this poorë folk there dwalt a Manne
Whome that was holden poorest of them alle:
For High God sometimë senden can
His grace into a littel ox's stall.
                    Geoffrey Chaucer, 1340-1400

Thine own heart makes the world.
                    Japanese proverb

12

EVEN THE LEGS SPOKE VOLUMES

Inch by inch as the church rose up before their eyes, the people would think of things sure to be needed for its greater beauty. And on almost any morning somebody's voice could be heard, hinting: "Man of God, when should we begin cutting doors for our Father's House?" The last of these reminders being: "Man of God, are you forgetting the Lord's Table?"

Their Man of God was pleased with this sense of urgency. For at first it had been hard enough to persuade his black congregation to give any time or service for the building of their new church. Indeed, there had been one Sunday, toward the beginning, when he found it wise to preach from the text: *They all began to make excuse*—so large did everybody's farm seem to loom, and everybody's own yoke of oxen, and everybody's own wife. He had developed an almost African sense of prolonging his story until his listeners could hardly conceal their mounting annoyance over a tribe so impolite as to ignore their chieftain's spreading of a special feast on a special table, only to have none of his tribe care enough to come. Here and there one or another of the congregation let out a sympathetic groan at the chieftain's disappointment, poor man! But when it began dawning on them that they were this indifferent tribe, their amazement and chagrin turned into other groans, many of which could not be uttered. This really was the reason why the table itself kept looming large in their dream of the finished sanctuary: the table for the Lord's own feast. They knew it should be something special. But nobody dreamed how especially special until a church across the jungle sent a delegate to attend the dedication.

For the drum call had sounded out its message:"God's House in this place is done! God's House is done! On Sunday we offer

it to Him! On Sunday!" But nobody expected that one of the delegates would arrive so early; much too early, really, since there
would still be four more sunrisings before the day of dedication
dawned; and it was, therefore, a hard thing to know what to do
with a delegate indelicate enough to become a four-day burden
on their hospitality. Until they discovered his intention. For it
turned out that he had brought them a drum.

"But we have a drum!" said the top deacon rather too bluntly,
being still bothered with this brother who could not tell Thursday
from Sunday.

But the brother bore no grudge. He simply pulled wrappings
off his gift, and everybody's heart stopped beating for a little moment in astonished admiration. For this was a carved call drum—
carved with jubilant little figures bent on hurrying, with exciting
gifts on their heads and in their arms, toward a church not unlike
their new church, steeple and all. At once the top deacon bowed
his head in acknowledgment of this superlative craftsmanship:
"So you are that carver of whom we have heard all our lives? Yes,
you must be the one for whose drums all the chieftains seek!"

"It is nothing. It is a small thing, until it speaks to you Sunday
after Sunday of brotherly love waiting for you far off, somewhere
else, among the men of my tribe who heard of your building. That
is why I came early. The men of my tribe thought maybe there
would be something not yet finished in the church, which I could
finish."

"Thank you," said the top deacon. "Thank you very much. But
everything is now finished and waiting. So your call drum will
be enough of a gift. It is a big honor you have done us in bringing
it, brother. And we will now put ourselves out to make you very
comfortable until the Lord's Day comes."

"Not at all! Not at all!" said the carver. "See, I have brought
bundles. This one is my own food for the four days. This one is my
mat to sleep on. I have been asking God to make you willing for
me to sleep on the floor of your church, so that I will be handy
when He tells me what to carve next. For of course He will know at
once what still waits to be done!"

Not a man nor a woman, nor the Man of God himself, could

persuade the little old fellow to consider bunking anywhere else. So they unlocked the new door and ushered him into the new church: "None of us have used our Father's House in any way, yet," the top deacon said, as if in warning.

Afterward, everybody liked remembering how the little stranger had slanted his head in real reverence, almost as if in the act of listening. Then he looked around him slowly. It was a lovely place, spacious and simple, with tall windows to show the great forests outside.

"Our men went deep in that forest to cut down the timbers to build this church," the Man of God explained. "They dragged in the great logs; and planed them down carefully; and did all the building, themselves. Our women wove the gorgeous curtains; they cut the grasses, and stained them, and wove the great Christian symbols which all church people use, the world around. Everyone was willing-hearted, as in the days when Moses lived, and the Children of Israel made God a house."

But it was almost as if the carver had not heard a single word; for he walked straight down the center aisle to the Lord's Table, and ran his hand lovingly over its wide smooth surface.

"*This!*" he cried, exultantly. Then he knelt and felt the great strong legs: "*And these!*" he whispered, almost as if in prayer.

Standing up again, he announced gently: "The Father has told me to carve it"; but added in a polite sort of agony: "Provided you will let me?"

Not once had anyone dreamed of a carved communion table. But then, not once had anyone dreamed of an artist like this one. All the top deacon could manage was a groan: "But is there *time* enough? For this is Thursday! If only you had come earlier!" For he was overwhelmed with pride to have a carver whom chieftains clamored for.

The white man, of course, knew nothing of chieftains and these tribal rumors of superlative skill; so with his practical white wisdom he put forth his objection: "But a communion table is not just a table, brother! It tells its own sacred story; by the very silence and simplicity it reminds us of the last supper, when Jesus was here among men."

"Yes, I know about that, too!" the carver nodded. "And every time I think about it, it hurts me very much. One of the men so bad that he soon sold Jesus! One of the men so bad that he soon denied he ever knew Jesus! All of the others so bad that they soon ran away and left Him alone! Like the men of my tribe. Just like the men of my tribe. We have found it so hard to eat with Jesus. We have found it so hard to stick close to His table. When I thought about how wrong this was, I learned Matthew, Mark, Luke and John by heart, to see how we could do better in my tribe. How is it over here in your tribe, brother?" he asked the top deacon, and as he asked he ran his hand again over the smooth wood. It was like a prayer.

The pastor was touched to hear his difficult deacon, so inclined to pride and boasting, confide in the carver: "We are the same over here, brother! We are just the same! When the men of this tribe started to build our Father's House, we were all so bad about working at it that our Man of God had to show us a picture of ourselves in the Bible. Perhaps you know it, also: about the big chieftain who gave a special feast, but everybody had his own excuse why he, of all men, could not come that day."

"I know that story!" the carver cried, and swept his hand across the table, somehow turning it instantly into acres of grain as he recited, graphically: "I have bought a farm—I go to plough it up!" Then he pranced three of his fingers off toward one corner of the table, and growled gruffly: "Whoa! Whoa! Three yoke of oxen!" Then he danced one finger daintily to the opposite corner and said in a mincing fashion: "Married a wife! Married a wife! Can't bear to leave her! Too soon! Too soon!"

The carver held his fingers poised experimentally at the table corners. A little silence fell on his spellbound audience. Then he nodded his head, and asked in a matter-of-fact voice: "Probably you think of this story on the Sunday when the Lord's Supper comes? It is the same with the people of my tribe, also. We have to pull ourselves outdoors to church by our ears! So God has been telling me that it would be wise to carve this story on your table."

"Yes," the deacon agreed. "That would be wise."

The white man sensed that they were using a sort of spiritual shorthand which they both understood instantly. He felt a sudden ignorance inside himself as compared with this modest and mystical stranger who drew from his bundle certain chisels and mallets, then dismissed everybody politely: "I will be very tidy here, since the place is holy—so do not trouble yourselves to think of me again until Sunday. I have all I need for food and bedding. If you could have a bowl of fresh water at the door, that would be all; except that you must pray for me every moment, so that I can hear God tell me how to carve His Table. For I must be kind to the wood, since the tree came from Him, first. I would never have thought myself, that a small seed could make a big mahogany tree! So God has still other wonders hidden in this wood. He wants me to find them at once. Thank you for letting me try!"

The white man and the deacon tiptoed to the door, wrapped in quietness and confidence. As they closed the church door softly, they saw the carver on his knees.

In the end the table spoke volumes! And it was all right. A processional of carved figures ringed the entire top of the table; along the center lay a farm, half of it with groaning grain, half of it with trailing vines; midway stood a farmer—a loaf of bread in one hand, a chalice in the other. There in the circle of figures around him, sat the plowman on one side with his three yoke of oxen—only the white man found it surprising that these beasts of burden were elephants; on the other side sat the bride and bridegroom. Each detail of the carving was exquisite: every stalk of grain was graceful, every angle of the arms and legs managed to look reluctant and indifferent to the feast; and on the vertical panel under the board appeared the significant words: "LORD, IS IT I?" Around the other three sides were the lame, the halt and the blind being brought in, with warm solicitude from the highways and byways by the servants; their very vigor and tenderness somehow conveyed the gospel words "and *compelled* them to come in"! On the vertical panel underneath these figures on three sides appeared the words: "GO HOME AND TELL WHAT GREAT THINGS THE LORD HAS DONE FOR THEE."

The white man found himself saying to the carver: "But Jesus said those words to a young man out of whom He had just thrown evil spirits!"

The artist ran his hand with strange sympathy over all the lame, the halt and the blind whom he had carved: "But all their lives, haven't these, too, had their evil spirits of complaining and resenting and bickering? Over in my tribe it does our invalids a lot of good to go home and tell what great things Jesus did for them in His hospital."

"Here, too!" the man of God agreed cordially. "I see now that you have chosen a really perfect reminder! I could wish, however, that our people could see both sides."

The artist was humble: "This is great kindness you give me. It lay in my heart, while carving, to wonder how it would be to turn the table each week, and fix it so that only on communion Sundays would the sentence haunt people: 'LORD, IS IT I?' All the other Sundays it would just give them a nice nudge to go home and tell about the Lord. Would that seem sensible to you?"

"Even more than sensible, my dear friend; I think it is inspired!"

The artist smiled a slow strange smile: "A man must not run ahead so fast that he gets in God's way! But it really seemed to me that He told me, Himself, that turning things around would be sensible."

The Man of God put his hand affectionately on the carver's shoulder: "Really more sensible than carving these four legs, dear friend! Look, the figures seem even more exciting than those up on the board itself; but alas! they are so near the floor that I have to kneel to see them properly."

"But is that so wrong a way to read the gospels?" the carver asked, as he too knelt down. Then he made his further explanation: "I only carved the legs for the children's sake—down low, where they live. God's word up on the table is too high for them to reach. They are not giraffes yet. Just little puppies. So on one leg I carved a child's story from St. Matthew—see: three Wise Men on elephants! a star! a stable! a baby! a mother! Then over on this leg, a story from St. Mark: a small girl sleeping! Jairus weeping! Jesus leaning over to say: 'Get up, little gazelle!' Now this third leg has the children's story from St. Luke: this hillside, with sheep! these shepherds, looking up! these angels, singing! down here in the village, this baby in this cowshed, sleeping! Over here, on the fourth leg, I carved all the names which St. John uses about Jesus—I hoped the children of your tribe could learn to find out for themselves what they are: vine! bread! shepherd! door! light! For it has never come over me before that *gospel legs* will be good for children to fall in love with, when they crawl around the floor while you preach. Or do the babies of your tribe sleep all through your sermons?"

"No, indeed!" sighed the Man of God, "They crawl—*how* they crawl!"

The artist smiled: "Then when I get back to my own town, it will please me very much on Sunday mornings to pray that the little ones over here may even learn to walk in church, hanging on to St. Mark and St. Luke to keep from falling."

"I will like to pray that, too," the white man said. "And it will also please me very much, brother, if you will offer your table to God in prayer, right now."

They were still on their knees beside the leg with the names from St. John, so the carver closed his eyes and said in his quiet conversational way: "Thank you for trees, Father. Thank you for hiding so much in the wood for a knife to dig out. Maybe You could fix it so that when the top deacon dies, and this Man of God dies, and when I die, this table can still live on and still speak to this tribe about the things of God. That is all. I am done talking. Amen."

The next day the dedication began with a thoroughly triumphal procession—the choir walking through the door and down the aisle chanted Psalm 43, with the congregation responding in this fashion:

Choir: O send out Thy light—
Congregation: Light we bring!
Choir: And Thy truth—
Congregation: Truth we bring!
Choir: Let them lead me—
Congregation: Feet we bring!
Choir: Let them bring me to Thy holy hill—
Congregation: Bodies we bring!
Choir: And to Thy tabernacles—
Congregation: Our Father's House we bring!
Choir: Then will I go to the altar of God—
Congregation: The Lord's Table we bring!

Choir: Unto God, my exceeding joy—
Congregation: Joy we bring!
Choir: Yea, upon the harp will I praise Thee, O God, my God—
Congregation: Music we bring!

And the stirring sound of the old drum and the new drum, coming through the door at that very moment, brought in all the latecomers also; so that there was hardly room enough for the immense congregation. Word about the Lord's Table had gone swiftly around town, and the curiosity was such that even the backsliders decided to return. Since there were not likely to be enough communion cups to go around, the wine was served in large green leaves. When somebody asked afterward: "But where did the leaves come from? We have never used them before?" the white preacher was touched by the top deacon's reply: "I saw the Man of God pick them up from the farm of the farmer who made excuses!"

The table had already begun to speak volumes.

AFRICAN CALL DRUM

It is Sunday! It is Sunday! Get awake! Don't sit down! Come to this good thing which won't come to you unless you come to it! Come to meeting, everybody! Come all! Don't sit down in your town today! The words of God have arrived! Come get them! No one else can get them for you! You must come! Sunday! Sunday! Come all!

from *Christian World Facts*

These things shall be: a loftier race
Than e'er the world hath known shall rise,
With flame of freedom in their souls,
And light of knowledge in their eyes.
New arts shall bloom of loftier mould,
And mightier music thrill the skies,
And every life shall be a song
When all the earth is paradise.

John A. Symonds; may be sung as a bass or tenor
solo, accompanied by drum beats—tune: "Truro"

13

UNLESS WE DINE ON TIPTOE

He was no longer at all young, and had become so painfully thin that he felt sure only his belt held his bones and his frame together—all as the result of too many concentration camps, too much moving from one to the other, too uncertain a diet. Yet here they all were again, routed out of their cold cells on this chilly February morning, apparently on their way to still another camp.

Well as he thought he knew Japan, from thirty years of residence, he recognized no landmarks; and could make no common sense out of all this useless tramping in midwinter through a frozen landscape to a place likely to be an exact replica of yesterday's camp. He tried praying, of course. For that had become his real dwelling-place these days: "The Eternal God is my refuge, and underneath are the everlasting arms." But this time all such reality had vanished. He was suddenly just a very old man; tottering, stumbling, chilled through and through. He found himself turning to the guard and saying quietly: "I don't seem equal to taking another step. This is the end! So just let me drop out here, and lie down and die."

"Walk on!" shouted the young Japanese, crossly; and prodded the old man's back with his gun.

So he walked on. For that was what voices of authority had been doing, lately. Their crossness was obeyed. Or else . . .

He dragged along dizzily, trying to remember when he had eaten last. But this was a foolish subject to think about, for it had been yesterday at noon—a thin, impossible watery mess which nobody could stomach. His ribs seemed to be caving in. His throat was dry. His bones ached. His feet weighed like pounds and pounds of lead. He wondered how a man would die while walking along in winter, drawing these short panting breaths, each so likely to be the last. He turned again to the guard: "I can't make it any longer," he said, in his dignified way.

"Walk on!" the guard thundered.

And he walked on. It was incredible where the strength came from. Incredible too about these fierce young fellows with their first authority, so firm and so ferocious. He could remember telling his denomination, on furloughs in America, that Japan was made up in equal parts of courtesy and charm . . . he tried marching in the warmth of those two words, and in the beloved practice of remembering in prayer certain Japanese Christians very dear to him. But one by one even their names now vanished into thin air: this freezing incredible air which seemed to cut his face in half and stab his very lungs. Without any of the cherished names in mind, a certain mood of despair seized him. He could hear his teeth rattling. Indeed, he shook all over.

Turning a third time, he apologized feebly: "Forgive me," he sighed. "I am too tired to go another step. It cannot possibly matter to you if I lie down here to die. One less mouth to feed. One less prisoner."

"Walk on!" roared the guard.

And he walked on. Bent over with weakness. Panting for breath. Staggering and swaying.

The guard touched him on the shoulder and said sternly: "You must walk on!" Then he leaned nearer and added in a whisper: "For we are coming to my grandmother's house."

This strange sentence seemed to make no sense. But because it was so utterly different from anything heard in the past six months, it was human enough to create hope. And in that spurt of hope, he walked on.

Presently he saw the guard dash into a small frame house by the roadside. He must have known exactly what he would find in there, for in no time at all he was back on the road. Going up to the old gentleman, he whispered: "Quick! fix your hands like mine."

As if playing Button-Button, the old gentleman cupped his palms together; and immediately the guard slipped his own clasped hands inside them, leaving a hot potato there, straight from his grandmother's hearth. Then with a world of liturgical

meaning he whispered two symbolic words: *"Take! Eat!"* and then
fell back into his usual place.

It was all so sudden that none of the prisoners noticed, nor any
of the guards. But the blessed warmth stole through the old gentleman's palms to his wrists; to his elbows; to his shoulders; and better
yet, to his very heart, as he realized in a wave of deep joy: "The
fellow is *Christian!* He was merely play-acting in all that earlier
gruffness, watched by his superiors. But if I live to be a hundred,
can I ever have a communion service as sacred at this—*'Take!
Eat!'?"*

He held the hot potato to his frozen lips, against each cold cheek,
each ear. Certain familiar and beloved words crowded back into
his memory: *"Ye who do truly and earnestly repent of your sins,
and are in love and charity with your neighbors, and intend to lead
a new life, following the command of God, and walking henceforth in His holy ways; draw near with faith, and take this holy
sacrament to your comfort; and make your humble confession to
Almighty God, devoutly kneeling."*

Every word but the last two had come true: he could hardly
kneel, of course; yet here he was—walking in newness of life,
henceforth! Was there some special way to walk to prove his
ecstasy, since he might not kneel? Out of his rich past came the full
meaning of what Emily Dickinson must have meant when she
said that God's table is too high for us unless we dine on tiptoe!
Yes, that was the way—to dine on tiptoe, reaching up and up to
the full measure of this Christian courtesy, this charming reverence
which a crude young soldier had managed to convey. It dawned
on him then that Japan would be safe in such hands, tomorrow. So
he partook of this strange and holy sacrament, to his comfort; and
went walking henceforth in holy ways . . . on tiptoe.

FOUR JAPANESE PROVERBS

One good word can warm three winter months.
Let men know by your own deeds who were your ancestors.
Everybody's voice is God's voice.

Sympathy is from above; respect is from below.

O Lord, let me ever take one bite at every meal in memory of Thee.
                                                    Maltbie D. Babcock

14

AND ALL THE BIRDS OF THE AIR
SAT ON THE BRANCHES OF IT

*(THE TREE OF KNOWLEDGE MAKES A PERFECT PEW
FOR THESE TEN SITTERS)*

Try it some Sunday.

Try sitting in the pew, looking about as usual: (how would that be anyhow—vivid? spellbound? with that glad-when-they-said-unto-me-come-let-us-go look? or glum? dumb? with that wild-horses-will-never-drag-me-here-again look?)

Try painting parishioners, preacher, and pews in your mind's eye as some preposterous new picture: four-dimensional! complete with sound strip! Perhaps copying our Lord's little masterpiece from Luke thirteen would be simplest: "Unto what is the kingdom of heaven like? and whereunto shall I resemble it? It is like a grain of mustard seed, which a man took, and cast in his garden; and it grew, and waxed a great tree; and all the birds of the air sat on the branches of it."

Try turning the pew into this big branch of the Tree of Knowledge. Let it sweep widely eastward and westward. Oh, wider than that! Be bold and extravagant about it. Then let the sparrow of the Psalmist come down and build her house on that branch. Let the swallow build her nest on it, with room for all her young. Let Shelley's skylark swoop down from heaven: Hail to thee, blithe spirit! Let Jeremiah's migrating birds lodge on it: "Yea, the stork in heaven knoweth her appointed time, and the turtledove and the crane and the swallow observe the time of their coming, but my people know not. . . ." Ponder what it is that people do not know! Then let Browning's little thrush give forth the proper sound effect: that's the wise thrush, she sings her song twice over to show she can recapture that first fine careless rapture! Ponder this, also. And from an old Irish anthem let "The Thrush in the Thorn Tree" be heard singing:

> I knelt to pray,
> Through storied pane the sunshine
>   spilled bright pools of colored light
> And all was still.
> I knelt to pray—to ask—to beg some boon.
> And then a throstle sang.
> In through the open windows, loud and clear and passing sweet,
> His message came:
> Do you—Do you—Do you
> Give Him thanks, give Him thanks
> As we do? as we do? as we do? as we do?
> God! God! God!
> To Thee be thanks, to Thee be thanks,
> For Sunshine and for Spring.
> I did it! I did it! I did it! I did it!
> Do you do it? Do you do it?
> He made you, He gave you Sunshine and Spring.
> Did you do it? Did you do it? Did you do it?
> Do it! Do it! Do it!
> Thank Him for everything.
> I knelt to pray.
> And nothing did I ask, nor boon, nor gift, but said:
> "We praise Thee, O God. We acknowledge Thee to be the Lord,
> All the earth doth worship Thee: the Father everlasting."
>
> A.E.R.H.; The Fellowship of St. Luke

Try hearing what cannot quite be heard as "all the earth doth worship Thee"; try seeing what cannot quite be seen on this same pew extending twenty-five thousand miles around the earth; try knowing what cannot quite be known, until the knowledge of God can cover the earth as the waters cover the sea.

Try letting the Bible leap off the lectern and fly to the uttermost parts of the earth. Try understanding that "all shall know Me from the least unto the greatest." Try saying with Ezekiel: "And I sat where they sat, and remained there astonished among them, seven days . . ." until the Tree of Knowledge can teach certain texts every Christian should know.

Do Ye Know That The Saints Are To Judge The Earth?
(1 Corinthians 6:2)

By sitting in Japan where Toyohiko Kagawa has sat, what days of astonishment! The early days, perhaps: when he first fell completely in love with Jesus Christ and discovered it would have to mean disinheritance from his aristocratic family, with all that meant of wealth and comfort and ease. See him choosing Christmas Day, in 1909, to move into a miserable room, 6 x 6, in the most miserable slum in Kobe. Sit with him and see him falling in love also with all the criminals, the poor, the sick. See him inviting one diseased beggar to share his room, his bed. See him contracting incurable trachoma from this undesirable guest. Learn how he came down also with T.B.; but continued working as usual, even with one lung. Overhear the astonished Japanese explaining: "He is so busy he forgets to die!" See him earning thousands upon thousands of dollars from the sale of his books, but keeping out only $60 a month to support himself and his family. Notice his solitary confinement again and again during the war years, when his public utterances against their bitter battles provoked all the military authorities. Sit in his lonely cell and hear him comment, quietly: "I could meditate with that wall!" Consider the case of Pastor Ai Pau, in Burma, during the occupation, when the Japanese garrison summoned him; deciding to be quiet about being Christian; turning cold when the Japanese officer asked: "Are you a Christian?" For better for worse, he found courage to say: "Yes sir, I am!" The officer leaned over his desk: "Ever hear of Kagawa?" For better for worse, he again managed to say: "Yes, indeed! I have several of his books, and even saved two of them, when we ran into the jungle!" The Japanese officer said: "Kagawa baptized me! I am a Christian, too." For richer for poorer, this marriage of true minds turned into a great conversation between pastor and general. Consider the more recent years when he has circled the globe, astonishing immense audiences out of their indifference by saying: "When Christians become dead in earnest enough to sell off even their house mats for the sake of their religion, Christianity will have power." See if you know why this Japanese saint can judge the earth, when he says of prayer: "You must rise from your knees with a tool in your hands." See if you knew what Thomas Kelly knew when he said that Kagawa is one "who knows the tendering of the Presence, a tendering which issues in the burden-bearing, cross-carrying, Calvary-re-enacting life."

The likelihood is that, reverberating the whole length of your twenty-five-thousand-mile pew around the earth, you can hear the echo:

> *"I know!"*
> *"I know!"*
> *"I know!"*
> *"I know!"*

OH THAT I KNEW WHERE I MIGHT FIND HIM! (Job 23:3)

By sitting in a bazaar in Burma, you can be astonished at Htingbai Gam. It was a noisy, disturbing place with a thousand fascinating sights. He picked a dozen things up. He tossed a dozen things down. And a book being duller stuff than anything else, he tossed a book down, also. But curiously enough, on his long walk homeward, one name from the pages of that book kept coming into his mind again and again: *Jesus! Jesus Christ!* He had no idea who He was; nor what the book was. And he fully expected to forget it.

But the next morning there it was: *Jesus! Jesus Christ!* He wondered again who He might be and what He had done to get into a book; but supposed the matter would end there. But no! He kept thinking of the name. He kept wondering. It lay in the back of his mind all day: *Jesus! Jesus Christ!*

The bazaar, of course, had moved on elsewhere; or he could have returned to pick up that dropped book, and satisfy his curiosity.

He began making inquiries; countless inquiries; and finally heard of a town ninety miles away where this book was sold. Probably you have never walked ninety miles to buy a book? Probably you have never walked ninety miles; period! But probably you have never been caught up by the strange and haunting beauty of the name of *Jesus! Jesus Christ!*

In any case, Htingbai Gam began this immense walk. Uphill. Downhill. Sun. Shade. Nights under a tree. Morning in search of food. Then on. On to find a book and a name.

At journey's end, there it was! They called it "The Bible," and it came in two sizes: one thick, one thin. Somehow the thicker book appealed to him more, the very size justifying the long, long trail awinding. He paid for it with delight: tucked it under his arm; and began the ninety miles toward home. The Bible grew heavier; the way seemed longer; his impatience grew greater; his one dream was to stretch out in the shade of his own roof to begin finding the lost name.

Probably this is the place to explain that Htingbai Gam had bought the Old Testament in his deliberate choice of the thicker volume. If you have sat down to blow the dust off Genesis lately, you realize what a stiff search lay ahead of the poor fellow, since paragraph after paragraph is solid with names: Abraham begat Isaac, Isaac begat Jacob, Jacob begat . . . begat . . . begat . . . begat . . . And since he was hunting for one particular name, it was only sensible to trace with his finger under each new name, row upon row upon row.

But the name of Jesus was not in Genesis.

Nor in Exodus. Nor in Leviticus. Nor in Numbers. Nor in Chronicles. Nor Psalms. Nor Daniel. Nor Hosea. Nor Malachi.

"That's odd!" Htingbai Gam thought to himself. "I have probably hurried too fast." So he plodded patiently from Genesis through Malachi again; without success.

By this time he realized that this Bible was not the Bible he had picked up in the bazaar, where the name of Jesus had come on page after page. The only sensible thing to do was to take it back and complain loudly about the mistake.

Therefore, he walked the same ninety-mile walk, all over again;

and complained loudly. Only to discover that the Kachin Bible is in two parts—the Old Testament, thick; the New Testament, thin. And he had deliberately chosen the thick book. This time he went home with the thin book, and eventually found Jesus Christ on nearly every page. An immensely more haunting person than he had expected. Forever doing beautiful deeds. Forever saying unforgettable words. Tragically killed by treacherous men. Marvelously made alive again.

Perhaps there is no way for Americans to sit where Htingbai Gam sat and feel the astonishment of knowing all this for the first time. A breathless knowledge leading to baptism. Even with his father threatening to kill him. Even with the necessity of leaving home. Even with slow years of study to become a preacher. Even with the Japanese army storming Burma, and all mission work stopping, as thousands of people marched northward with Stilwell into India.

But Sara Htingbai Gam stayed behind, teaching and preaching. Then came a day of dreadful disaster in his life, when he and his people were making salt; a great gale of wind suddenly blew down a great tree, breaking the young pastor's leg in such painful fashion that nobody knew what to do for the violent swelling, the terrible torment. When it seemed certain that Htingbai Gam was dying, one of his elders prayed for the beloved pastor, reminding God how much the whole tribe needed him; and when the breath of life returned, everybody knew that God must know how deep their need was. For a whole year they saw this patient lying there, unable to take a single step; yet always able to open his Bible and make a certain name become clearer and dearer.

Today his leg is still as crooked as can be; but he goes limping from town to town with his matchless news! As you sit in the pew where he sits, you can hear the echo of those who now know where to find the Helper he had found:

"I know!"
"I know!"
"I know!"
"I know!"

Now Learn a Parable of the Figtree: When His Branch Is Yet Tender, and Putteth Forth Leaves, Ye Know That Summer Is Nigh.   (Matthew 24:32)

The Poo Tai people in northern Siam have never had evangelists, Bibles nor churches. But one cheerful old man named Nai Hak, who had never been away from home, somehow received a gospel of Matthew. He said a traveler gave it to him, telling him that it was a pretty good book to read.

So Mr. Nai Hak read it. It proved so unusually good that he read it again. And this time it seemed so unbelievably good that he felt everybody else ought to hear it at once. So, without either suggestion or pressure, this wise old man in the East would hurry out right after breakfast to do what none of the three wise men in St. Matthew's gospel seem to have done—since we have no record that either coming to the stable nor going home again did they tell anyone the story of Jesus. But Mr. Nai Hak never stopped! He was over eight-four, and very deaf; but his eyesight was good and his feet were nimble, so he never stopped going through his village to read his delightful book.

It was a government official who brought news of this activity to a Bible Society agent, and before long an evangelist traveled over to meet him. Nai Hak had gathered from St. Matthew that one day in seven was the Sa-ba-ra-to, so he did no work on it. But when the Sabbath came, and the evangelist held the first worship service in that home, Nai Hak had never heard a hymn before, he had never heard a sermon before, he had never hear a prayer before. Yet it was all entirely familiar. For the prayer he found in Matthew six, at once. His tattered old copy had even been re-covered to keep it from falling to pieces, he had used it so long and so hard; but nothing the evangelist told him sounded strange, and when the word "baptism" was explained, the astonishing old gentleman knew at once that yes, he was ready! The moment the service was over, he led the visitor from his home to a mountain pool, and there the saintly Nai Hak—whose name means Mr. Love—entered the blessed company of all true believers, which he had already done so much to increase.

There are many passages in his old copy of St. Matthew which you might quote if you could sit where he sits, but for anyone who from total ignorance turned into total fruitfulness, surely our Lord Himself would say once more: "Now learn a parable of the figtree; when his branch is yet tender, and putteth forth leaves, ye *know* that summer is nigh . . . even at the doors."

Probably you can almost hear the leaves of some tree in Siam clapping its hands in endless encore the whole length of the pew:

> *"I know!"*
> *"I know!"*
> *"I know!"*
> *"I know!"*

YE KNOW THE GRACE OF OUR LORD JESUS CHRIST, THAT, THOUGH HE WAS RICH, YET FOR YOUR SAKE HE BECAME POOR, THAT YE THROUGH HIS POVERTY MIGHT BE RICH. (2 Corinthians 8:9)

It is when a tremendous text like this one vibrates the length of a pew that all mild mediocre worshipers need to fall to their knees in reverence over discovering that seated near by is someone whose life resembles that of Jesus Christ. Even to the darkness of His face—which a man from India has. Even to the skill of healing in His hands—which Dr. SubbaRow also had.

Even to giving up riches and becoming poor—which Dr. Subba-Row also did.

Quite literally the "Tree of Life" and the "Tree of the Knowledge of Good and Evil" grew side by side in his career. The "evil" came early in the life of Yellapragada SubbaRow, when his favorite older brother died, and he wondered how he could ever live on, without him. He was just about going to bury himself from the world as a priest in a Hindu monastery, when he met a Christian missionary who said: "But how much greater to offer all you have for God to use right here in the world of men, who suffer just as your brother suffered."

This fired the young man's imagination. His brother had died of a disease called sprue. Very well—he would study medicine and find a cure for sprue! And this is exactly what he did do. Spending long years of study in Madras and London and Harvard. Then fifteen years as a professor in Harvard Medical School. Then on to the Lederle Laboratories in New York, where Dr. SubbaRow became director of their mammoth research work, with as many as three hundred assistants under him. It was here that he discovered the cure for sprue, and with his own money sent the drug to India, where it wiped out the disease from which his brother had died.

It was about this time that a young minister met him. Gordon Torgersen had a genius for sharing spiritual ideas adequately; Dr. SubbaRow had a heart ready for these new depths of the riches of Jesus Christ. It became a rare friendship. The man of world fame, known everywhere for the discovery of aureomycin, learned much from the man of God whose church he joined. It astonished Dr. Torgersen to discover that Dr. SubbaRow kept giving away all the money he made, wanting everything to go for God's work—relief abroad; medical and ministerial students in this country; he poured it all out, wanting nothing whatever for himself.

And then he died. The newspapers said that he was one of the greatest medical research men of the century. Prominent scientists from all over the world came to his funeral. One of them said: "He was more like Jesus Christ than any man I ever met."

But was it not because Dr. SubbaRow knew so perfectly the divine grace and the divine poverty of his Lord, that pew after pew at his funeral could respond with reverence:

"I know!"
"I know!"
"I know!"
"I know!"

I Know Whom I Have Believed, and Am Persuaded That He Is Able to Keep That Which I Have Committed Unto Him Against That Day.   (2 Timothy 1:12)

Back in the year 1928, how little this Chinese mother had actually committed to her Lord, she would be the first to recognize now. But in 1928 she was attending the Jerusalem Conference and wrote to her little son: "Today I was suddenly so homesick for you, my darling, that I knelt in the streets of Jerusalem, and put my arms around a little Jewish boy your size, and kissed him. God keep you safe till I come back."

Human nature being what it is, this was entirely too much for young China to take. He sat down at once and wrote bluntly: "I have put my hand down on this paper and outlined it. I have put my foot down on this paper and outlined it, too. So the next time you feel like kissing a little boy, you can just kiss my hand and my foot until you get home. Your loving son."

When twenty-three years had come and gone that youngest boy had grown up, of course; and his older brothers even more so. All of them became as conspicuous in their profession as their mother had been in hers: each of them in public life. But when times began changing in China, when loyalties began shifting, over a year ago their mother invited her sons to a family dinner party. It was an immensely gala affair: all the fine china, all the brass candlesticks, all the best silver. Nobody could guess what it meant, since it was nobody's birthday or anniversary; yet everybody's favorite dish was served.

After dinner their mother locked all the doors, pulled all the curtains, looked behind all the screens, and then said in a low firm voice: "I realize that these are strange days in our country. I realize that you face curious choices on every side. But I trust that every son of mine is remembering that his Christian belief is a sacred trust from God Himself. As your mother who bore you in pain, and brought you up with care, I expect you to keep absolutely true to the beautiful faith you have had in Jesus Christ. Never to let anybody tamper with it, now or later."

"But, mother, we would lose our jobs!"

"We would land in jail!"

"We could lose our lives!"

She looked at them quietly: "Some things are more precious than life. Shall I remind you that our Lord lost His life precisely because He never wavered from obedience to God? 'Thy will be done,' were His words. Was it any easier to say that in the streets of Jerusalem then, than now?"

They explained to her carefully that sometimes they really had to do the most ridiculous little deeds or say the most ridiculous little words; not that any of it meant a single thing. Not even skin deep.

"Thank you for telling me frankly," she said in her beautiful quiet way. "I am the one nowadays, who is still holding your hand and your foot, Youngest Son! And now let me ask you for dinner again next Thursday; in fact, every Thursday; so that we can keep in touch with one another and with God. I will even serve your favorite dishes again."

But the next week the table itself looked curiously bleak and bare, decorated only with a radish, a beet and a knife at each son's place. They looked in high amusement at such a practical joke; but she said: "No, it is far from funny! Have you ever noticed that radishes and beets are shaped like the human heart? So now it would please me to see you cut your radishes in half."

When this was done she said quietly: "As you see, somewhat red on the outside; but white all the rest of the way, inside. I am praying that this may be the symbol for my sons! And now, if you will kindly cut the beets in half also."

When each young man held both slices in his hands, she shuddered and said: "Red! Red through and through! Your fingers are stained! Your knives are stained! There are red spots on the tablecloth! So perhaps you will tell me frankly: how was it this week with you—a radish, or a beet?"

Suppose you sit where she sits every Thursday night, listening for the quality of their answers—colder; more secretive; open; warmhearted; always waiting for their tones of Christian belief:

> "*I know!*"
> "*I know!*"
> "*I know!*"
> "*I know!*"

THE PEOPLE THAT DO KNOW THEIR GOD SHALL BE STRONG, AND DO EXPLOITS. (Daniel 11:32)

On a world-encircling pew—twenty-five thousand miles in length—any concern which can leap oceans and lodge lovingly among alien people to prove their common love of God is sure to be an exciting exploit. And none could be more thrilling than the House-of-Loving-Your-Neighbor which Japanese Christians built in Peking.

For when the Japanese army in 1931 took over Manchuria and bombed Shanghai in 1932, all Japanese Christians were deeply disturbed. But it was the women who said: "Let us do more than sigh and lament! Let us send the Chinese something better than bombs!"

They chose a small delegation of women to go to Peking, representing the women's department of the Japan Christian Council and the W.C.T.U. And down in the most sordid slum section of Peking, near the old Yungting Gate they found the need: for the place was jammed with beggars, coolies, half-naked laborers, wandering children, disreputable outcasts. It was noisy with crowds buying secondhand clothes from rickety old stalls or half-rotten food. In the midst of all this din and bustle, where not a green thing had ever grown, the Japanese women built a neat little two-story house, with a clinic and a doctor and a nurse; with playrooms for children and sewing rooms for women. While beside the side door they went to the immense expense of digging a deep well.

This was perhaps the most astonishing part of their gift to Peking! For up until then the Chinese living in that slum area had had to buy from pushcarts dragged through the streets until the water was tepid and tasteless. But water from this deep new well was cool and pure, and free! All day women came with kettles and pails. All day their curiosity was such that they stepped indoors a moment, lingering to learn what the Japanese meant when they said that Jesus was the water of life.

Back home in Japan the church women gave enthusiastically toward the upkeep of this little House which could make their love bridge the China Sea and help new neighbors to know their God!

"I know!"
"I know!"
"I know!"
"I know!"

THAT YE, BEING ROOTED AND GROUNDED IN LOVE, MAY BE ABLE TO
COMPREHEND WITH ALL THE SAINTS WHAT IS THE BREADTH, AND
LENGTH, AND DEPTH, AND HEIGHT; AND TO KNOW THE LOVE OF
CHRIST, WHICH PASSETH KNOWLEDGE. (Ephesians 3:17-19)

Perhaps this is the most astonishing pew of all. Still the same
25,000 miles, as all the other pews are. Yet somehow broader
—the *breadth* coming from being asked rather suddenly to stretch
the imagination to take in all people which on earth do dwell.
Very well. We will try!

And somehow longer—the *length* coming from being asked to
go so far from home, and to stay away for so long a time: still for
the sake of brothers never seen. All right. Count on us!

And somehow deeper—the *depth* coming from our horrible
homesickness and hunger in this barren place: we had not known
it might bring us so close to starvation and death.

And somehow higher—the *height* being our utter astonishment
at being chosen from among all the sons of men for this experiment; we felt taller. We grew gigantic. But also humbler, knowing
ourselves as only we can know ourselves . . .

Have you guessed that all this is actual preamble? That the
United States Navy actually sent actual officials to an actual island to ask an actual tribe to leave that island voluntarily, promising them another island, far off, at a safe distance: so that their
Bikini could be bombed, and the explosion studied.

It has never been explained to this day why the Navy might
not have experimented with the other island and let the people
of Bikini stay where they belonged. But when the request to let
themselves be moved elsewhere came to them, out of the blue;
and when the tribe had met to vote on this total upheaval, their
chief reported to the United States Navy:

*"We love our homes. It will be hard to leave our native land.
But if our going will help to preserve world peace, we will do it
gladly!"*

This is a more historic statement than any church pronounce-
ment made since Pentecost. For here were one hundred and sixty

simple-hearted Christians gladly giving up their homes for the peace of the world.

Suppose that next Sunday morning, on every pew in Christendom, the sitters were required to copy Chief Juda's twenty-eight historic words over and over and over during the usual sermon period—would a shiver go the length of the pew, the way it used to in a certain traffic court where the judge required the careless drivers to copy ten times the dreadful magazine article entitled *"And Sudden Death"?*

The sequel to Bikini is an unforgivable piece of civilized carelessness; for when our Navy called at the island of Rongerik six months later, to see how the transplanted tribe were getting on, their spokesman said: "My name is Philip. Now I shall tell you something of myself. We"—sweeping his arms to include the tribe—"are very hungry. We have nothing to eat, yes. This is a very poor island. We have not enough coconuts, no. For many days now we eat nothing but fish."

So that it passes knowledge how we have overlooked, in our own day, this people rooted and grounded in love, able to comprehend with all the saints what is the breadth, length, depth, height of those who know the love of Christ. But each breeze that sweeps the ocean brings tidings . . .

> *"I know!"*
> *"I know!"*
> *"I know!"*
> *"I know!"*

WE KNOW THAT WE HAVE PASSED FROM DEATH UNTO LIFE, BECAUSE WE LOVE THE BRETHREN. (1 John 3:14)

There are always enough ways of loving to show how far one has passed from death into life. But of all the people sitting on the pew around the circumference of the Christian world on any Sunday morning, the Africans seem to have gone further.

The black women of Dondi were astonishingly practical about their love. Long after it had happened, they heard that the Village of King George in England had been badly bombed by his enemy.

So everybody brought an offering on the Day of Prayer to help the homeless people in London. And when they sent the King their $11.12, they wrote him this letter:

We send you our warm greetings with the hope that you are well. We are well. We have heard of your hardships you are seeing and of your distress of mind. And so we, the women of our Lutamo Church, said: "We will send a little gift to help our children there who have been left orphans because of the war." Our friends, the main thing is this, namely: Even though you have many hardships still have faith in the Lord Jesus, praying to Him with perseverance day by day. Our friends, even though we do not see one another face to face, yet we can know each other through the conversation of our hearts. And now, our friends, we close with very great love. Farewell with love. We are,
The Women of the Church of Christ at Dondi-Lutamo

Certain African laymen were equally practical in their affection, and even more brave—since no man knew what might be required of them. For when they heard that their white missionary lay seriously ill in the little mission hospital, they ran all the way to the surgeon to say eagerly: "We have just heard that our friend is sick! So if you need any skin or any bones or any blood, we want you to know that we are waiting right here at the door!"

Any such love from black men to white men has its own angle of devotion, of course. But as between one black tribe and a black enemy tribe any element of paternal gratitude is absent. And it caused an immense stir of astonishment in a mission chapel, when an older man arrived late, one Sunday morning. Without sitting down, he interrupted the service by announcing that a village down the trail had been badly robbed, their trees and gardens burned, and many people injured. He suggested, therefore, that all the women leave church at once to prepare bundles of fruit and yams and peanuts, with bandages also; and that all the men should then carry these bundles down the trail.

A younger church member sprang to his feet and shouted across the church: "Sit down, brother, you must be crazy! That village over there has always been our bitter enemy! They have stolen my own food, my own animals, many a time!"

But far from sitting down the old man stood his ground: "It

says in the Bible to love your enemy, to do good to them that curse you. And that this is the way to turn enemies into friends!"

"But we will miss the sermon, if we do as you say," the young man stuttered.

"That will *be* the sermon, brother! That will be the sermon."

The preacher had never had a service get out of hand with such Christian common sense, half the congregation agreeing that the plan was reasonable; the rest half-hearted and reluctant. He dismissed them all with a swift blessing, and had the joy of seeing a long processional start fairly soon—a bundle on every man's head, a smile on most of the faces. Only the cross young man was crosser than ever: "We shall see what we shall see," he growled in his contrary fashion. "They will beat us up! They will chase us out! We shall look like fools!"

"We shall look like friends!" the old man insisted. "Then it will be with them as it is with us. Until now, they have only *heard* that we are Jesus Christ's men. But they have no idea what that means. But when we come marching up with such gentleness, our spears at home, then they will know what we know."

And that is just what ran like a whisper from person to person:

> "*I know!*"
> "*I know!*"
> "*I know!*"
> "*I know!*"

I KNOW THAT ALL THINGS WORK TOGETHER FOR GOOD TO THEM THAT LOVE GOD, TO THEM WHO ARE THE CALLED ACCORDING TO HIS PURPOSE. (Romans 8:28)

Of all the sights she saw in Germany at war's end, a relief worker says that by far the most astonishing was the one and only door left upright in a certain badly bombed section of Berlin. Not only was the door itself surprising, but every day, and all day, a little dog sat waiting patiently for that old familiar door to open as usual. At intervals barking, to remind the family he was there.

Nothing could have bound that neighborhood more closely into a purpose than their attempts to convince that dog that nothing was left—*nothing!* That the walls were gone forever. That the ceilings were all mixed up with cellars. That the family was gone. Dead! Never to return. And nothing left. Nothing!

But the dog knew better.

The door was there, wasn't it? The door that had always opened to let him in? So he sat and barked occasionally, as polite dogs do. Women came out of the rubble of their patched-up cellars to argue with the little creature in soft German: There is no more family! No more house! No more food!

But the dog knew better.

So he barked.

And the bark broke everyone's heart. It was the days of fifteen hundred calories or less, especially less; so everyone was desperately hungry. Nonetheless, they could not stand that anxious bark, that eager tail. So that there was never a day when the saucer on that doorsill was not filled, as the women found themselves moved by a common compassion . . . lest tenderness die out on earth, and they commit the final horror of denying man's ultimate guardianship of total helplessness.

For piece by piece the awful news leaked out. The camps! The tortures! Decent people had not dreamed such dreadful deeds could happen. The refugees poured in, more than any ruined house could hold; but these people were starving and destitute. Church women of all ages stood all day on winter street corners holding cups to collect *pfennigs* for the care of refugees; money was scarce, and it took a day to collect even a dollar, a penny at a time.

"But this at least we can do for each other," they said . . . lest Christian tenderness die out on earth.

Mercy Bags were hung on church door knobs to collect all possible leftovers, for the sake of the strangers within their gates . . . lest tenderness die out on earth.

And in the summer of 1951, a mammoth crowd of four hundred thousand Christians gathered in Berlin. Bishop Dibelius told them it was *Funf vor Zwölf:* Five minutes of twelve . . . lest Christian tenderness die out on earth. Once again they had their own missionaries present from Africa and Asia, sitting in the same pew: all of them knowing that all things can work together, if . . . tenderness does not die out on earth.

"I know!"
"I know!"
"I know!"
"I know!"

FOR I KNOW THAT MY REDEEMER LIVETH, AND THAT HE SHALL STAND UPON THE EARTH. (Job 19:25)

One of the astonishing places where our Redeemer now stands on the earth is over the harbor of Rio, where, on a peak of Corcovado—rising sheer from the sea, twenty-five thousand feet—stands the hundred-foot statue of Christ: the figure oriented north and south, with arms outstretched from east to west. Illuminated at night, and visible far out at sea, there the silent figure stands: in the shape of the Cross: in the shape of a plus sign, also.

That was a wise little girl who saw a cross in a sanctuary and was curious enough to inquire: "Why do they have the plus sign in church?"

They have it because it adds Kagawa of Japan+Htingbai Gam of Burma+Nai Hak of Siam+Yellapragada SubbaRow+a Chinese mother of high valor+Japanese women building their house of Chinese friendliness+men of Bikini suffering to add peace to the world+people of Africa also in dead earnest over this peace +women in Germany adding tenderness=all of this to equal the Mystical Body of all True Believers: on your pew, each Sunday.

For "all shall know me, from the least to the greatest." But lest you miss the message of their stories, at least remember that the Christ over Rio is a *mosaic:* thousands of tiny triangles of different-colored native stones were brought from every part of Brazil —to symbolize by their very colors that there is no place for race or class distinctions in their nation, neither Indian, Negro, nor Portuguese. To symbolize, also, the separate and distinct regions represented—each with its own history, culture, economy, dreams.

Yet from the city, looking up, the figure sems to be carved from one piece: *"Father I pray that they may all be one, even as Thou and I are one; I in them and Thou in me, that they may be made perfect in one; that the world may know Thou hast sent me. . . ."*

Up from the streets of Rio and from the pews of the churches sounds a chorus of Portuguese voices:

"I know!"
"I know!"
"I know!"
"I know!"

And much of this chorus will be due to the amazing activity of Hugh Tucker, known the world over as "The Man Who Sold a Million Bibles in Brazil."

But selling Bibles was only a beginning with him. For he saw the ships of all nations anchored in the harbor of Rio. He saw sailors from Portugal, England, France, Italy, Spain, the United States, and the Orient. Homesick fellows wandering the streets with no place to go except a saloon. Hugh Tucker rented a house and put up a sign: "SEAMAN'S HOME." Ten thousand sailors a year walked in and out his front door. Each with a Bible.

But one house was nothing at all to the man who walked the streets of Rio hearing men cough, seeing them weak and crippled and hopeless. Dr. Tucker took pictures. He showed his pictures all over town—to the mayor; to the Board of Health; in public schools; out on public squares: "See! Here are the sick in our town, and we do nothing!" The city authorities gave him money to build a hospital for those with tuberculosis.

But what were two houses? When on every street he saw listless children too tired to play, to stupid to study. *"Malnutrition!"* he said, and approached the gas company for stoves to put in a cooking school, to teach the mothers of Rio that pickles and coffee could not make a child healthy.

But this was a mere side issue, too; as he went selling Bibles he saw so many rags and tatters that one day he walked into a sewing machine company and talked the manager into sending machines for a sewing school, so that mothers could learn how to make cheaper new clothes with neatness and dispatch. This done, he saw how riotously reckless it was for the children of Rio to play out in the thick of traffic. He appeared before the mayor to beg for a corner of a beautiful park for children to play in. The mayor was reluctant, and made a proviso: only if you would provide the equipment! Dr. Tucker, keeping his eyes open, saw some old streetcar tracks being torn up and hurried to the Traction Company to ask for them.

"What for?" asked the manager.

"For swings and teeters and slides!" Dr. Tucker replied, describing his dream.

But the manager made the dream come true in a finer shape, by offering to buy in New York all the new equipment which Hugh Tucker felt a playground needed.

This, of course, is only part of his continued story. They still say of him in Rio that he was "like the love of God walking around on two feet"—*for all shall know Me from the least unto the greatest.*

It still happens along the length of the pew every Sunday: all the little pieces coming together once more+*I in them+they in Me—He has not left Himself without a witness in any nation.*

God writes straight on crooked lines.
Brazilian proverb

God has written one line of His thought upon every people.
Giuseppe Mazzini

I am the man who, when Love lectures in the heart, takes notes, and then retells the lessons to the rest of men.
Dante

Friend, let this be enough.
If thou wouldst go on reading,
Go and thyself become
The writing and the meaning.
Johannes Scheffler

Note: The telling of these ten stories may become a public worship service if (1) at the end of each of the stories the Speaker will ask the various pews to affirm in unison the words "I know!"—entire front row repeating the words, then entire second row, etc., etc. to last pew where (2) a soloist stands ready to sing, instantly (tune: "Bradford" by Handel)

> "I know that my Redeemer lives,
> And ever prays for me;
> A token of His love He gives,
> A pledge of liberty."

15

... OR A REASONABLE FACSIMILE THEREOF!

(ON BEING CONTENT WITH NOTHING BUT "A SPEAKING LIKENESS" IN PRAYER)

You have seen this amazing sentence in advertisements of certain firms offering prizes to winners of contests: "and be sure to enclose four labels off our packages, or a reasonable facsimile thereof." Yet how can even the most reasonable facsimile prove that you have ever tasted or handled or even owned that particular brand? By looking around America, it becomes obvious that just such long distance imitation has become typical of whole areas of our life: Woolworth carrying a reasonable facsimile of Tiffany jewelry; the Bargain Basement carrying a reasonable $19.98 facsimile of the exclusive $195 model from the Green Room upstairs. All in order that rather a poor lady may have the stylish satisfaction of considering herself a reasonable facsimile of a fastidious figure of fashion. Even if no damage is done by trying to look like "The Real Thing" or "Almost As Good As," the fact is that the dullest person knows it is done to deceive.

But let such a practice slip over into the realm of religion and ethics, and even a General will acknowledge on V-J Day: "Our trouble is basically theological." It is, indeed! And echoing down the nineteen centuries of Christian history there comes the voice of One who cannot be deceived, for He knows what is in man: "He that hath ears to hear, let him hear what the Spirit saith unto the churches"—like a conversation in parentheses, really: small staccato sentences, brash and secret on the human side; penetrating and stern on the divine side. The Psalmist had his own interpretation of all this when he wrote: "Thou hast set our iniquities before Thee, our secret sins in the light of Thy countenance. We spend our years as a tale that is told." A tale . . .

About Business and our unreasonable facsimile of genuine workmanship: ("Watch me 'get by' this time, too!") ("Thou fool! this night, thy soul!")

About Brotherhood and our unreasonable facsimile of equality: ("Just between you and me, my dear, she doesn't quite know her place!") ("Father, I pray that they may all be one, even as Thou and I are one.")

About Peace and our unreasonable facsimile of goodwill on earth: ("Who do they think they are, anyhow, daring to criticize our country?") ("My peace I give unto you; not as the world gives, give I unto you. Let not your heart be troubled.")

About Worship and our unreasonable facsimile of someone "lost in wonder, love and praise": ("I have kept all these commandments from my youth up. What lack I yet?") ("Go, sell. . . . Come, follow. . . .")

About Prayer and our unreasonable facsimile of someone "practicing the presence of God": ("Father, I thank Thee that I am not as other men are! I give tithes! I pray twice a day! I! I! I!") ("I have somewhat against thee: thou has lost thy first love.")

Prayer, then, becomes the crux of our trouble—for until we are honest enough to discern the "facsimile" trends in our spiritual behavior, we cannot expect to have our prayers answered, or even to call them prayers, since their basic insincerity threatens our very life—as the Spirit said to the churches: "Thou hast a name that thou livest, but are dead." And we are sometimes too eager about the *name;* too inert for the *life.* The old Roman motto *"Esse quam videre"* (meaning, "To be, rather then to seem to be") is the essence of the matter, for St. John says of our Lord: "As many as received Him, to them gave He power to become sons and daughters of God." And there is nothing facsimile about being that son or daughter. There is no "seeming to be." You are! "Beloved, now are we the sons of God," was said to men in prison, in a nasty mess of politics, nationalism and class rivalry: *"Now* you are a bit of God Himself! It is no longer you that lives, but Christ that lives and breathes and moves through you."

It is a stupendous sentence; and could bring us a revival if even twelve disciples in every local church could begin acting as if they believed it was their truest and most exciting discovery.

But the very rudeness and crudeness of our present way of praying proves how little we have let this power and this glory sweep through us. Merely say that lovely phrase: "practicing the presence of God," then ask yourself how it would feel to be granted as interview in the White House and—midway of a conversation with the President—yawn, and nonchalantly drop off into deep sleep, the last little sentence left dangling in space. The next morning how red your face would be: "What on earth can he be thinking of me?" The likelihood is he would understand perfectly how little you valued the experience; otherwise you would have been on the very tiptoe of expectancy. For what he said to you would be something to tell your children's children and all your neighbors—jubilantly, forever after.

Step number one, therefore, is to enter into His presence with joy! The Psalmist adds another clue: *"with singing"*—and it will be a new day for us when we learn how to walk to the rhythm of majestic hymns which voice the superlative strength and yet the matchless tenderness of our Father, forever concerned, forever working close beside us in this family Business.

As Nels Ferré learned to walk—and sing—when nobody thought that he could possibly manage his new post at the time he became a professor at Andover-Newton Theological Seminary: lame as he was, crippled as he was. Another professor had offered to call for him daily; but the very first morning, it had looked as if even this was going to be a tough assignment, as Dr. Ferré made his slow and painful way down the front steps to the automobile, then attempted the difficult climb into the car itself. His forehead was wet with perspiration, his face twisted with the tension of realizing that the same ordeal must be met in reverse at the other end of the ride. Climbing out. Walking. Climbing steps.

The other professor was hardly prepared, therefore, for Dr. Ferré's request, a little later, that instead of stopping at this own front walk the next morning, he stop two houses down the street. He managed that tedious trip triumphantly; and suggested the following week that he be picked up four houses down the block. The following week, he suggested the next block. And this lengthening-out process continued until the climax when Nels Ferré said: "Don't call for me at all! I'm hoping to make it, on foot!"

It was a jubilant journey, where every inch of the way was a matter of controlling every ounce of energy. So that when he reached the entrance to the Seminary his face was radiant; and to everyone's surprise, he lifted his arms to high heaven, singing with Scandinavian fervor:

> A mighty fortress is our God,
> A bulwark never failing,
> Our helper He amid the flood
> Of mortal ills prevailing.

If this is step number one to enter God's presence with joy and singing, then ask yourself a further disturbing question. How would it be never to meet a certain friend without handing him a limitless list of things you needed? Or, having received them, never to meet him with a gale of gratitude positively blowing you eagerly toward him to try to utter your unutterable words of sheer delight? It would turn your tryst into a begging bowl: not even a reasonable facsimile of appreciation. Obviously, when prayer gets out of focus in this way, the other basic business of actual Worship, actual Brotherhood, actual Goodwill, and actual Labor is thoroughly bankrupt, too; which accounts for so much of our modern absorption in the mere facsimile features of worship.

And all the time there is the one aspect which sons and daughters could cultivate with increasing care, which is—A Speaking Likeness! But to speak like Jesus, you will need to pray like Him. John 17 gives the pattern of His private prayer; it is very simple, very searching, and very sacred. Study it, phrase by phrase, to see how far you are from being even reasonable facsimiles of that amazing oneness your Elder Brother felt toward His Father and yours. In almost every phrase recapture His own major concerns. Understand what He meant by verses 16 and 18: "I pray not that Thou shouldst take them out of the world. As Thou hast sent me into the world, even so have I also sent them into the world." For here is enough of the Speaking Likeness to show what evangelism ought to mean for each Christian in each denomination this coming year: all His Business, all His Brotherhood, all His Goodwill to be incarnated once more in a child of God. To be! Rather than to seem to be! To be, even for a brief moment, in the heart of the Eternal. To be a part of His ritual of remembrance. To be His word made flesh again. To breathe a promise; to receive a promise; and to have both of them identical would mean that at long last you had become like a footnote on verse 8: "For I have given them the words which Thou gavest me"—a Speaking Likeness! "Open Thou my lips, O Lord, and my mouth shall show forth Thy praise."

When we consider the manifold weakness of the strongest devotions in time of prayer, it is a sad consideration. I throw myself down in my chamber, and I call in and invite God and His angels thither, and when they are there I neglect God and His angels for the noise of a fly, for the rattling of a coach, for the whining of a door; I talk on . . . knees bowed down as though I prayed to God; and if God and His angels should ask me, when I thought of God last in that prayer, I cannot tell.
                                                    John Donne 1573-1631

Father, give to Thy child that which he himself knows not how to ask. I dare not ask either for crosses or consolations; I simply present myself before Thee, I open my heart to Thee. Behold my needs which I know not myself; see and do according to Thy tender mercy. Smite or heal; depress me or raise me up: I

adore all Thy purposes without knowing them. I am silent; I
offer myself in sacrifice: I yield myself to Thee; I would have
no other desire than to accomplish Thy will. Teach me to pray.
Pray Thyself in me. Amen.

Thomas à Kempis

16

THE GRANDFATHER CLOCK
STRIKES THE HOUR

This is romance too good to be true. For who would expect anything of a bondswoman sent over from England to serve seven
years in a convicts' prison? Not that Mollie Walsh ever stole anything in her life. Not that Maryland liked being used as a penal
colony by the British, either. But in the year 1700 that was the way
things were.

And when Mollie Walsh's seven years were up, she left prison
with a Bible as her sole possession brought from England, plus a
small amount of cash. So who would expect anything to come of it
—such as the entire city of Washington, D.C.? such as America's
first clock to strike the hours? such as America's first almanac?
Obviously she must have done a whole row of enterprising things.

The first night out of prison she sat on a log by a spring, praying
for an ax so that she could start clearing way the undergrowth, in
order to lay claim to the cleared earth. In the morning she found a
tomahawk by her spring, where Indians had come for water.
Using it was such a tough job that she knew she needed help. So
this resourceful woman went down to a Maryland port and bought
two strong Negroes just arrived from Africa on a slave ship. But
one of them proved a total loss, since he sat idly under a tree all
day, refusing to do a stroke of work. Yet when she fed both these
men, the man who did all the work promptly gave his share to the

lazy fellow. Not speaking their language, Mollie Walsh was certainly puzzled by such irregular behavior, until by makeshift signs she managed to make out that the unbusiness-like "Banneky" was the son of an African chief, and therefore it would be beneath him to stoop to day labor.

A woman who had had such ups and downs found it immensely romantic to find that she owned such a distinguished personage; and made up her mind that she would distinguish herself by sensibly marrying into the family! It surprised Banneky completely to discover that now all this cleared land was suddenly his; that this new log cabin was his; that this energetic woman was his; and that she had freed him. From that moment on he started working with total enthusiasm as a freed man could, knowing that the future was his to make as he wanted it. But who could have gussed, even then, that his future could ever include that clock! that almanac! and that Capital of the entire United States.

This marriage had worked out so well that when Mollie's daughter grew old enough to marry, Mollie went down to the same Maryland port and bought another black slave as a husband for Mary. When they had a little son named Benjamin Banneker, the clock, the almanac, and the Capital were all about to become true.

For Benjamin Banneker was born with a genius for figuring things out and thinking things through. It was a Quaker, met by chance on a country roadside, who opened up to the little black boy an opportunity for schooling. But from that time on it was his own delight in drafting and surveying that led to his particular future.

For by the time he had made the first clock ever to strike the hours on the North American continent, the hour it struck was 1791, and Thomas Jefferson had invited Pierre Charles L'Enfant to come over from France to examine and survey and make maps to lay out the new site for a Capital along the shores of the Potomac River. But this well-known French engineer was an eccentric genius, and even after an expensive year with extravagant fees, he refused to show to Mr. Jefferson any of his surveys or maps.

This seemed so arbitrary and arrogant that Mr. Jefferson and the Federal Commission dismissed him, sending him back to France. And he sailed away with all the plans in his pocket!

All such a complete disappointment to the Commission, that Thomas Jefferson could hardly believe his ears when a Negro draftsman stepped forward and explained that Major L'Enfant had employed him to help do all the mechanical drafting of these maps; consequently, they were very clear in his memory, almost as if still painted on his eyelids, and only needed time to be set down on paper "if Mr. Jefferson so wished, Your Honor!" Thomas Jefferson was overwhelmed with surprise and delight that plans which had been paid for at such a huge cost by his poor young Government were not lost, after all. He gave Benjamin Banneker three days to reproduce them.

But Mr. Banneker preferred doing his drawings at home with his own drafting implements. So Mr. Jefferson loaned him a horse for this long journey. The story of that trip is actually as exciting a part of American history as Paul Revere's more publicized ride! For both Thomas Jefferson and our own nation nearly lost the desired plans for their Capital that night. Since those were the days when no Negro was allowed to ride a horse after dark. But Benjamin Banneker's ride was of necessity a long one, so that when darkness had fallen and he was seen galloping past a tavern, certain gentlemen saw him, leaped on their own horses and chased him.

Mr. Banneker was over sixty years old at this time, so that the adventure takes on even more pluck when we realize how quick-wittedly he plunged his horse into a near-by river, persuading this strange beast to swim across, by himself swimming beside him, uttering encouraging words—although completely uncertain about what might happen on the other shore in the blackness of night: could he find a road? would he meet trouble there, also? But he rode safely home. Drew his plans. Rode back to hand them to Thomas Jefferson in person, three days later, as requested.

And now, two hundred years later, those are the very same streets where senators stroll, and congressmen, and lobbyists, and tourists, and all that host of Negro citizens who may not dream that every inch of the ground they walk on is sacred to the memory of a skillful Negro whose first striking clock and whose first almanacs were also this black man's gift to their native land, and his.

Perhaps the hour has now struck, therefore, when his native land could not do better than to follow a suggestion in his almanac for 1792: *"Let the following sentence be inscribed in letters of gold over the door of every house in the United States:* 'THE SON OF MAN CAME INTO THE WORLD NOT TO DESTROY MEN'S LIVES BUT TO SAVE THEM.'"

For this is the romance too good to be true: that the grandson of a free Negro convict should choose from his grandmother's only possession the one verse which alone can save all of us, now.

We are tomorrow's past. Even now we slip away like the pictures painted on the moving dials of antique clocks . . . a ship, a cottage, sun and moon, a nosegay. The dial turns, the ship rides up and sinks again, the yellow painted sun has set; and we that were the new things, gather magic as we go.

Mary Webb

However good a clock may be, we must wind it up daily, and he who takes good care of his heart, will, as it were, wind it up toward God night and morning.

St. Francis de Sales

When the clock strikes, or however else you shall measure the day, it is good to say a short ejaculation every hour, that the points and returns of devotion may be the measure of your time; and so do in all the breaches of thy sleep, that those spaces which have in them no direct business of the world may be filled with religion.

Jeremy Taylor

17

EVERY TWO MINUTES: THE XYZ OF ABC

(ELEVEN BABIES GREW UP AND SPOKE THEIR MINDS)

Alphabetically, this title is no more mysterious than the moment when you are about to become a parent—

X = Unknown quantity: The child (boy? girl? The world waits!)
Y = You (and you wait!)
Z = Zero Hour ("almost any minute now," the doctor says.)
A = A
B = Baby
C = Comes.

But the birth which seems altogether momentous to your family is a mere mathematical detail that day, when 69,999 other babies will also have been born; which equals a city the size of Macon, Georgia, or Charleston, South Carolina.

For every two minutes another XYZ, another ABC! With 70,000 new cradles endlessly rocking. And the next day another 70,000, endlessly rocking. Or a total of 25,000,000 XXXXXX a year. But on no day will there be 70,000 new cups of milk! or 70,000 new loaves of bread! So that too many of these little Unknown Quantities will go through life hungry. Only one out of twenty will have the chance to be born in the United States or Russia; two-thirds of them will be colored; their chances of being born in China are one out of four; in India, one out of nine.

Think what miracles could happen if every little X born this day could have a Y to whom an angel had appeared, announcing: "You are to be the mother of a Saviour!"

Emily Dickinson would have felt that this was a reasonable expectation, for she wrote from Amherst, Massachusetts, that the Madonnas she saw were those that passed the house every morning on the way to their work, carrying little Saviours in their arms.

It has been said that when God wants an important thing done in His world, or a wrong righted, He goes about it in a roundabout fashion. He never lets loose thunderbolts nor stirs up earthquakes. He simply has a tiny baby born: X. Often in a very obscure home, of a very humble mother: Y. And He puts His idea into that mother's heart, so that she can put it later into a cradle song or a story; then God waits: Z, for the ABC to come true again.

For the momentous events of His world are not battles nor conquests nor dictators nor earthquakes. The momentous events of His world are babies. They are His earthquakes: 70,000 a day to shake old things out of place, and jolt new things into position. And wise men have found many ways of stressing this; e.g.—

Socrates felt so strongly about the high value of X: The Unknown Quantity, that he felt the first step in any new society was to banish everybody over ten years of age! Older than ten they would be spoiled by bad habits, false beliefs, dreams of greed, and lost in a hopeless fascination for all successful wrongdoers! And as if to prove what he meant he wrote: "The children now love luxury, they have bad manners, contempt for authority, they show disrespect for their elders, and love chatter in place of exercise. Children are now tyrants, not servants of their households. They no longer rise when elders enter the room. They contradict their parents, gobble up dainties at the table, cross their legs, and tyrannize over their teachers." (If Greece was like that, two thousand years ago, produced by older people, what would this ancient philosopher say to parents in the nineteen fifties?)

The Jewish Talmud would not have agreed: "The world exists for the sake of children." The ancient Aztec priest had his own formula to be chanted over each new little X born in Mexico: "You are born into a world of suffering; suffer then, and hold your peace!" But a tree was always planted when an Aztec child was born into the world, this tree bearing the infant's own name. Kabir, of India, would have understood this when he wrote: "God, whose expansion the three worlds are, is contained in the tiny seed of the banyan tree."

The Omaha Indians pray for each newborn X: "Ho! Ye Sun, Moon, Stars, all ye that move in the heavens, I bid you hear me! Into your midst has come a new life. Consent ye, I implore! Make its path smooth, that it may reach the brow of the first hill!"

What does the Catholic priest mean by breathing lightly upon an infant's face, slapping his cheek softly, putting a grain of the salt of wisdom on his lips, anointing his breast and the crown of his head with the oil of the Catechumens and finally pouring the baptismal water? Why does he hint to the parents, Y, that they recite the Credo, renouncing Satan's pomps; and, on taking the lighted candle, heed the words: "Receive this burning light and keep this baptism so as to be without blame." The word is *christen*: *made Christ's*. (And the secret symbol for Christ in the early church was X!)

Martin Luther knew this need for renewal when he wrote, in his day: "Strange that every twenty years God builds Himself up a new church out of a new generation of little children."

Jonathan Edwards knew this even more achingly when his people in Northampton drove him out of the church which he had served for twenty-three years (eager to get him away from their Massachusetts community, but forced to listen to his farewell sermon): "We have had great debates how the church ought to be regulated . . . but the regulation of your families is of no less, and in some respects, of much greater importance. Every Christian family ought to be a little church, consecrated to Christ, and wholly influenced and governed by His rules, and family education and order are some of the chief means of grace. If these fail, all other means are likely to prove ineffectual. If these are duly maintained, all the means of grace will be likely to prosper and be successful."

In the thirteenth chapter of Judges there were two such parents: Y, to whom an angel had foretold the coming of a son: X. Before the Zero Hour: Z, Manoah prayed: "O Lord, I pray Thee, let the man of God whom Thou didst send come again unto us, and teach us what we shall do unto the child that shall be born." It would be

enlightening to know what "child guidance" was given! For Sam-
son, their son, turned into a self-willed X, of whom we read: *"at
times* the Spirit was with him."

To which Dean Faulkner of Fisk University has given us the
perfect Negro commentary: "You can't no more give your children
what you ain't got, than you can come back from where you ain't
never been."

And every day of the year, 70,000 new XXXXX, who can't be
given what YYYYY haven't got! In Madagascar the birth notices
are eloquently phrased: "We have the honor to announce that Mrs.
Y. lives anew." For, as the French say: "It is the men who make the
roads, but it is the women who teach the children to walk on them";
to which the Chinese could add: "When the child goes away from
home, it carries away the mother's hand."

Over thirty years ago a famous Australian clergyman, named
Boreham, wrote a number of provocative essays, one of which said
that in the year 1809 everybody was preoccupied by the terrifying
speed with which Napoleon Bonaparte was sweeping across
Europe like an earthquake, ripping whole countries apart. So
nobody paid any attention whatever to a few obscure babies born
into the world that same year; Dr. Boreham mentions some of them
—Abraham Lincoln, William Gladstone, Charles Darwin, Alfred
Tennyson, Oliver Wendell Holmes, Edward FitzGerald, Edgar
Allan Poe, Fanny Kemble, Felix Mendelssohn, Frédéric Chopin,
Cyrus McCormick. Dr. Boreham lets this impressive list speak for
itself; adding that by 1814 Napoleon had been completely de-
feated.

But meanwhile the eleven babies had become five years old,
still well under the age of ten when Socrates would have banished
their elders! Imagine these eleven being called together, years
later, into a "British-American Committee Meeting of Famous
Babies Born in 1809"—the enterprising chairman, eager to have
the Minutes made memorable, might ask each member to bring
in writing some significant statement from his or her printed works.

It is delightful to wonder whether an American President or a
British Prime Minister or a Poet Laureate would be called on first
to make his statement. But if this were some early "White House

Conference," one fancies that the chairman would open the meeting by mentioning the well-known fact that whenever anybody said in Benjamin Franklin's presence: "What's the use of *that*?" Franklin's inevitable reply was: "What's the use of a newborn babe?" Knowing full well that all the hope of tomorrow was wrapped up in that child! Therefore, he took pleasure now in presenting the President of the United States, born in the year 1809: Mr. President!

Imagine *Abraham Lincoln* unfolding his long awkward frame as he rose from his chair, holding three items in his hand: the Bible he used to read as a boy, by the light of the fire as he lay on the hearth, in his log cabin days; a certain pious book his stepmother once gave him, on the flyleaf of which he had written:

> Abraham Lincoln
> His book and pen,
> I will be good
> But God knows when.

The British-American Committee of Famous Babies Born in 1809 would grow limp from laughing. For they would all guess that Mr. Lincoln's third statement would be some marvelous evolution out of any such reluctance, into the more God-like beauty of: "With malice toward none; with charity for all."

International protocol would indicate that *William Gladstone* should arise next. Everybody would remember about this Prime Minister of England that he and his wife were in the habit of going out on the streets of London at night to befriend fallen women and other lost souls, giving sanctuary in their own home. So curiosity mounted high about what clue Mr. Gladstone might offer for such Christ-like concern over those in trouble at home and abroad. He would then sum up his entire viewpoint by reading his statement: "The great thing in life is to discover in what direction God Almighty is going in the next fifty years."

Charles Darwin would be called on next, for he had already rocked every thinking person by his *Origin of Species,* and there was immense curiosity, therefore, over any statement he might make. He would begin by saying that when he first went to

Pategonia, for instance, he had decided that these people were surely the lowest of the low, and that no power on earth could ever possibly lift them higher in the scale of intelligence or kindliness, out of their early savagery. Yet when he went back later, and saw what Allen Gardiner had been able to do in Christianizing these primitive pagans, he wrote in his diary: "The missionary's work is an enchanter's wand!" (In an aside to the British-American Committee of Famous Babies, it is to be hoped that he would also mention that from that good moment onward he had made an annual contribution toward this missionary work!) But as his real contribution for the Committee's consideration, he would offer the following: "Among the scenes which are deeply impressed on my mind, none exceed in sublimity the forest primeval undefaced by the hand of man. No one can stand in these solitudes unmoved, and not feel that there is more in man than the mere breath of his body."

Undoubtedly a sigh of relief would sweep around this roomful of Famous Babies: so Darwin *does* believe in God! For they had all wondered ...

When the chairman would come to introduce *Alfred Tennyson,* it would be natural for him to quote Thomas Carlyle who had recently said: "Alfred is always going about carrying a little bit of chaos, and trying to turn it into a cosmos!" Would the Poet Laureate of England therefore share with the Committee of Famous Babies Born in 1809 any significant verses which would clarify how chaos could become cosmos?

Alfred Tennyson's choices might well have been these three:

> The Lord let the house of a brute to the soul of a man,
> And the man said: "Am I your debtor?"
> And the Lord: "Not yet—but make it as clean as you can,
> And then I will let you a better."

A murmur of protest might go the rounds: "Fancy such a good man saying *that!*" Whereupon this good man would quote his own idea of the evolution of XYZ:

> Where is one that, born of woman, altogether can escape
> From the lower world within him, moods of tiger, or of ape?

Man as yet is being made, and ere the crowning Age of ages,
Shall not aeon after aeon pass and touch him into shape?
All about him shadow still, but, while the races flower and fade,
Prophet-eyes may catch a glory slowly gaining on the shade,
Till the peoples all are one, and all their voices blend in choric
Hallelujah to the Maker: "It is finished. Man is made."

The Famous Babies would clap and nod approvingly; then the
third quotation would somehow sum up everybody's dream:

> One God, one law, one element,
> And one far-off divine event
> Toward which the whole creation moves.

The next speaker, *Oliver Wendell Holmes*, was such a wag that
he would be unable to resist reading, in Mrs. Kemble's honor, an
early poem of his own, to show how brilliantly women had
managed to evolve even from the days of his own boyhood when a
favorite aunt of his had described her life at boarding school:

> They braced my aunt against a board
> To make her straight and tall;
> They laced her up, they starved her down,
> To make her light and small;
> They pinched her feet, they singed her hair,
> They screwed it up with pins—
> O, never mortal suffered more
> In penance for her sins!

Mrs. Kemble's curls would probably bob in high amusement
over each cheek; but the Autocrat of the Breakfast Table would
calm everyone down by reading: somewhat more steadying state-
ments:

> Life is painting a picture, not doing a sum!

> Sometimes a person's mind is stretched by a new idea,
> and never does go back to its old dimensions!

> Fame is the scentless sunflower,
> With gaudy crown of gold
> But friendship is the breathing rose,
> With sweets in every fold.

The axis of the earth sticks out visibly through
the center of each and every town and city.

Build thee more stately mansions, O my soul,
As the swift seasons roll.

Edward FitzGerald would be called on next. Holding his well-known copy of *The Rubáiyát of Omar Khayyám*, he would read solemnly his own forlorn version of the XYZ of ABC:

> The Moving Finger writes; and, having writ,
> Moves on: nor all your Piety and Wit
> Shall lure it back to cancel half a line,
> Nor all your Tears wash out a Word of it.
> With earth's first Clay they did the last man knead,
> And there of the Last Harvest sow'd the Seed:
> And the first Morning of Creation wrote
> What the Last Dawn of Reckoning shall read.
> Yesterday *This* Day's madness did prepare
> Tomorrow's Silence, Triumph, or Despair:
> Drink! for you know not whence you came, nor why:
> Drink! for you know not why you go, nor where.
> Yet, Ah, that Spring should vanish with the Rose!
> That Youth's sweet-scented manuscript should close!
> The Nightingale that in the branches sang,
> Ah whence, and whither flown again, who knows!
> Would but some winged Angel ere too late
> Arrest the yet unfolded Roll of Fate,
> And make the stern Recorder otherwise
> Enregister, or quite obliterate!
> Ah Love! could you and I with Him conspire
> To grasp this sorry Scheme of Things entire,
> Would we not shatter it to bits—and then
> Remold it nearer to the Heart's Desire.

Great gloom would settle down on all the Famous Babies, which *Edgar Allan Poe* would do nothing whatever to lift when he read mournfully: "Quoth the Raven: 'Nevermore!' " or made his contribution about fame: "*Glitter*—in that one word how much that is detestable do we express!" It would take *Fanny Kemble,* the actress, to win the Committee by saying that it was precisely through the glitter of the stage that she herself had managed to remove some of the gloom from mankind—might she be permitted to remind all these contemporary "Babies" that while playing in America she had fallen in love with a certain Southern gentleman; had gone to his plantation; had been horrified and sickened by the things she saw; had left her husband; had returned to England; and although she could show no immortal literature known the world around, still she had written thousands of letters against slavery, to Kings and Queens and Prime Ministers, and well-known Americans! So that, long before the Proclamation of Emancipation, her own "moving finger having writ, moved on" and agitated some more, and then again some more, and some more, seeking to re-mold this sorry scheme of things nearer to the heart's desire!

At this point the chairman would introduce *Felix Mendelssohn*, who, with perfect timing, would sit down at the piano and restore everyone's soul by singing from his own oratorio *Elijah:* " 'O that I know where I might find Him, that I might come into His presence! . . . . If with all your hearts ye truly seek Me, ye shall ever surely find me!' thus saith our God."

It would, therefore, have been an extra boon of beauty to have *Frédéric Chopin* follow Mendelssohn with certain quietening Etudes; which would make the British-American Committee ready for *Cyrus McCormick* of International Harvester fame—who might have the common sense, at this point, not to brag of his famous invention, about to revolutionize harvesting around the world, but to content himself by quoting Ralph Waldo Emerson: "The name of Jesus is not so much written as ploughed into the history of mankind."

And now that the Famous Babies Born in 1809 have long since gone home; now that seventy thousand new babies are being born every day, twenty-five million a year; now that we know that "you can't no more give your children what you ain't got, than you can come back from where you ain't never been"—the major question about every X is: What has his Y got to give him? Now that Z has arrived? Now that ABC is here, 70,000 strong? Now that every day is Mother's Day, and Father's Day, and Children's Day, rolled into one?

Now that that teen-ager over ten is known to be consuming each week 190,000,000 candy bars, drinking 130,000,000 bottles of soft drinks, chewing 230,000,000 sticks of gum, licking more than 13,

000,000 ice cream cones, *what else* is this child over ten to receive out of his allowance from Y this year, to turn him into such an X as the twelve famous ones born in 1809?

Did Socrates have the right answer?

Or Jonathan Edwards?

Is there a Y in any American town teaching some new little X this definition of the *Bible,* printed in the new Russian *Dictionary of Foreign Words:* "A collection of different legends, mutually contradictory and written at different times, and full of historical errors, issued by churches as a 'holy' book"?

Or is there some Y canceling out this sacrilege by doing what Jacob Tobiasch did (becoming both *Mamusha I Tatush,* both mother and father, as in "New Babes in Old Woods"); or some other Joe Lucas ("Cleveland Had Ten in a Row") or another Walpurgis in East Germany ("Other Broomsticks, Other Witches") or another African carver concerned that children love Jesus Christ ("Even the Legs Spoke Volumes") or other Chinese parents and teachers ("More Little Gray Homes in the West"; "The Leaves Are for the Healing"; and the Chinese mother giving radishes and beets on Thursdays: "All the Birds of the Air Shall Sit on the Branches")? Are there other X's as remarkable as Dick Willenzoom ("Better than a Finger in the Dike") or Benjamin Bannekar ("The Grandfather Clock Strikes the Hour")? and when there is a new slaughter of new Holy Innocents is there some Y to take this sorrow as it was taken in Oregon, England, India and Switzerland ("Intolerable Compliment")? Suppose all these more recent parents could also be assembled in a committee meeting, the time would surely be ripe for some modern Manoah to pray:

O Lord, I pray Thee, let the man of God whom Thou didst send, come again unto us, and teach us what we shall do unto the child that shall be born.

THE COMICS
Herod was frank. He didn't play a game.
He didn't dress a soldier as a clown.
"Slaughter the innocents"—the order came

Brief, to the point, against the luckless town.
But whoop-la! how today we kill the young
Dressed in gay garments in a circus ring!
From net to net the little minds are flung.
Live marionettes are jerked upon a string.
We blow desires up like bright balloons
And burst them in our disillusioned air.
We neon-light our brothels and saloons,
And jazz the crooked pathway to "the chair."
The smallpoxed pages have a sticky hold
That kidnaps with a poisonous embrace.
And little children's lives are bought and sold
Two for a farthing, in the market place.

Edith Lovejoy Pierce, from *Wind Has No Home*

Brain of the New World, what a task in thine,
To formulate the Modern!
By vision, hand, conception on the background
Of the mighty past, the dead,
To limn with absolute faith the mighty living present!

Walt Whitman

18

SEVEN FOR A SECRET

I saw seven magpies in a tree,
One for you and six for me.
One for sorrow,
Two for joy,
Three for a girl,
Four for a boy,
Five for silver,
Six for gold,
Seven for a secret that's never been told.

OLD ENGLISH RHYME

Unless a person lives in Baltimore there might be no way of hearing anything about Kenneth Smith's surprising secret. For a motorman on the least important streetcar route in town is not employed for his dramatic use of seven idle minutes every once in a while during his day; nor is it required of him that when he loops the loop at the end of his line, he leave that loop a thing of beauty and a joy forever. Almost nobody rode as far as the loop, anyhow, since it was a dismal dump heap, deep in a forest of red oaks, birch and poplars until the oval is reached where the car must loop the loop; giving Mr. Smith his seven-minute wait.

At first, those seven minutes must have seemed rather long in such a God-forsaken half-acre plot, with nothing to do but walk around, kicking at brambles and underbrush, watching his watch. But when his secret suddenly obsessed him, seven minutes flew by like the wind, and Mr. Smith had all he could do to get going on time. For the secret was to do something with that oval! First to pull the weeds out. Then to get at the underbrush. Then to start planting seeds. Then to haul water to sprinkle them. How about grass seed, too? Of course! More seven minutes of stooping and strewing the seeds in ground made ready in some previous seven-minute stop.

In this private enterprise, his public job of running his No. 24 route from the water tower out to the end of Roland Avenue turned into a mere interval between plantings. As a rule, all passengers would desert his car long before Lake Avenue, so that he was free to think up plans: What next? What next? After his flowers were planted, Mr. Smith invested his seven brisk minutes in making cinder paths through this garden, having had to haul the cinders secretly on earlier runs. Always interrupted by that necessary dash back to the water tower, and the return along Roland Avenue until he could take up the secret where he had left off. Another inspiration was to edge the cinder paths with bricks. Good! So he hauled the bricks. Next: why not whitewash some of them? Fine! So he hauled the whitewash.

Later still, the dream of a barbecue pit—if a person were on a picnic, wouldn't that be ideal? Of course! Therefore, dig the pit. In the end the secret leaked out when Kenneth Smith was able to persuade the Baltimore Transit Company to put up a tall pole to fly the American flag. That day (it was July 11, 1942) a public neighborhood ceremony was held, and everybody began walking along the cinder paths, admiring the flowers, enjoying the grass, and making plans to use that wonderful barbecue pit, themselves, before long. Every clear day thereafter, Mr. Smith saw to it that the American flag went up at sunrise and came down at sunset, even although he lived far across town on Oak Hill Avenue.

When this had been going on for three years, the *Baltimore Evening Sun* thought the whole affair amazing enough to send a reporter to look into it. The reporter found the half-acre loop blooming with brilliant Mexican roses, petunias and zinnias.

"We got over having iris and violets in the spring!" Kenneth Smith explained, not wanting some of his earlier favorites to go unmentioned.

But nobody has yet said what everybody must be thinking: that here is the secret anybody could share to advantage. The secret which Abraham Lincoln knew when he said of himself: "Die when I may, I want it said of me by those who know me best, that I always plucked a thistle and planted a flower where I thought that a flower would grow."

God works in moments.

French proverb

God works in a little hour.

Spanish proverb

God expects a little help.

Irish proverb

God is a good worker but he likes to be helped.

Basque proverb

Joy is the gigantic secret of the Christian.

G. K. Chesterton

. . . and there was not a man to till the ground. But there went up a mist from earth, and watered the whole face of the ground. And the Lord God formed man of the dust of the ground, and breathed into his nostrils the breath of life; and

man became a living soul. And the Lord God planted a garden
eastward in Eden; and there He put the man whom He had
formed.

Genesis 2:6-8

FOR THOSE WHO DIED THAT THE DESERT MIGHT BLOOM.
Sign at Boulder Dam, in memory
of the 89 men who died, building it

19

SATURDAY'S CHILD WORKS HARD

FOR A LIVING

The likelihood is that if Saturday's Child should recite through all
of the old English rhyme until he reached his own particular birth
day, he might sigh in dreary fashion: each of the earlier days would
sound much more blithe and debonair, as if tossed off in one first
fine careless rapture. Whereas he! he! he! must work hard for his
living, earning every penny in the pay envelope Saturday night.
So that anyone inconsiderate enough to provide him with a Bible
verse as the world's best religious philosophy of work would find
him resenting John 18:37—"To this end was I born, for this cause
came I into the world."

"*What?* Forever and a day to collect fares in a crowded bus?
forever and a day to stuff identical objects into endless rows of
identical boxes? forever and a day to dictate dry-as-dust letters to
dry-as-dust customers about dry-as-dust orders for dry-as-dust
items? forever and a day to ring doorbells and demonstrate
vacuum cleaners to cross reluctant housewives? forever and a day
to sell Gent's Haberdashery to men with little taste and less cash?
forever and a day to be everlastingly nagged at home to fix the fur-
nace, shovel the walks, mow the lawn, water the flowers, put up the
screens, wipe the dishes . . . the same old dishes? No, no! Surely I

was born for something more heroic and world-shaking than this! Surely for a more memorable cause came I into the world!"

Saturday's Child would feel deep within himself that his was a vastly more exciting self than such endless drudgery would demand. And he would be quite right about himself. But dead wrong about the drudgery. For of course he does have a riotously rich and rewarding personality: the only one of its kind in all the world! Which is precisely why he should apply it to his tedious tasteless task, until he can discover how dramatic it is to say of his job: "To this end was I born, for this cause came I into the world—to bear witness to the truth." The truth that, as a luminous person, *any* dull duty can be raised to another level.

Saturday's Child would stand in need of some new design for living, of course; and acutally it lies right at hand in the remainder of the old nursery rhyme about the seven days. Suppose that he could be persuaded to devote to his own self the descriptions hinted at for each earlier day in the week as it came around; suppose that every Monday through a whole year he could walk down the front steps on his way to his work, reciting as a ritual:

Monday's Child is fair of face—

It might stand brooding over with alarming bluntness by anybody working hard for a living: "Your face is your fortune." Suppose, therefore, that Saturday's Child spent each Monday thinking of faces; collecting clichés is educational: "Sourpuss!" "Old pain-in-the-neck!" "Killjoy!" "Wet blanket!" "Iceberg!" "Nose in the air!" "Stony stare!" "If looks could kill!" "Conceit written all over him!" "Cat-that-swallowed-the-canary look!" "Never really listens to a thing you say, always looking over your shoulder for somebody more important!"

Or would the cause for which a Christian came into the world be more accurately described by such instant impressions as: "Goodwill written all over him"? "Looks at you as if you mattered"? "Ever notice how he welcomes people"? "Notices little things and thanks you"? "That million dollar smile"? "You can always catch his eye"? "Always time to listen"? "Doesn't turn up his nose indifferently"?

In other words, by deciding deliberately on Monday what adjectives should be written on his workaday face, many a Saturday's Child could dispel the dullness from his daily duties. Other men have done it under other difficulties: *Jesus*—"He was transfigured before them and His face did shine as the sun"; *Stephen*—"And all that sat in the council, looking steadfastly on him, saw his face as it had been the face of an angel"; *Peter* and *John*—"Now when they saw the boldness of Peter and John, and perceived that they were unlearned and ignorant men, they marvelled; and took knowledge of them, that they had been with Jesus"; of all the *disciples* "God working with them"; "Who is the health of my countenance, and my God"; "They looked unto Him and were radiant, and their faces were not ashamed"; "Seek ye my face . . . Thy face, Lord, will I seek!"

Tuesday's Child is full of grace—

All over our country certain socially ambitious persons go to a nationally advertised dance studio daily and acquire enough grace to dance by Saturday night! It may take considerably more than six Tuesdays to acquire the contagious charm that overflows into active goodwill, or the joyous abandon that melts from the atmosphere anything awkward or chilly. But it has been done. For although in every business there are places where angels fear to tread, employees still are forced to go there no matter what the climate. Let Saturday's Child try Tuesdays for learning how! As a Benediction before Business there is no ritual more redeeming than the constant remembrance of: "The grace of the Lord Jesus Christ be with you all, Amen . . . be *with* you all, Amen . . . be with *you all*, Amen."

Mark Twain once said to a friend: "Take out your mind and dance on it, it's getting caked up!" Tuesday would be a perfect date for mastering such agility.

Wednesday's Child is full of woe—

Secret spiritual ventures rarely proceed without hitches. On plenty of Mondays poor Saturday's Child may "lose face." On plenty of Tuesdays his grace may seem positively elephantine. The one prophylactic procedure is to turn every Wednesday into a

Wailing Wall by reciting every woe to himself, on that day only: all the abominable blockers-of-his-path; by name, of course. All the unfair assigners-of-unjust-extra-duties. Also by name. All the deliberate misdoers of misdeeds. By name. Until they are out of his system, by the sheer amusement of wallowing in wrongs on Wednesdays only; when suddenly he should sense the wry wisdom in the old Hebrew saying: "Woe to him who goes supping sorrow with a long spoon."

It was James Kwegyier-Aggrey who learned the hard way that *laughing is the way to go through life*—for he had real woes for real wailing: a Negro. Brilliant. Perceptive. Sensitive. And constantly slighted. But with a matchless capacity for forgiveness and mirth. When somebody asked him if he would choose to be a Negro again, provided he were to be reborn, his answer was arresting: "Yes! And I would beg God to send me back blacker than this!" This is the wisdom of working wrongs out of the system.

John Steinbeck did much the same thing in his *Grapes of Wrath*, where Ma Joad *made laughter out of very inadequate material.* And the sacred writings of Sufuism ask: "Are you less than a piece of earth? When a piece of earth finds a seed, that is Spring; it gains a hundred thousand friends."

Every business in this nation needs such quickening life.

Thursday's Child has far to go—

Which gives Saturday's Child a day for dreaming: for longing to improve his skills: for "showing himself a workman who needeth not to be ashamed." Fifty-two Thursdays a year from breakfast to bedtime will not be nearly enough for the ambitions and dedications and insights needed. The Jews have always felt that every trade was a kingdom. But kings do not reign by watching the clock; nor by listening for the five o'clock whistle.

Once when Albert Schweitzer was up on the roof of his hospital in Lambaréné, repairing it, he called down to ask a young Negro to hand up some tools on the ground. The African said, with dignity: "Sir, I am a scholar! I do not do day labor!" Dr. Schweitzer looked at him, gently: "Yes, I had a try at that, too. But it did not take!"

Nothing is too lowly to do when it needs to be done. For just as a watchmaker makes a watch, in a far more delicate fashion the watch also makes the watchmaker: his painstaking precision in placing wheels within wheels, his expert knowledge of each detail, knowing that where only a tiny cog is needed only a tiny cog will do. But how many a Thursday it took to master all this. His perfection made up of trifles; but the perfection itself no trifle. By far the best appraisal the Carpenter made of His craft was summed up in the sentence: "My yoke is easy, and my burden is light"—it was unthinkable that the yokes He turned out should chafe or rub or bruise.

But this is a slipshod generation: "I can get by with it." "While his back is turned." "The boss will never notice." "Up to his old tricks again." "It won't show!" "Who cares?" "I should worry!"

But Saturday's Child *should* worry—every Thursday. For God is his only Employer! And he probably has "far to go" to match His divine dependability, His absolute orderliness, His creative craftsmanship. "Every man's work shall be made manifest: for the day shall declare it, because it shall be revealed by fire; and the fire shall try every man's work of what sort it is."

Friday's Child is loving and giving—

This is a still further discipline for a worker to learn. Much as Gandhi used to learn it; for his office consisted of four bamboo poles with a bit of thatch overhead and the Mahatma's desk underneath. On the two posts on each side of his desk he had two pictures—one a copy of Ford Madox Brown's painting of Christ washing the disciples' feet; the other a crucifixion scene, by an old master. Gandhi always said that he liked to do his office work and letter writing within sight of Christ serving and Christ suffering. Friday is certainly the day of days to dedicate to this remembrance.

How was it when Christ was here among men? Not a disciple would do that lowly business of washing another's feet; and it must have scandalized them to see their Lord wrap the towel around Him and kneel so humbly. It is a religious philosophy of work which nobody wants to learn, even yet.

The Turks have said this in a proverb: "Working is half religion." But the medieval monks said it better: "To labor is to pray." And centuries earlier a Chinese philosopher taught the people: "Wherever you go, employ all your heart." While out of primitive Africa comes an old Bantu proverb: "Not to help a person in distress is to kill him in your heart."

Why is a day for loving and giving harder to enjoy than a day for woe? or for grace? or for going places? Is it not reckless to be selfless when others are selfish? to "employ the heart" when others are heartless? to stoop to do the dirty work when everybody may step all over him?

It is for this that Saturday's Child has been given a day of rest, about which his rhyme has the most picturesque description:

And the child that's born on the Sabbath day
Is fair and wise and bonny and gay—

Here, then, is his reason for being glad when they say to him: "Let us go into the house of the Lord." For fairness, wisdom and gaiety are fabulous features—out of this world, really, and never found in any pay envelope on any Saturday night; yet he needs to earn them all, weekly. Emerson could have told him how: "Life consists in what you are thinking about all day."

But if *thinking* is to remake his career, let him try giving a day apiece to those simplicities of face and grace and woe and loving and giving personified in the Man who said of Himself: "My Father worketh hitherto, and I work." Moreover, He was tempted in all points as Saturday's Child is. But without sin. So, the more tedious his task, the more stimulating his insights. For there is no limit to what God can do with a life wholly dedicated to His purpose.

A man I know has made an
altar of his factory bench,
And one has turned the counter
in his store
Into a place of sacrifice and
holy ministry.
Another still has changed

his office-desk
Into a pulpit-desk, from which
    to speak and write,
Transforming commonplace
    affairs
Into the business of the King.
A Martha in our midst has made
Her kitchen-table into a communion-
    table.
A postman makes his daily round
A walk in the Temple of God.
To all of these, each daily
    happening
Has come to be a whispering from
    the lips of God,
Each separate task a listening-
    post,
And every common circumstance
A wayside shrine.

           Edgar Frank, in *The Christian Century*

20

OTHER BROOMSTICKS, OTHER WITCHES

(THE GRAMMAR OF THE GENTLENESS OF GOD PUT TO USE IN EAST GERMANY)

A broomstick began it. An old dilapidated affair which was an absolute abomination for a thorough German hausfrau to use, with its last straws threatening to drop off the end at the least sweeping. But when a woman has lost something priceless, she does just what the Bible housewife did—she sweeps her house till she finds it. And although in East Germany it would be sheer recklessness to call in any neighbors to rejoice publicly over this particular finding, still, there were quieter private ways to set the beautiful news circulating. But it had been heartbreaking enough to discover them.

For the thing Fraulein Walpurgis had lost the previous year had been her schoolteaching job. Therefore, all her income. Therefore, all her status in town. Therefore, all her popularity with her pupils. Therefore, all that jubilance which makes a woman get up gladly in the morning to face the new day, and go to bed happily each night over the joy she had had, now that the war was over; now that even from rubble one could build a new world in Germany.

But now, this new rubble! For the previous year she had picked up her broom and started to sweep, on the night before the first of May, getting ready for Wilhelm's arrival from Frankfurt. And then the last straw really did happen—for each frail little wisp at the end of her broom came loose, and fell on the floor, every-which-way. She would have liked to cry, for it seemed like the end of the end. She had been picking up these last straws when Wilhelm burst in and shouted: "Porgie! Do you put on some comical charade, maybe? Is it that you play a witch, riding your broomstick in honor of this special date, maybe?" For there she was—still clinging to the useless handle, held sidewise as she stooped to pick up the straws on the floor.

She stood up and kissed him soberly: "This date is the end of my world, Bruderchen! For today I have lost my job! And today this little old broom chooses to come to pieces, also, with no money now to buy another! I think I shall go out of my mind! Everything is all rubble again, worse than before. I think I shall go crazy!"

He sat down heavily and pulled a card out of his pocket: "Then I must give you the little placard used all over Frankfurt am Main recently; I brought it as a name-day card to show you what Goethe wrote, over a hundred years ago. Read it, Porgie; for over in Frankfurt these days we quote it all the time as we rebuild Goethe's old house."

She took the small placard and read it aloud:

> Should you find in ruins what once you built
> Set busily to work and clear the rubble;
> Make new schemes and think of better measures.
> Should this world ever get out of joint

> Or be cleft asunder of its own will,
> You will build it again for eternal joy.

"Good, isn't it?" Wilhelm asked.

She nodded her head, but all she said was: "I think maybe I will go crazy. How can I sit home quiet when there is so much to say?"

"Tell me what happened," he said then, realizing the trouble was total, and intolerable.

"Just as in Russia, now here, no child under sixteen must hear any religious talk. Just as in Russia, now here, our new East German textbooks say: *'Of course there never was such a person as Jesus Christ. He was a myth conjured up by a group of people in order to deceive and exploit the ignorant. Little by little intelligent people are getting rid of this superstition.'* The Herr Prinzipal said in his most awful voice: 'And so, Fraulein Schmidt, you refuse to teach this textbook?' And I answered: 'Ja! I refuse!' So out they have kicked me. And now never again can I say to the children the very things that need to be said; now, more than ever. I think I will go out of my mind! The other teachers laugh up their sleeves: 'She knows too much about God, that one!' they say. I think I shall go crazy! It is the old German proverb come true for me: 'He who has God for his friend, has the world for his enemy.' "

Wilhelm leaned over and wagged a finger at her: "Would that the good Herr Doktor Martin Luther could be here to tell you that this is no new thing in the world, meine liebe Porgie! Would that he could tell you his parable of Hell—how on a certain day some devils went down to report to Satan. Number one Devil boasted: 'When I was up on earth, your majesty, I managed to get a lot of Christians chained to a ship as galley slaves, then I had the ship wrecked, and drowned all the Christians!' But Satan simply shrugged his shoulders: 'So you drowned only their bodies, and not their souls?' Number two was a little less sure of himself: 'When I was on earth, I arranged to get lots of Christians thrown to the lions and eaten alive!' But Satan simply shrugged his shoulders: 'Ja? So you had their bodies chewed up, but not their souls?' The number three Devil hardly dared to brag: 'Sire, I got a good many Christians burned at the stake!' But Satan again shrugged his shoulders: 'Ja? so you let their bodies get charred to cinders, but

not their souls?' The number four Devil came forward: 'Your
majesty, when I was on earth I dressed myself in Sunday-go-to-
meeting clothes; and, looking very handsome, I went to church.
Up stood a really charming Christian Madchen and told how much
she loved God. So I turned and smiled pityingly at her stupidity!
She said that she followed Jesus Christ every day. So I snickered
out loud! Then she began to pray in public. So I just laughed my
head off! I tagged at the heels of that Madchen morning, noon and
night; and every blessed time she said a single Christian thing, I
ridiculed her, and made fun of her, until at last I put out her fire;
and killed her soul!' And instantly all Hell broke loose with cheer
after cheer. So you see, meine kleine Porgie, as in the days of
Martin Luther, so now!"

Fraulein Walpurgis looked at her brother crossly: "I am not your
congregation in Frankfurt, Wilhelm, that you should preach sermons at me, as if in public! And do not quote me Martin Luther
any more. I love him. But he is of yesterday. Today, I think maybe
I will go crazy! With nothing but a broomstick left."

Wilhelm was holding the broomstick, and he said compassionately: "I must quote Martin Luther once more, Liebechen. For he
it was who said: 'I have had many things in my hands, and I have
lost them all; but whatever I have placed in God's hands, that I
still possess.' Had you thought of placing the broomstick in God's
hands, Porgie, to see what He can make of it?"

She looked at him sternly: "So you still talk fairy tales when I
think I must be going crazy?"

He looked back at her just as sternly: "Then why don't you go
crazy? It is a wonderful idea! Just softly and gently and nicely go
out of your mind, and start talking all sorts of quiet nonsense. Day
in and day out, a sweet harmless sort of babbling nonsense and
fairy tales. I have an old lady like that in my parish in Frankfurt.
She got that way being frightened nearly to death during the night
bombings. So she just quietly went out of her mind. Nobody
notices a thing that she says any more, for it hardly makes sense;
except, of course, the children in the neighborhood, who find her
entrancing. They stand in a row with their hands behind their
backs, spellbound. Nobody else in all Frankfurt is as fascinating

to them, so by all means, go crazy, Walpurgis! It's your one way
now to keep on saying whatever comes into your blessed little old
head to say. The grownups will think you harmless; the children
will find it delightful. By the way, Liebechen, can you still whittle?"

"Of course, I can still whittle, Wilhelm! You taught me yourself!"

"Then let us cut up this broomstick into sections so that you can
whittle them into figures. And all day long, in your harmless crazy
way, you can mutter and murmur harmless foolish things about
the dolls you make. Then they can go flying over town in the hands
of a little child, who will cherish the enchanting flow of meaningless words so full of your beautiful meanings. Porgie, it was awful
when I came in, to be so poor that all I had to give you for your
name-day was a Goethe card from Frankfurt! But now that I am
rich enough to give you back your own broomstick, couldn't you
whittle the old forgotten story of your namesake, the real St. Walpurgis, perhaps? I am suggesting that you be 'a fool for Christ,' as
the Apostle Paul once wrote. Couldn't you think up all sorts of
roundabout delicious ways to talk and talk, aimlessly? guilelessly?
cryptically? deeply? It is the valley of the shadow of death, once
more. But Thy rod and Thy staff they confort me. Here, meine
Liebe, I hand you your crosier!"

A look of curious peace came over her face as she took the
broomstick and kissed it: "So! So I lost something; and I have
swept my house till I find it! Wilhelm, Wilhelm, how you have
preached! And how I can practice that sermon! 'A fool for Christ':
that will be the one right way." She looked across to her brother
and broke out laughing: "It will be so dangerous! And such fun!
Wasn't I full of myself when you came in?"

Wilhelm had his own reply to that one: "May the preacher quote
the good Herr Doktor Luther once more, perhaps?"

"Ja! The congregation is now quite willing."

"'If anybody should knock at the door of my heart and asks who
lives here, I should never think of saying: Martin Luther lives here!
but I should say: Jesus Christ lives here!'"

"Ja, that will be how we can do it from now on; He and I. And
these poor little East Zone infants."

"Walpurgis Night, when the witches used to fly! Well, other witches, other broomsticks, is your answer from now on. You looked just like one, when I first came in."

"That early Walpurgis was patron saint against all magic arts. That, too, must be my task. And now I have remembered the best thing of all, St. Walpurgis is actually represented in sacred art carrying a crosier in one hand! Thy rod and Thy staff they comfort me—Wilhelm, you have added life to my years."

"Life, and danger, and joy, and peace!" was his answer. "To-morrow we must think up how to go about it. I hope this can be the best name-day you have ever had."

"Then let us pray that my next one may be better still."

In the end it was not hard to plan. Her first step was somewhat disappointing, for she went to the library, anxiously looking up every scrap of information about her famous namesake, only to find she was discarding more than she kept in her notes: *b. 780.* (Never mind that one; dates won't matter.)—*b. in England.* (Annoying fact; throw out.)—*d. of a W. Saxony under-king.* (Unpop. idea in this atmosphere!)—*niece of St. Boniface, Apostle to the Germans.* (Mercy no! omit! omit!)—*who invited W. come Germany with other Eng. nuns to help him civilize the fierce Teuton women —as hopelessly uncouth and ferocious as their men.* (Too frank; rephrase, rethink, retell at own risk.)—*on voyage to G. violent tempest; sailors in panic; W. knelt on deck; instant calm. Therefore all sailors venerate W. Now patroness of storms, sailors, hydrophobia.* (Risky drama to give children!)—*lived out her life in neighborhoods totally idolatrous, many attempts on her life and that of her two brothers—monks, near by. Later some would-be murderers convicted.* (Comforting for me; but why put destructive ideas in some E. German heads?)—*Last years of her life, W. spent as head of her brother's monastery.* (Delete! Woman less conspicuous in this sad age.)—*wrote life of her brother in Latin; therefore first female author of England and Germany.* (Makes me feel inches taller to be named for her; but keep this news dark, too.)—*after death, portions of her bones given to Cathedrals in Cologne, Antwerp, Furnes.* (Too graveyardy and scary and Walpurgis-Night-Witchery for my small neighbors.)—*beloved patroness of Eich-*

stadt, Oudenarde, Furnes, Antwerp, Groningen, Weilburg, and Zutphen. (Omit! any woman conspicuous in seven cities would attract too much top Red Police inspection.)—*major traits: virtue, sweetness, intelligence, grace, gentleness endeared her to all.* (Retain. But how endow a broomstick doll with any of this?)

Fraulein Walpurgis went home from the library, discouraged, to share her findings with Wilhelm. He looked over her notes and said: "Scrap all the biography! Your one hint is in the last line, here—somehow it must be the grammar of the gentleness of God which your dolls teach, without once mentioning God. 'Thy gentleness hath made me great' is your Saint's motto! So now see what grammar you can learn to croon witlessly, du kleine ex-teacher of grammar, du! When I get back to Frankfurt, I shall think of you as sort of a German Caedmon; for if that poor limited cowherd could start chanting the Scriptures in his mother tongue for the first time in English history, what can't you start chanting for the first time in German history, three hundred years later, meine Porgie?"

It was curious, in the end, to discover that all her real mesmerism must lie in monotonous repetition—not only did it seem more aimless, but also the words somehow sang themselves home and lodged in the memory. She sat all day by her open window carving her broomstick sections. Wilhelm had shown her how innocent and wistful the planes of a face could be—the high cheekbones were the secret, and the set of the deep eyes, with their merest dab of forget-me-not blue. His first larger Walpurgis doll, in a long blue robe, became her model, the smaller dolls being exact copies, their dresses long, like nun's habits; but of a blue so royal that no one would ever connect it with cloisters or chapels.

The first young neighbor lured to the window, asked the inevitable question: "What are you making, Fraulein Porgie?"

This first chanting proved the strangest experiment of her entire life, so much depended on how the child took this weird incantation, on several keys; monotonous and meaningless: "*I* love gentleness—*he* loves gentleness—*she* loves gentleness—*you* love gentleness—*we* love gentleness—*they* love gentleness—" all the time her hands were busy.

The little girl stood rooted with suspense: "What makes you sing,

Fraulein Porgie?" She knew that never again would she make a direct answer; so, as if she had not heard, she made the tall Walpurgis doll slowly bow forward on her face; then she made both of the smaller replicas, now ready, slide across the table to lean forward also, and lie face downward—all to the much lower meter of: "*I* love gentleness—*he* loves . . ."

Instantly the little neighbor tiptoed through the open door and whispered, "Why do they lie on their faces, Fraulein Porgie? Are they going to sleep? I can sing the little song to Stalin, from our Day Nursery," and she flung back her head to sing the well-known words: "Close your little eyes! Fold your little hands! And give a little thought to Stalin!"

"Ach, du liebes Gott!" Fraulein Walpurgis groaned silently, looking at this little heathen in her home. With instant ingenuity she stood all three dolls upright on their wooden bases, and chanted her declensions with a very wide-awake variation: "I *will* love gentleness only—he *will* love gentleness only—you *will* love gentleness only!" And so to the end . . . "See what you can make of *that*, my infant!" she thought.

The child was overwhelmed with delight to be given one of the smaller dolls when it was time to go home; her eyes were like saucers as Fraulein Walpurgis held the doll close to her own lips and murmured her grammar all over again into the little wooden ear, more softly than ever. As she handed the doll over to its new mother, she had the final inspiration of placing her finger on her lips, to indicate a conspiracy of secrecy. The child nodded in delight, feeling that this made it all just right. Instantly she put her finger on her own lips, and tiptoed thoughtfully down the porch steps, her broomstick doll clutched with deep tenderness. By the time she reached the sidewalk, the spell broke, and she raced down the street shouting to her friends to come out and see what she had.

This did it!

From that moment on, the little plan worked perfectly, with an awed little audience always on hand, watching the carving, the sewing, the robing, the bowing; all to the rise and fall of the endless mysterious murmur. Any child who had not received a doll earlier,

knew he or she was entitled to one. The entire circle waited for
the final initiation, when their Fraulein Porgie would whisper the
passwords more softly than ever into the ear of the departing doll;
then put her finger on her lip. Everybody did this also, then, with
a shiver of delight over their secret.

Grownups merely shook their heads with a sad sort of smile:
"Poor soul! Once a grammar teacher, always a grammar teacher!"

Then one day an alien element burst in. A noisy girl came by,
shouting: "Let's all go down to the Platz! The boys are marching
down there in their white shirts, getting ready to parade in Berlin!
They are holding their fists over their heads! The drums are thump-
ing! It's wunderschön! Come on, let's go!"

Fraulein Walpurgis held her breath: new Teutons being trained
in new fierceness! But would her small enchanted circle ever stay
with her, with such excitement in the air?

In the twinkling of an eye she reached under the table for the
short sawed-off broomstick sections; one by one she banged them
down on the table and thumped them with military precision
across to a corner large enough to form them into a martial forma-
tion. It was noisy and almost brutal. At the same time, with her left
hand, she bowed the tall Walpurgis gently forward in prayer. She
had never been more astonished than when a dozen small hands
instantly reached forward, and of their own accord very reverently
laid all the dressed dolls forward on their faces also, in the ritual
none of them understood but which somehow spoke to something
deep inside.

Fraulein Walpurgis turned her usual chanting into a low melan-
choly moan; she herself swayed from side to side as she let out the
agonized words, almost as if they were being torn loose: "I *must*
have gentleness—he *must* have gentleness—you *must* have gentleness!"

This despair was so obvious that one little guest began to pat
her sleeve: "There! There, Porgie—it will be all right!" All the
little neighbors crowded around her in sympathy, and in tune with
her moaning they kept saying: "There! There, Porgie! There!
There! There! There!"

Until, like Walpurgis of old, she prayed that she too might be inducting Teuton women into that Realm of Gentleness which is, after all, the Kingdom of God on earth.

One must carve one's life out of the wood one has.

German proverb

Are you in earnest? Seize this
very minute:
What you can do, or dream you
can, begin it;
Boldness has genius, power and
magic in it.
Only engage and then the mind
grows heated;
Begin and then the work will
be completed.

Johann Wolfgang von Goethe

Every spirit builds itself a house, and beyond its house a world, and beyond its world a heaven. Know then that the world exists for you. For you is the phenomenon perfect. What we are, that only can we see. All that Adam had, all that Caesar could, you have and can do. Adam called his house, heaven and earth. Caesar called his house, Rome. You perhaps call yours a cobbler's trade; a scholar's garret. Yet line for line and point for point, your dominion is as great as theirs, though without fine names. Build therefore your own world. As fast as you conform your life to the pure idea in your mind, that will unfold into great proportions.

Ralph Waldo Emerson

21

CLEVELAND HAD TEN IN A ROW

Every so often other businessmen endow chairs in schools or colleges, for some reason or other. But Mr. Lucas endowed ten chairs every year for twenty-six years! In all Cleveland there were literally no chairs to compare with them—not so much for scholarship's sake, perhaps; but who else had ever maintained ten such serious seats of learning side by side in a *store* for more than a quarter of a century?

Nothing on earth could persuade Mr. Lucas that maybe eight chairs would do. Or even seven. Or six.

"Ten!" he would always reply with emphasis. And since he took any financial risks involved, ten there always were—somewhat high and lifted up, as shoeshine seats should be, complete with two brass footrests in front of each chair, and even more complete with one Negro boy also in front of each chair, ready to say: "Shine 'em up, sir?" when customers came in the store. The ten boys being the real reason for the ten chairs, of course. Since eight could easily have cared for the trade. Or even seven. Or six. But Joe Lucas kept the number permanently at ten for twenty-six years; and nothing on earth could get him away from Cleveland. Certainly not a vacation: in all that quarter of a century he never left his ten chairs. And certainly not an invitation to leave them permanently, to better his own status. This moved him least of all. There was the dizzy day when Booker T. Washington himself came to Cleveland and tried to persuade Joe Lucas to become his private secretary.

"Man alive! Look how you are wasting that superb education of yours!" the famous Negro urged. "Think what a place of prominence you could make for yourself among our race. Has any colored man like you any business to hide himself away in a shoeshine stand like this?"

"Yes!" said Joe Lucas. "Yes, I do have a business here! Just look

156

at these ten boys, Dr. Washington—every one of them is attending school. I arrange their hours, so that some can go to high school, some to college, some to night school. I have it all figured out that the earnings from this stand can pay the bills of ten boys at a time. When anyone graduates, then I fill up his place with another Negro boy, so there will always be ten boys and ten chairs. And I aim to do this as long as I live! Thank you kindly for honoring me with this invitation, sir. But I figure out that maybe nobody else in Cleveland will lift a finger to take care of ten boys a year if I'm not here to see to it."

So, year after year there were ten chairs standing, ten scholars studying, ten Negroes shining, ten customers smiling, and occasionally, in idle moments, ten voices humming:

> I got shoes, you got shoes,
> All God's children got shoes;
> When I get to Heaven
> Going to put on my shoes
> Going to walk all over God's Heaven.
> Heaven! Heaven!
> Everybody talking about Heaven
> Ain't going there . . .

But not a person in all Cleveland doubted that Joe Lucas would go straight there, the year that he died. Newspapers wrote up his extraordinary career with unusual enthusiasm: "For more than a quarter of a century this unknown, unsung colored man in our midst kept ten boys in school. His business had no other purpose."

And surely nothing on earth could have persuaded Joe Lucas to leave Cleveland permanently except his last great call to: "Arise, shine! Thy light is come, and the glory of the Lord is risen upon thee."

> *Nor knowest thou what argument*
> *Thy life to thy neighbor's creed hath lent.*
> Ralph Waldo Emerson
> *God be in my head,*
> *and in my understanding*
> *God be in my eyes and in my looking.*

God be in my mouth and in my speaking.
God be in my heart and in my thinking.
God be in my end, and at my departing.

                              Sarum Primer, 1558

22

NOR SIT IN THE CHAIR OF PESTILENCE

Half the cruelty in the world comes from our inability
to put ourselves in the place of others.

                              JOHN FISKE

Not being Catholics, most of us are unaware that in their Douay
version of the Bible, the first Psalm is much more tragically translated into English than our milder Protestant phrase: *"nor sitteth
in the seat of the scornful"*—for in the Douay Bible the words read:
"nor sat in the chair of pestilence." Scorn is deadly enough! But
pestilence is virulent business! For nobody wants to mow down his
neighbors into their graves. Or does he?

For news came up from Nicaragua, a while ago, that in the town
of Managua there had been for many a year the good old Spanish
custom of placing chairs on the sidewalks at sunset time, so that
ladies might sit and watch all the world and his wife walk by. So,
after the day's work was done, picture them out there in a row,
gossiping gaily behind flirtatious fans, and saying this or that, as
ladies do, the planet over.

This may have been all very well in the days of oxcarts and
donkeys, but now that bicycles, autos and trucks jam the streets,
the chief of police grew alarmed by the mounting toll of deaths due
to pedestrians mixed up in traffic. Therefore, he caused signs to be
placed at the street corners of Managua ordering the inhabitants
to remove all chairs from all sidewalks. But *The New York Times*
(February 13, 1941) reported that the ladies of Managua were

about to protest this edict, on the ground that it was their oldest social custom; and it was almost unthinkable to give it up—hadn't all their grandparents before them sat there on these very same chairs?

So ... dowagers drew up to the curb on their heirlooms; pedestrians dodged in and out of danger, doomed to violent death; and people who had always done what they had always done, kept right on doing what they had always done, in the way they had always done it.

But ... out in the thick of the traffic there would often be bitter turnings of heads, and the question: *Is it really nothing to them as people go plodding past, each with his sandals of pain?*

From serving in stores: standing, waiting, bending, lifting things up, opening, shutting, spreading things out, explaining, endorsing, persuading, selling, not selling, putting things back, lifting more boxes, spreading things out, holding things up, selling, not selling: *is it really nothing to them as they sit in their chairs?*

From building a building: stooping, shoveling, straightening-up, straining, balancing, carrying, climbing, setting-down, returning, stooping, shoveling, straightening-up, straining, balancing, carrying, climbing, setting-down, returning, stooping: *is it really nothing to them as they sit in their chairs?*

From teaching school: listening, explaining, asking, correcting, scolding, writing, parsing, erasing, spelling, erasing, adding, erasing, dividing, erasing, correcting, correcting, correcting, standing, standing, standing: *is it really nothing to them as they sit in their chairs?*

From fitting fine frocks: kneeling, shortening, pinning, lengthening, ripping, pinning, rising, basting, sewing, ripping, kneeling, shortening, pinning, lengthening, ripping, pinning, rising, kneeling, kneeling, kneeling: *is it really nothing to them as they sit in their chairs?*

From looking for rooms: walking, ringing, knocking, climbing, inquiring, offering, dickering, descending, departing, walking, searching, ringing, knocking, climbing, inquiring, offering, dickering, descending, departing, walking, searching, walking: *is it really nothing to them as they sit in their chairs?*

Not that they were bad sitters, at all. Nor do they all live down in

Nicaragua. For over in England they had this same old British custom—Shakespeare having had a character plagued with "the disease of not noting, the malady of not marking!" And Elizabeth Barrett Browning wrote a poem about this very thing:

> Good Christians who sat still in easy chairs,
> And damned the general world for standing up—
> Now may the good Lord pardon all good men.

And of course the Psalmist knew them only too well in his day: "Such as sit down in darkness and rebel against the word of God."

He might have been remembering Egyptians in easy chairs: for if Pharaoh ordered a double number of bricks one day, by evening if any were lacking, a child was torn from its Jewish mother to replace that missing brick. And Jewish builders, building houses, were compelled in place of a shortage of bricks to bury their children alive in the walls! So that the Talmud had a verse which read: "When the toll of bricks is doubled, Moses comes."

And how about the Chairs of Pestilence on Nazi sidewalks in Germany and Poland during the last war, when six million Jews walked past on their way to gas chambers and torture? What were the citizens thinking? (Those who protested being sent to torture, themselves.)

Or, worse yet, how about these same Chairs of Pestilence along all the streets of America now—FOR GENTILE CLIENTELE ONLY!— where Christians sit rocking today on their heirlooms, while fifty-seven anti-Semitic organizations flourish before their eyes?

For any Gentiles who worship the Lord in the beauty of holiness, the Jewish Talmud has certain texts which would make startling signs for policemen to nail at street corners:

> If I am here, then everyone is here.

> In every place where you find the imprint of men's feet, there am I.

> If thou hast taken up God's trade, put on His livery also.

> Who practices hospitality entertains God Himself.

> **The table at which strangers eat becomes an altar.**

But three who have eaten at one table, and have said over
it words of Torah, are as if they had eaten at the table of God.

Or, in somewhat less spiritual mood, these practical Hebrew
proverbs: "He threw my coat out-of-doors, I happened to be in it";
"Each of our miseries is a piece of the Golden Calf."

Remembering this Golden Calf, it is disconcerting to discover
that far from worshiping only in the beauty of holiness, this glittering beast has been our real national idol whenever others have
been forced to stumble through our streets: past a row of chairs on
our sidewalks. As Tennyson made Ulysses say: "I have become a
name for always wandering with a hungry heart." How they must
have wondered as they wandered!

For in the seventeenth century, it was John Eliot's own Christian Indians who were driven by force from their New England
villages, their homes burnt to ashes; their new little churches, also.
What in the world were white Christians thinking when these
darker Christians filed sadly past?

In the eighteenth century, it was David Brainard's Indians
driven as far west as Kansas by the advance of white Christians
settling down on white chairs on white sidewalks. While up in
New England, Massachusetts placed a bounty of $75 on each
Indian scalp. Later that same year the reward had to be raised
to $400; and on August 22, 1722, Jeremiah Bustead of Boston en-
tered in his record book the strange words: "This day 28 Indian
scalps brought to Boston, one of which was Bombazen's [a Christian mission Indian] and one was Friar Rasle's [a white Catholic]."

In the nineteenth century, it was the entire Cherokee Nation
being driven from ancestral homes in the Smoky Mountains,
rounded up by the United States Army in the winter of 1838 in
North Carolina and Georgia, forced along the "Trail of Tears"
westward to Indian Territory—to make room for more white chairs
on more white sidewalks, in spite of all that Samuel Worcester
tried to persuade Christians to do.

In the twentieth century, it was turning Indian Territory into
the State of Oklahoma, allotting the best lands for white settle-
ment, and the poorest lands for Indians. All of this misery being a
piece of Golden-Calf worship. But hardly the Christian way to

make straight through the desert a highway for our God, with 372 Government treaties broken; and right before our own eyes, the past few years, Navajos dying of malnutrition.

No wonder our Lord painted His last judgment in six shockingly simple scenes of the Stranger as Himself—

1. The Stranger faints in His tracks: did you ask Him in for a meal?
2. The Stranger is dying of thirst: did you rush in the house for a cup of cold water?
3. The Stranger has no place to rest: did you ask Him to come indoors?
4. The Stranger is shabby and shivering: did you give Him that extra suit?
5. The Stranger is knocked down by the traffic: did you hurry to call in His sickroom?
6. The Stranger has been arrested: did you go straight to His prison cell?

Robert Browning put this unforgettably into words:

> For contract our infinite senses
> We behold multitude; or expanding, we behold as One,
> As one man all the Universal Family; and that man
> We call Jesus the Christ, and He in us, and we in Him,
> Live in perfect harmony in Eden, the land of life—
> Giving, receiving, and forgiving each other's trespasses.

But out in the thick of the traffic the tramps are thinking: "*When?*" While up on their chairs on the sidewalks the Golden-Calf followers inquire with crestfallen voices: "*Who?*" In Sweden they have an old saying that God often goes about in worn-out shoes; which India alters to read that even Buddha was once a cart horse. While Aesop, slave and Negro, went even further when he said that the Creator of men did not mix clay with water but with tears.

This, then, is the tale of those tears. Unhappinesses usually edited out of schoolbooks, not being particularly creditable; yet caused by Christians on sidewalks who might be woefully shocked to discover that instead of singing: "O come, let us worship!" they are really chanting: "O come, let us make a Communist!" By keeping some miserable fellow off of, and out of, and away from, their private property: their sacred Golden Calf. Sociologists all agree that Negrophobia and anti-Semitism come from a sense of deep insecurity of some sort, which the person overcomes as soon as his ego finds somebody lower down his social scale toward whom he can feel superior.

India seems to have thought through this psychological bias, centuries ago, and to have fashioned it into a legend: "When men said to the Scare Crow: 'Do you never tire of standing all day in this field?' the Scare Crow made answer: 'The joy of scaring is deep and lasting, and I never tire of it!'"

From Simon Legree with whiphand over black slaves to the Ku-Klux Klan in our day, *this joy of scaring* seems to have written the history of Negroes in America. Scare Crow and Jim Crow are pathetically alike, especially to the person inside that old coat. But among the quiet ladies it has been merely the first nine verses of the second chapter of James in action: under my footstool, out of sight, out of mind ... the traffic is plenty good enough ... my chair! my sidewalk!

What matter if all the early wealth poured into the making of the Golden Calf came from the hands of slaves? Perhaps the only real wealth has been the lavish outpouring of patience on patience, forgiveness on forgiveness, adjustment on adjustment, waiting on waiting: "Nobody knows the trouble I see; nobody knows but Jesus."

And the reason He knows is that He often goes about in worn-out shoes, mixing mortal clay with tears not water, noticing that the only two places where His black children can turn for immediate acceptance on an equal basis are the Roman Catholic Church and the Communist party. Side by side, kneeling with white men for communion. Or side by side, plotting with white men to overthrow the government. What virulent business quiet ladies do undertake at sunset time, on sidewalks! Abraham Lincoln commented on it as long ago as 1858:

And when by all these means you have succeeded in dehumanizing the Negro, you have placed him where the ray of hope is blown out as in the darkness of the damned, are you quite sure that the demon you have roused will not turn and rend you? What constitutes the bulwark of our liberty and independence? . . . Our reliance is in the love of liberty which God has planted in us. Destroy this spirit, and you have planted the seed of despotism at your own doors. Familiarize yourselves with the chains of bondage, and you prepare your own limbs to wear them. Accustomed to trample on the rights of others, you have lost the genius of your own independence, and become the subject of the first cunning tyrant who arises among you.

But Indians and Negroes are only one part of this Scare Crow policy. In 1924 our Government saw fit to pass a Japanese Exclusion Act, which denied to the Japanese the same kind of quota system which white European immigrants had. This greatly humiliated the Japanese—to be considered more undesirable than illiterate peasants; and it has been quoted in our papers that on December 8, 1941, in Tokyo, Admiral Tojo rubbed his hands together in pleasure over the success of Pearl Harbor, saying: "Now we are beginning to get even!" For scarecrowism can work both ways. And this leaped instantly to everybody's mind: "Lock them up! Get them off our streets!" Immediately nearly one hundred thousand Japanese were rushed from American cities to be interned in Relocation Centers. Of course, nowadays, the Supreme Court admits that this was a sizable case of national hysteria. But it took all kinds of forms. Perhaps the single instance of the Reverend Mr. Toru Matsumoto illustrates it best. He was a Japanese pastor who was working with his denominational Mission board in New York, living in the suburb of Larchmont. Victory gardens were popular just then, and Mrs. Matsumoto had planted one, assisted by her little son, Tadashi, known as Teddy.

But one June morning in 1941, the police called up to tell her that during the night every vegetable in her particular patch had been torn up and broken in pieces by somebody wearing Number 12 shoes. She took the news with such beautiful bravado that the police were stirred by her serenity, and the local paper wrote a special editorial to Teddy, likely to become as classic as the famous one to "Virginia" who had asked about Santa Claus:

We're sorry about your garden, Teddy.
You worked hard on it and the beans and cabbages and tomatoes

and strawberries were just beginning to flourish. The rows were neatly laid out and there weren't any weeds. You and your mother have worked hard on it all through the spring. And then someone sneaked in during the night and ripped it all to pieces.

Whoever did it, Teddy, didn't understand about you. They didn't know that your father was tortured in Japan for opposing the military government and for preaching world peace. They didn't know you are an American citizen because you were born, four years ago, here in the land of the free and the home of the brave.

Those are two good words: "free" and "brave." They mean you are free to live in America and plant a Victory garden, but they also mean you have to be brave enough to put up with a few people you meet here and there who aren't real Americans—the kind of people who trample a little boy's garden because his name is Teddy Matsumoto.

As you grow up, never forget what your mother said when she heard about it: "I can't hate anybody. I just feel so sorry for them because they don't know what they are doing."

That is an echo of something said by One a long time ago who suffered at the hands of cruel, unjust people. So, if you want to grow up to be a real American and a real Christian, Teddy, be like your mother.

And remember another thing. What has happened to you often happens to people who plant seeds in this world. It happened down through the generations to those who tried to plant love and understanding and tolerance in the world. Just when the plants begin to grow, someone who doesn't understand tramps in and ruins the garden. But they have kept planting and each time more of the seeds survive.

So get to work and plant your garden again, Teddy, and one of these days you'll reap a harvest.

Two sequels to this story are worth noting. The first one: wonderful! For before sundown the gardeners of Larchmont were so aroused by this pestilential scaring in their town, that they took the best plants from their own gardens and replanted every inch of Mrs. Matsumoto's vegetable patch. Which meant that she was almost better off than before—with taller, finer, riper things to eat, and this reassuring evidence that the sidewalks of Larchmont were lined with matrons who had no intention that this gallant little lady should be mowed down! But . . . the second sequel was a letter to the same newspaper, signed by a Jew, telling how long he had lived in Larchmont, what troubles he had had, but that no matter what had happened, nobody had ever rushed forward to help him: so why all this to-do over a Japanese enemy alien in wartime? Obviously he felt that his coat had been thrown out-of-doors, and he happened to be in it.

During the war years, our government evidently took to heart its lesson about how the Japanese Exclusion Act had rankled in Japan, perhaps precipitating Pearl Harbor. Therefore, on its own initiative, a law was passed writing off an even older but similar Chinese Exclusion Act. This decision caused wide rejoicing among the Chinese already here, and produced the desired effect in China.

With their long background of patience, industry and culture the Chinese had proved splendid citizens, of whom one likes to think that the Wong family in San Francisco are typical. For Jade Snow Wong was a fifth daughter in this strict Chinese household and when she wrote a book recently, called *Fifth Chinese Daughter,* her family gave a ceremonial dinner and her father made the following prayer:

King of Kings in heaven, we are gathered here in thought of a book which is being read throughout America. This book was written by a Chinese—my fifth daughter, Jade Snow. Father in heaven, I acknowledge to You that this book was not written through my wisdom in training that daughter, nor because of her special talent, but only comes from Your blessings and Your continuous graciousness. Our family is indebted to the inspiration of Christianity for the happiness it has experienced in America.

This is so much the gracious way everyone loves America to be—a distinguished Chinese girl graduating from Mills College, writing a book, and being honored in San Francisco—that it is hardly bearable to read in the papers that an equally distinguished Chinese young man, graduating from Earlham College, is deliberately dishonored in this same San Francisco by the deliberate vote of 174 deliberate neighbors who haven't a thing in the world against him, they say; except that they worship the Golden Calf more than they love either God or man.

Mr. Sing Sheng had been a former intelligence officer with the Chinese Nationalist Government; but that day was over, of course; and here he now was, twenty-six years old, married to a Chinese-

American wife, with a two-year-old son, and another baby expected soon. The Shengs were in need of a larger house, and found a little white cottage with charming pink shutters. Mr. Sheng had made his down payment of nearly three thousand dollars and was buying his furniture when the neighbors objected to having Chinese on their street, lest it lower real estate values. For a while he considered moving in, anyhow; if he did, what would happen? The neighbors said children would break his windows and throw garbage all over the place. Mr. Sheng wondered how children would dare be so primitive unless their parents let them do such things: was this the way democracy worked? Then Mr. Sheng had a fine democratic idea of his own—have the neighbors vote whether he should move in or not: he would let their vote control him. Ballots were sent to every household, and he wrote each householder this personal note:

Before you reach any decision as to how you will vote in the ballot, allow us to tell you our opinion. The present world conflict is not between individual nations, but between Communism and democracy. We think so highly of democracy because it offers freedom and equality. America's forefathers fought for these principles and won the independence of 1776. We have forsaken all our beloved in China and have come to this country seeking the same basic rights. Do not make us the victims of false democracy. Please vote for us.

But the real estate man wrote to the owners also: protect your property! So when the votes were counted 174 objected to having a non-Caucasian neighbor, only 28 voted "Come," while 14 had no idea, one way or the other.

After the votes were counted, the little Chinese wife cried softly as her husband stood up and said to the neighbors: "Let us hope that your property values go up every three days."

A few years ago, when church leaders were meeting to talk about the Point IV program, a layman named Ronald Bridges led in prayer in words to grip all who heedlessly sit while the world passes by:

Almighty God, our Father, we are respectable people gathered here. Forgive us. We are men of rectitude and good standing in our communities. Forgive us. Fill us, engulf us, sweep us away with the tides of Thy spirit, that we may live in righteousness. Search us out with all the hounds of heaven when we hide from Thee in our respectability. Send legions of angels to beleaguer us when we make stand against Thee in the round tower of our good works. Forgive us, Lord, when we are stupid and insist on doing that in Thy name which is not Thy work. Forgive us when we invoke Thy name to assert our vanity and our prejudice. Forgive us, Lord, for our impatience with the movement of Thy hand among events. Teach us to wait Thy time and to move in the rhythm of Thy purpose. Help us to stand rigid—inflexible against all evil, all cruelty, all hatred in the name of justice. But remembering our sins, we humbly ask to know the mystery of mercy that we may yield a little in Thy time and for the sake of Thy Son, Jesus Christ. *Amen.*

All the mischief in the world is done by one thing: the inability to remain at rest within one's own room.

Blaise Pascal

EARTH FORGET NOT THE BLOOD SHED ON THEE!

Words chiseled on the tall stone pillar in a green meadow in Germany where once stood the dreaded death camp of Bergen-Belsen

I see myself now at the end of my journey; my toilsome days are ended. I am going now to see that head that was crowned with thorns, and that face that was spit upon for me.

John Bunyan

But you must learn, you must let God teach you, that the only way to get rid of your past is to make a future out of it. God will waste nothing.

Phillips Brooks

23

THIS CARPET IS STOLEN DAILY

This carpet gets stolen somewhere, every day! Until the robber has now become Public Enemy Number One—armchair detectives please take notice; for it is high time the fellow got tracked down, and arrested.

Naturally any carpet whisked off from under people's feet must be very valuable stuff; undoubtedly an heirloom; with plenty of history behind it. Although not even Thomas Jefferson guaranteed that it would be *magic:* for on a magic carpet a person flies through the air with the greatest of ease. But he who runs may read that such would be a mere fairy-tale fabrication. Whereas our carpet which gets stolen every day is a tangible, visible, literal, woven affair—with warp and woof and woolen pile, where actual feet of actual Americans have stood safely on its actual nap.

And although puns are utterly beneath contempt, still, what neater word than "nap" could properly describe the forty winks which certain Americans must be indulging in while this daily theft takes place right under their toes?

By far the most absurd of these affairs happened in Washington, D.C. at the Statler Hotel. The day that it happened the large lobby was covered by a stunning carpet—on a white background there were huge gray ferns crossed by equally huge black ferns woven in a very sweeping, spectacular design, pleasing to the eye and creating a perfect perspective.

Certain workmen, at the side entrance, said to certain guests: "Pardon us, would you kindly stand aside while we roll up this carpet—we are sending it to the dry cleaners?" The guests obligingly stepped to one side, and the whole width of the carpet was rolled up in a business-like fashion as far as the place where the next group of guests had to be approached similarly; they complied similarly. Then—rounding the corner—the workmen reached that part of the lobby known as "Front" where mail clerks, registration clerks, bell hops and guests created a busier atmosphere than ever. But even there the same polite request received the same polite response; one of the hotel managers removing himself promptly as the gigantic roll snowballed in leisurely fashion across the floor, then swerved toward the side door where it had started its career. And so, out of sight.

But not out of mind. For the bare floor reminded everybody that they were waiting for those dry cleaners to finish their job. But as the first week stretched into the second week, and then into the third, considerable impatience began to be aired; at first they had merely realized that in wartime no plant could finish work with normal speed. But then everybody at the Front Desk was asked daily: "When do you suppose our carpet will come back?"

As a conversation piece it became a distinct success—everybody topping everybody else's story about slowness with a better one. But finally a manager spoke sharply to the head housekeeper about it. And she, even more sharply, replied that somebody had taken it upon himself to get the job done—right over her head; for she herself had never authorized any dry cleaning. And then, of course, the ghastly truth began dawning: nobody had authorized such cleaning! It was simply a smart stunt in stealing. One way to whisk something desirable in Washington right out from under the tourists in town at the time.

Wiser and sadder, the Statler substituted the equally spectacular carpet you may have seen recently in its lobby, with great crimson blocks surrounding great green leaves. But if your curiosity should get the better of you, a remnant of the old white carpet can still be seen in the Verandah Room: for this is a luncheon and cocktail lounge, with such a multitude of tiny tables that any thief would think twice before troubling to move them aside while rolling up the carpet. So here you can see the original design—that sweep of the graceful gray fern crossed by the beautiful black fern: now symbolic of something stolen from underfoot. And stolen daily.

It makes strange reading in the newspapers. What is so rare as a day in June, 1951, for instance, when practically the same thing happened one noon in the Brown Hotel, in Louisville, Kentucky. For all on this summer's day the Lions Club had planned to give a luncheon in honor of Miss Bettye Foster; she had just won first prize in their essay contest on *Why I Love America*. It was really a charming bit of creative writing, in which Bettye, who was thirteen, had said with touching enthusiasm: "America is like a mother into whose arms I can flee for protection. Therefore I have a right to love that which protects me. . . ."

The only trouble being that on that June day, Bettye was not allowed to flee over the white carpet of the Brown Hotel into the arms of her American fathers to receive their prize—for Bettye was a black fern, as it were! And the management refused to allow any luncheon to be given for any Negro on their premises: This is a white carpet, we are taking it up to clean it! Please step aside, Bettye Foster. An essay is one thing. Blackness is another thing.

Also in June that same year a similar theft developed into an international incident in New York State, in a suburb called New Rochelle, where Bloomingdale's have a branch store. Three well-educated ladies from India, whose husbands were United Nations delegates from Pakistan, went shopping that June afternoon, wearing their gorgeous oriental saris. A corner cop saw them go into Bloomingdale's, and said to himself: "Gypsies!" So he called the police station. Instantly two detectives dashed over in their squad car. They discovered two of the "Gypsies" in the gift department; the third—more suspiciously still—was looking at spoons in the silverware department. So the detectives did their duty as they saw it, arresting all three ladies, removing them at once to the police station from the White American's floor. The ladies were most indignant, exploding into their exquisite crisp English: "Disgraceful!" "Outrageous!" "Scandalous!" "Incredible!" For Mrs. Shafia Faroog is wife of the second secretary of the Pakistan delegation; Mrs. Rahat Said Chhatari's husband is also a delegate, and her daughter Nadira was with her.

The policemen kept explaining sheepishly: "But we thought you ladies were Gypsies!"

Whereupon Mrs. Chhatari asked icily: "And what's wrong with Gypsies? They're as good as Americans, aren't they?"

And the next thing anyone knew the entire Pakistan Delegation wrote from the United Nations, demanding an official apology. At which memory the police still shake their heads sadly, and say, "Just the same, Gypsies do steal things!" With no knowledge at all of ancient Gypsy history—traceable through Hungary, Poland, Rumania, Bulgaria, Yugoslavia, France, Russia: with its curious word "*Patteran*," where beloved roads are marked by little trails of crossed leaves and grasses left behind them—probably carefree gray ferns crossing lighthearted black ferns on many a path, in a ritual too ceremonious to be pulled to pieces ignorantly: since it deserves reverence, if only for surviving so many centuries unchanged.

When June, 1951, had turned into July, the carpet was stolen again in Illinois, in a place known as Cicero. Here a Negro named Clark had rented an apartment and moved in his furniture—but it seemed that in Cicero black ferns may not cross gray ferns on a white background; and a regular riot started. Young hoodlums threw all of Mr. Clark's furniture out of the windows; smashing them, of course. This proved to be such great sport that they threw everybody's furniture out of everybody's windows, wrecking the whole place. The following evening curious grownups gathered in a circle, to see what might happen next; and the police just let things happen.

Mr. Clark is a man of immense moderation; a graduate of Fisk University, and unwilling to cause any fuss. From all over the country indignant white people began mailing him money to buy new furniture, and a town in Connecticut offered him a safe home and a good job—laying down anew their own carpet of human rights: black *and* gray, *on* white! He said he would like to come later, but felt it would be better to stay in Cicero longer, until people could see how wrong they had been.

By the time July, 1951, had turned into August the same old theft took place, in an even sadder way at an even worse moment, in Sioux City, Iowa. But this episode was so widely written up in all the nation's newspapers that you may recall reading about Sergeant First Class John R. Rice, the Winnebago Indian killed in action in our army in Korea. His body was brought home for burial in August, his widow had bought a cemetery lot, the funeral itself was over, the mourners were leaving the grounds, when suddenly the superintendent of the cemetery discovered that the soldier was an American Indian. He stopped the burial instantly, since the cemetery was for Caucasians only.

Early the next morning when the President of the United States read of this undemocratic and unpatriotic act toward a war veteran, he was thoroughly shocked, and wired Mrs. Rice at once that her government would authorize burial of her husband in Arlington National Cemetery, all transportation charges to be cared for, including that of herself and her family. What a curious memory it will be for these three little Indian children growing up on the Winnebago Sioux Reservation—Pamela, five; Jean, three; Timothy, two—to know that a soldier good enough to die for democracy abroad, was not acceptable enough to lie in death side by side with white men.

And although this was the episode which received the widest publicity, identical incidents happened two years before and the year after. For in February, 1949, Private Felix Longoria was killed in action in Korea, but was refused burial in his home town of Three Rivers, Texas, because he was an American of Mexican descent—this time also, the Arlington National Cemetery caught up the lack of patriotism by opening its gates. And in January, 1952, a private cemetery in Phoenix, Arizona, had denied a plot in the veterans' section of their cemetery for the body of Private Thomas Reed, killed in action in Korea; for five weeks his coffin was kept waiting while the white trustees tried to "clarify their policy" about burying Negro soldiers in their veterans' section . . .

What a carpet Christian Americans do pull out from under any feet which are not white!

Surely we might talk more convincingly about democracy abroad if we recalled more frequently the story of the day when St. Francis of Assisi called on the Sultan, hoping to convert him. The Sultan was enchanted to notice that the carpet in his throne room was completely covered with crosses: which meant that if Francis refused to walk over them, it would be an unforgivable insult to him, as sovereign; whereas, if Francis should walk over them, would it not be an unpardonable insult to his God?

The Sultan was completely taken aback, therefore, when St. Francis walked blithely toward him over all the crosses in his delightfully debonair stride, with no hesitation whatever. The Sultan called his attention at once to the way he had openly dishonored his Lord. The Little Brother of the Poor never even looked down as he answered: "But your majesty is forgetting that my Saviour was crucified between two other crosses! It is, therefore, over the crosses of these two thieves that I have just walked to bring you the magnificent news of my Lord's resurrection and matchless love for you, and for all men everywhere."

These thieves that seek to steal the carpet of matchless love for all men everywhere—who are they? *The Book of Common Prayer* has the only answer—

Against Thee, my Lord and against Thy whole Body Mystical have I sinned and done this evil in Thy sight. In Thy Church so fitly framed together in the unity of the Spirit, every secret sin committed is an offense against the whole. For Thou livest in each soul of Thy redeemed, and dost suffer in each for every wrong which is done against God. No man liveth unto himself but all live to Thee, and Thou art glorified in Thy members or crucified by them, according to Thy will. I come to Thee, my Lord, to Thee whom I love and whom I have wounded. In Thy pity receive me; in Thy mercy, hear me; and in Thy love forgive all my sin. Through Jesus Christ our Lord. Amen.

There is, however, one further solution—desperate and dramatic. Perhaps only a Cleopatra can bring it off, successfully. And yet, remembering how dramatically actual thieves got away with an actual carpet at the Statler, who can say that it can't happen here? Cleopatra wanted to have an audience with Caesar, and he refused it. So she had herself rolled up in a priceless carpet, which was then carried into his presence as a gift. When it was unrolled, up rose Cleopatra from the middle of it. Herself the gift! This is, of course, the one haunting hint in the above prayer in which you say to Almighty God: "Thou livest in each soul of Thy redeemed, and dost suffer in each for every wrong."

To feel *yourself* denied shopping privileges, as a gray fern on a white carpet in New Rochelle. To feel *yourself* denied burial, as a black fern on a white carpet in Phoenix. What is it but the Golden Rule in action—your neighbor as yourself? Or perhaps that exciting word "empathy," which identifies you instantly with the other person in a less superior mood than "sympathy" implies. Recently Robert Oppenheimer put it in a quotable phrase: "The best way to send knowledge is to wrap it up in a person!" How is the carpet in your town today?

You ask what you can do? You can furnish one Christian Life!
Phillips Brooks

If thy heart were sincere and upright, then every creature would be unto thee a looking-glass of life, and a book of holy doctrine.

Thomas à Kempis

If a stranger sojourn with thee in your land, ye shall not vex him. But the stranger that dwelleth with you shall be unto you as one born among you, and thou shalt love him as thyself.

Leviticus 19:33, 34

Broad is the carpet God has spread,
And beautiful are the colors He
has given.
O God, whatever road I take
Joins the highway that leads to Thee.

from the Persian

24

THREE SUCH COMFORTABLE MEN FROM
THREE SUCH COMFORTABLE HOUSES

Of these three comfortable men it can be told briefly that one paints, one plays the piano, and one started out to be a priest, but changed his mind. Actually, you know all three very well indeed—both their three comfortable faces and their three comfortable addresses. But the thing they did one day when they got together publicly in Europe, is so uncomfortable to recall that nobody even tries, any more. But there is no excuse to write FINIS as if the short story were over, when it still goes on and on, each chapter ending with the words *"Continued in our next."* Then our *next*. And our *next*.

In private life, however, our three comfortable men are pleasant enough to meet. Take the painter. A delightfully talented genius, with a round cherubic expression of absolute goodwill on his face. And a mind of such brilliance that when he speaks, great rolling sentences sparkle forth in such torrents of majestic English that more uncertain people straighten their spines, tighten their belts, jut their chins forward, and grow nobler by the minute . . . *"Blood and sweat and tears,"* he said. And this was just what they gave. *"We will fight on the beaches, we will fight on the streets,"* he said later. And that was just what they did.

He started painting about thirty years ago when his countrymen put him out of his comfortable government post, preferring to let somebody run things for a while. Time hung heavy on his hands; so he bought both paint and canvas. Dipping his brush cautiously that first day, he laid his first timid dab of paint on the canvas; about the size of one Boston baked bean. But a lady standing by said: "No! No! Winnie, like *this—*" and she made wide sweeping strokes which created cloud effects at once. So that is the way he has been painting ever since. He is unusually good at it. National art galleries buy his pictures. People crowd to his public exhibitions and say: "Good, isn't it?"

But the one thing to be noticed is that he does either still life (lovely flowers in lovely vases) or landscapes with here a tree and there a tree; here a hill; there a lake; a house or two. But never any people on his pictures.

But do not be deceived. The people are there, all right. Eight and a half million of them. Right there! With one stroke of the brush, one stroke of the pen. It is horrible to be the critic who can tell you where to find them! For in every one of his landscapes there must be some hole down which he drops these people; then forgets them. Eight and a half million down a hole. And still there. Forgotten.

We know all about holes in our country. Only a few years ago a little girl named Kathy Fiscus was playing all over the landscape near her home. Nobody knew a hole was there; but she fell in by mistake. People hunted all day until they heard her calling up the shaft. Her mother shouted: "Kathy, are you down there?" and her little frightened voice called back: "Yes, I am!" Everybody read it on the front pages of their papers. Even in New York. Even in London. All sorts of men tried all sorts of schemes to get Kathy out. But the shaft was old, the walls were narrow and crumbling. All over our nation people walked slowly past newsstands to glance at the Last Edition: "KATHY STILL THERE; RESCUE TOO PERILOUS." Australia cabled for news: "KATHY SAFE YET?" England cabled. Radios announced:"NOT YET! TOO RISKY!" And when they did get Kathy out, she had died from lack of air. The whole world mourned. For sympathy can cope with one small girl. *With a name. With her picture in the paper.* Everybody becomes her parents in the most haunting and unabashed sentimentality. Men cried in their offices, unashamed: "We didn't save her, after all," they said one to another.

"*We!*" A thousand miles from the scene. But there in that hole every minute all day. Breathless for air. Hungry for food. Frightened to death. And saying, in the end: "*We* couldn't save her!" It is the best thing about the human race: to be able to say "We." But the worst thing, too. Or why should eight and a half million children down a hole be forgotten before the page is turned?

Even our painter forgetting them.

He wrote a book called *Painting for a Pastime* in which he said that whenever he looked at a wall or a flat surface he always amused himself by trying to see how many delicate tints and colors he could distinguish, asking himself: did they come as reflections or from natural hues? But he never wrote a word about eight and a half million facing the flat surface of their home in a hole; rain-soaked, smoke-charred, blistered from bombing.

He put it down in black and white that pigments were nice stuff to handle, "*if it does not retaliate!*" As if it could fight back, when it got good and tired of a hole in the ground, biting the hand that fed it all that drab paint. But he closed by adding that when he gets to heaven he plans to spend his first million years painting with a much gayer palette than he used on earth—orange and vermilion would be his dullest shades thereafter; and beyond them a dizzy riot of tantalizing tints to tease his *"celestial eye,"* etc., etc. But God requires of men on earth a "terrestrial eye"; and suggested to another writer that he paint a picture for a religious man to pay attention to:

"So I returned, and considered all the oppressions that are done under the sun: and behold the tears of such as were oppressed, and they had no comforter; and on the side of their oppressors there was power; but they had no comforter. Wherefore I praised the dead more than the living which are yet alive" (Ecclesiastes 4:1, 2).

Those eight and a half million living, whom—by the stroke of a brush, by the stroke of a pen—the painter had authorized to be moved in any old boxcars from one part of Europe to some other part of Germany, dumping them into any old hole of any old landscape. Such an incredible thing for a comfortable man to do. Especially one anticipating the penetrating pleasures of a "celestial eye" through aeons and aeons of eternity.

Or consider the comfortable man who plays the piano. He spent almost three years, recently, making his comfortable house more comfortable, until he could feel proud of 1600 Pennsylvania Avenue. Now musicians, of course, are sensitive souls; and he was especially sensitive when a certain critic wrote a certain piece for the newspapers saying that the daughter of this pianist did not strike him as much of a singer. Instantly this comfortable man sat down at his comfortable desk and took pen in hand to lambast this miserable critic for daring to make his comfortable daughter uncomfortable. Yet with the same kind of stroke of the same kind of pen he himself signed away all possible comfort for eight and a half other million other uncomfortable daughters and their parents and their grandparents from that day forth and forever.

It may be all very well to play "Home Sweet Home" on his own comfortable piano. But what song is he teaching all those eight and a half million voices to sing in their discomfort? And if he doesn't happen to like the way they sing, would he dare to criticize . . . remembering how fathers are; for in eight and a half million people there might be a million irritated fathers to rise up against him. Or are they rising, anyhow?

One way to gauge the magnitude of that earlier stroke of his pen is to imagine his signing a mandate that all of Manhattan, New York, must be moved tomorrow morning out to Manhattan, Kansas.

Manhattan, New York, would rise up in wrath: "But you can't do that. There are eight and a half million of us!"

"I know that perfectly well. And I *can* move you! By the stroke of this pen I have made it an Agreement. Get ready to leave at once!"

This bitter exodus would begin in the twinkling of an eye. Too much must be left behind. Too little could be carried by hand. Every inch of the journey westward in boxcars could cause new indignation to rise, new fierceness to fester.

And Manhattan, Kansas, could become suddenly thick with tragedy, too: "But, Mr. President, we are only eighteen thousand souls in this town! How can we ever take in eight and a half million refugees? And have you forgotten our floods these past summers? The mud is barely swept from our cellars—our walls are too discolored to be decent, so how can we ever cope with a mob of complaining newcomers?"

"You can and you must cope! I have signed the ultimatum."

"But why do you do it, Mr. President? There's no earthly logic in it!"

"There is every earthly logic in it! Aren't both of your names 'Manhattan'? Very well, what could be more rational than putting you two together?"

What indeed?

Except that nobody could sing "Home, Sweet Home" any more; "how shall we sing the Lord's song in a strange land? By the flood waters of Kansas we sat down and wept when we remembered Manhattan, New York, and the Hudson. We hanged our harps on the Kansas willow trees, and complained bitterly: they that carried us away have required of us a song, and they that wasted us required of us mirth, saying: Sing us one of your songs from the east . . ."

But suppose they should go even farther east than the comfortable man from the comfortable house at 1600 Pennsylvania Avenue had intended; suppose they should adopt the chant of the Villain of this piece, and in their mounting bitterness could only be consoled by shouting, shoulder to shoulder:

> Arise, ye prisoners of starvation,
> Arise, ye wretched of the earth,
> For justice thunders condemnation,
> A better world's in birth.
> No more tradition's chains shall bind us,
> Arise, you slaves, no more in thrall!
> The earth shall rise on new foundations,
> We have been naught, we shall be all.
> Toilers from shops and fields united,
> The union, we, of all who work;
> The earth belongs to us, the workers,
> No room here for those who shirk,
> How many on our flesh have battened!
> But if some noisome birds of prey
> Shall vanish from the sky some morning
> The blessed sunshine still will stay.
> 'Tis the last final conflict,
> Stand each one in his place!
> The International Soviet
> Shall save the human race!

The comfortable pianist would wring his hands uncomfortably, and call Long Distance across the Atlantic to the comfortable painter: "The people are out of hand! But how could we have foreseen this calamity?" And the comfortable painter would look down the hole in his charming landscape for the first time, where eight and a half million people were milling around, facing rain-soaked walls and charred timbers, singing the same mad song; and he would shout across the Atlantic: "Well, we only did it because Josef Vissarionovich Dzhugashvili wanted retaliation for what the Nazis had done to him. How it must please him all over again, to see that now we too are the ones being hated. How it must please him!"

And of course it did please the third comfortable man very much. In 1945 it had been a lovely little plan to get rid of eight and a half million bothersome people from countries he had just gobbled up. This meant a lot of extra space for his own poor devils to move into. And now, of course, he seemed to be growing popular with all those displaced persons. Well! Well! how uncomfortable they must be! And his eyes would sweep around the comfortable palace where he lived. It was, indeed, an immense place to sweep! For nowhere else on earth is there a more stunning sight than Red Square with its mile and a half of brick walls—twelve feet thick, sixty-five feet high, spaced at intervals by high towers, each roofed with brillant green tiles. Inside those beautiful old pink walls, built back in the days of Columbus, stand several imposing cathedrals, great imperial palaces, many monasteries, convents, and so forth. Compared to such ancient magnificence, 10 Downing Street and 1600 Pennsylvania Avenue seem almost like simple summer cottages-by-the-sea.

One of the five great entrances into the Kremlin used to be called "The Spassky Gate"—The Saviour's Gate; with a sacred picture of Christ placed there in the year 1647; and until the Russian Revolution any man who walked through that gate had to remove his hat. But now, of course, this third comfortable man had long since forgotten that he himself ever intended to be a priest; and the picture of Christ has long since been taken down; and the compassion of the Saviour for those in tragic tribulation has long since stopped troubling Joseph Stalin, just as the beauty of sound had stopped pleasing his predecessor, for it was Lenin who said: "I can't listen to music too often. It upsets your nerves, and makes you say stupid nice things, and stroke the heads of people who create such beauty. But now you mustn't stroke anyone's head, you might get your hand bitten off. You have to hit them on the head." (Mr. Winston Churchill, painter, please take notice.)

Perhaps that was why Stalin had liked signing the Potsdam Agreement. By the strokes of three pens three comfortable men reduced the territory of Germany and swapped immense populations almost overnight . . . people herded like cattle into boxcars or wagons, dumped at journey's end into this reduced territory of Germany, crammed into cities which were already rubble, to share houses which had no roofs with people who had no food, no room, no patience. Never before had three such comfortable men made any blot in history more barbarous or brutal. And why were these particular people uprooted and expelled? For a reason no more reasonable than the sudden moving of Manhattan, New York, into Manhattan, Kansas, would be! For it was *name* only that was used as the excuse: these people in the new countries Stalin had seized were Germans; therefore, they belonged in Germany. But any possible connection with Germany was often over three hundred years old: some great-great-great-grandfather who had moved into Poland or Czechoslovakia, perhaps. But an ancestor nobody knew. With a language none of his descendants could speak. There was the extra tragedy that whole groups of these new Protestant refugees were pushed ruthlessly into areas of Germany which were wholly Catholic—and vice versa; so that even the solace of familiar worship was denied in this living agony which went on and on; and still continues. Children running wild, joining juvenile gangs; family life deteriorating from the friction of overcrowding; morals desperately loose.

But it was Thomas Jefferson who said once that *"it is part of the American character to consider nothing desperate!"*

Therefore, if this chapter seems like a nightmare there are always other pens and other comfortable people with more conscience, and—by now—more perspective, on the international scene. Nobody needs to be a painter to deal promptly with this landscape. Nobody needs to be a pianist to change the tune. But everybody does need to be a priest, and not quit before taking orders.

For where is the Protestant who does not prize the phrase "the priesthood of every believer"? Where is the Protestant who has not always known that Christianity is simply a Spassky Gate through which he comes and goes, removing his hat in reverence; and, for the Saviour's sake, seeing in all forgotten men His beloved face, His beloved form? Doing for Him, belatedly, each and every compassionate deed which three comfortable men forgot. Learning to say *"We"* even at long distance from that landscape: *"We* got little Kathy out of that hole in time, thank goodness!"

We!

We . . . and Church World Service!

For Church World Service has become the uncomfortable conscience of the world at work in Europe with loving-kindness: undoing past misdeeds by maintaining necessary welfare and resettlement services, distributing relief materials provided by aroused Christians everywhere—food, clothing, medicine, shelter. Limited, alas! by the stroke of your pen. For even as you sign your name, the God whose eyes go to and fro across every landscape, is reading the stubs of the checkbook to see how warmly you are saying: "*We!*"

GREAT POWERS CONFERENCE

The blind men add the figures, draw the maps.
The deaf men blow the bugles, beat the drums.
And peace becomes a wavering perhaps,
And war a tidal wave that goes and comes.
The legless men march forward to success,
The armless men cry: "Victory within reach!"
And life becomes a length of more or less,
With sure uncertainty for all and each.
The men without a heart dispense relief,
The mindless men devise the master plan.
The perfect government ensues, in brief
The Commonwealth of Man without the man.

Edith Lovejoy Pierce, from *Wind Has No Home*

Suppose some brother or sister is ill-clad and short of daily food; if any of you tells them, "Depart in peace! Get warm, get food," without supplying their bodily needs, what use is that? So faith, unless it has deeds, is dead in itself. Someone will object, "And you claim to have faith!" Yes, and I claim to have deeds as well; you show me your faith without any deeds, and I will show you by my deeds what faith is! You believe in one God? Well and good. So do the devils, and they shudder. But will you understand, you senseless fellow, that faith without deeds is dead?

James 2:15-20, Moffatt translation

25

NOT EVEN GRANDMA MOSES COULD PAINT
SIX SUCH SKIES WITH ONE BRUSH

Where there is heart room, there is hearth room.
OLD GAELIC SAYING

There is, of course, nobody quite like her. But not even Grandma Moses could paint six such skies with one brush as she usually does in her pictures: *"that way,"* she says, "you save paint!" But even though she was brought up on a dairy farm in Vermont, she could not possibly cope with the six skies over Ethar Milliken's dairy farm in Maine at one stroke—from one dip of blue! For some of the skies would be too red, and some too gray, and some too black. But how lovely to turn the delightful old lady loose on the scenes of his childhood: for, man and boy, he has lived in Kennebunkport, where this entire story took place.

Now that Grandma Moses has become everybody's darling, the thing to acknowledge is that all she actually does is to paint things that make all the rest of us homesick; for instantly we think to ourselves: America used to be just like that! And we wish to goodness that it could all come true again—even to this lump in our throat, this tear in our eye, this tenderness in our heart. But good as Grandma Moses is, Ethar Milliken can go one better! For he makes all those homespun, warmhearted, everyday, sensible scenes come literally true for dozens of homeless people on this heartless earth. Until he is more than a lump in the throat, more than a tear in the eye, more than a tenderness in the heart. He is a practical dairy farmer with a pair of sensible hands; and so he simply did what Ornan did back in Old Testament days when King David wanted to buy Ornan's threshing-floor for a place of worship: "Take it!" said Ornan.

And: "Take it!" Ethar Milliken also said, eventually. But, before that day, let us set Grandma Moses to painting his six scenes. It is said that she has the most unorthodox way of beginning a picture— far down in the left-hand corner! Which causes other artists to hold their breath, wondering if she has any notion of how things are going to come out—for to begin at the center, and plan in balanced patterns, left and right, would seem so much safer. But since all her pictures turn out so utterly safe, and people dart through her scenes with lively briskness, let us trust Ethar Milliken to her care, and see what turns out . . . beginning down in that left-hand corner where she is painting in a crab apple tree with a yoke of oxen tied to the trunk, and the matchless Maine woods in the background of a rambling Maine farmhouse close to the road. Mr. Milliken will tell her, as he told us, that that was his first memory of this charming place. Plus the notion then and there, to own it some day! So that as this first picture spreads upward and right-ward, only Grandma Moses could manage to put in (somehow or other) the fact that he did buy that farm! that he did move in! that he married his schoolteacher! that her father on a near-by dairy farm invited the two of them to come on over to live in his house so that Mrs. Milliken could keep house for him, too . . . and, if they would come, then he would leave them his farm and his dairy, in his will. Which must all be conveyed in paint in one picture, to account for Mr. Milliken's owning two farms. You will realize, at once, with what a debonair flourish Grandma Moses could sweep all this in, on the one canvas—convincingly and adequately.

But scene two would be altogether different, done in violent scarlets and reds, vicious tongues of orange flame licking through the marvelous hemlocks and pines, with all the farmers dashing hither and yon, doing this or that in frantic haste—all to no avail. For the year would be 1947; and that fire was of historic propor-tions, as every newspaper in the country said in tall headlines: "TERRIBLE FOREST FIRES SWEEP MAINE WOODS." But how could you know, until Grandma Moses painted it, how ghastly and grotesque the blackened tree stumps would loom in the background? And how could you know that Ethar Milliken had dangerously over-exerted himself in the endless efforts to beat out those fires threatening his trees? And how could you know, unless Grandma Moses painted a cross section of his second farmhouse, that he would have to lie quietly on his back a whole year, to mend that tired heart and to lie there looking at his own gray ceiling?

Ceilings are none too companionable to stare at for a year. Too gray and too flat. Someone really ought to invent home movies to be shown on sickroom ceilings! But Ethar Milliken did not need *gadgets*—a missionary magazine was plenty good enough. For there was an article about refugees in Europe, millions of them—homeless, hopeless, hungry; herded into concentration camps, waiting for some country to offer them new homes and new jobs. But countries were slow; and offers were few. This was all the movie Mr. Milliken had! But he played it and played it, back and forth across his ceiling. Their misery. Human beings like himself. Decent farmers like himself, without farms. Without *hope* of farms.

It was then, of course, that his other farm began to flicker and beckon across his ceiling.

Maine farmers do not do dramatic things. They are quiet, law-abiding conservative men—of course they do dreadfully dramatic things when disaster sweeps through the Maine woods. But for a farmer to lie in bed and see on the ceiling a lot of refuges crossing the Atlantic Ocean for no other purpose than to live under the roof of his other farmhouse, *that* is totally thrilling stuff for a farmer to dream up. But he liked it so well that he asked Mrs. Milliken what she thought of it.

And she thought well of it!

Only Grandma Moses would know how to do that dramatic decision in her lovely undramatic homespun way: the quiet Millikens of Kennebunkport, Maine, thinking yes! Why NOT reach across the Atlantic and fill up their empty farmhouse? Seemed like sheer common sense, any way you looked at it!

The next picture certainly ought to be the Europe of the refugees. And one supposes that Grandma Moses would be hard put to it to know how to make it hopeless enough, overcrowded enough, with hairbreadth escapes from occupied lands—often right under the noses of dreadful guards at the frontiers. Often in boxcars, crowded like sardines, with no water, no food, no privacy, no sanitation. And sometimes no engine! The boxcar waiting on some siding, day after day. The forlorn passengers collecting roots for a thin soup. Begging food from villages which themselves had no food.

The old lady might well say: "Look here! I'm ninety-one, and in all my born days I never heard tell of such goings-on! You quite sure of your facts, Mr. Milliken?"

And he would be quite sure! He would show pictures of a room where sixty refugees slept; a blanket on a sagging cord the only partition from all the next-door families.

" 'Taint decent!" the old lady would say sharply, and dab on more misery, more queued up with tin soup bowls, waiting for more refugee soup. " 'Taint wholesome!" she would say sourly, looking into that mammoth kettle with such watery measly stuff floating around it: "Fit to turn a decent person's stomach!" she would surely add.

All of which meant that by contrast the next scene became gay and giddy with the kind of action she understood best. There might be a corner showing Mr. Milliken offering his farmhouse to two big Boston churches, in the hope that they would want to sponsor the project (but they turned him down) and in the end it was the Baptist State Convention of Maine that decided, yes! they would love to make such a glorious share of the Kingdom of God come true in the state of Maine. So then the beautiful excitment began—the sound of the scrubbing brush heard all over Ethar Milliken's Freedom Farm; the sweet smell of soapsuds; the aromatic smell of paint; the swish of paper-hangers (who were simply Kennebunkport housewives in kitchen aprons), a riotous hammering up on the roof where Baptist parsons were replacing shingles, looking on a Monday, in overalls, as they never looked on a Sunday; in their pulpits. Neighbors with sewing machines ran up curtains. Neighbors with pantries brought over jams and preserves to line the shelves for the refugees. Baptist young people of the state said a farm was not a farm without horses . . . so Grandma

Moses would please oblige by hitching both of those they bought
to a tree, or in the barn, as seemed best. These same young Baptists
of the state knew there ought to be cows on the landscape. So they
collected enough funds to buy two. Laymen hung heavy winter
clothing in the clothespresses. Women's missionary organizations
made sure that there was warm clothing for women and children,
too. From Kittery to Caribou, food and furnishings and farm
equipment poured into Freedom Farm—everything from goats and
chickens to bedsprings.

And then the three Parnas came! Ants and Agnes, from Estonia,
with their little daughter, Lembi, who had almost lost her sight
from malnutrition in the camps abroad, where the only food had
been a constant serving of ungarnished oatmeal, oatmeal, oatmeal—as thick and rubbery as glue. All of this after their forty
days' escape across Europe in a boxcar, with no food but raw po-
tatoes. To the three of them the cleaned scrubbed farmhouse was
a fairy-tale bit of sheer enchantment . . . Mrs. Parna walking
around the eleven rooms and managing to say in English: "Is nice!
Is nice!"

Then later Mr. and Mrs. Wassily Gontschar from Ukrainia. Mr.
and Mrs. Mykola Wolotschaj of Poland, with their son, Ivan.
Surely only Grandma Moses could make those strong and radiant
Slavic faces seem to say the things they did say: "People all so
good! So good!" And Mr. Gontschar, sighing: "Here is very nice.
Have never been so nice as here!" All told, more than twenty-eight
of these displaced persons from overseas have come to live in this
rambling old farmhouse, built back in the days when tall sailing
ships and hardy sea captains carried the name of Kennebunkport
to every corner of the earth. But Grandma Moses would wonder if
any commodity had ever been quite so thrilling as this work-bee of
the neighbors and this gratitude of the newcomers! She would
have the time of her life painting their first Christmas—each family
going off to the woods to cut down and bring back its own tree for
its own celebration. Probably the old lady would ask Ethar Milliken what he would like to do *now*? To which he might say to her,
as he did to us: "I wish all twenty-eight were where I could put
my arms around them all!"

And this only Grandma Moses could do—making it seem quite possible for one pair of arms to encircle even those who had moved off to fine jobs and safe dwelling places: with blue skies from her paintbrush! And that special American lump in American throats, which carries us back to our homespun past when this kind of hospitality was the kind of thing we did best . . .

But are there really no other old ladies in this big land with paintbrushes poised to reproduce this same vigorous scene in the place where *they* live? Are there no other scrubbing brushes ready to make spotless some *other* idle farm in some other state? Is there no other Ethar Milliken with such a rich love for Jesus Christ that he sees in every stranger a friend in need of a roof and a bed and a meal? For it was Robert Browning who wrote:

> We're made so that we love
> First when we see them painted, things we have passed
> Perhaps a hundred times, nor cared to see:
> And so they are better painted—better to us,
> Which is the same thing. Art was given for that;
> God uses us to help each other so,
> Lending our minds out.

So we lend you the mind of Ethar Milliken, pro tem, now that you have seen him painted. For you may not have a farm, or furniture, or even funds—but surely you are not such a nonentity that you have no friends to stir up! Someone who may *have* a farm to connect up with someone who *has* funds, so that other State Conventions can be prodded into reproducing all of Grandma Moses' blue skies over all of Ethar Milliken's kind of new friends. We lend you his mind! For the scene is reproducible in any corner of any map!

> *Come, I will make the continent indissoluble.*
> *I will make the most splendid race the sun ever shone upon,*
> *I will make divine magnetic lands,*
> *With the love of comrades, with the life-long love of comrades.*

*I will plant companionship thick as trees along all the rivers
   of America.
And along the shores of the great lakes, and all over the
   prairies,
I will make inseparable cities with their arms about each
   other's necks,
By the love of comrades, by the manly love of comrades.*

Walt Whitman

*He is base—and that is the one base thing in the universe—to
receive favors and render none. The benefit we receive must
be rendered again, line for line, deed for deed, cent for cent,
to somebody. Beware of too much good staying in your hand.
Pay it away quickly in some sort.*

Ralph Waldo Emerson

26

NEW BABES IN OLD WOODS

So many times history does repeat itself. Its worst self! Once before, it had been a man named Moses who had led the children of
Israel out from a place of desperate danger toward the Promised
Land. But this time, three thousand years later, the name of the
new emancipator was Jacob, and he led his little flock of one
hundred and eighty children through ten thousand miles of terrible
trouble in the most unexpected fashion. He had supposed an hour
would do! But it took all of three years. And actually is not ended
yet, for some of them.

The Bible takes us step by step through all the mounting reluctance which Moses felt when God first called him to take up just
such leadership. But Jacob Tobiasch had literally no time to hesi-
tate on that horrible June morning in 1941 when, out of the clear
blue, the Nazis began pouring down bombs on the city in Soviet
Poland where Mr. Tobiasch was spending his vacation.

It may have been because he was a schoolteacher that, the moment the bombs began falling, he began wondering about what was happening to a summer camp for children not far from where he was staying. Whatever "call" God sent him, therefore, he certainly answered at once, by going straight to the camp directors and offering his services. They decided that the quickest but most important thing he could do for them was to escort certain of the children on the short train ride back to their parents. An hour would see the job done.

You may have had entire care of one hundred and eighty children on a train at some time in your own life. If so, you will know how distracting it can be at the best of times to count noses, count tickets, count baggage, count money, count questions, and on this particular ride, count *stops*. Those sickening jerks every ten minutes or so, when the train would lurch to a standstill; with the thud of enemy planes to be heard overhead, and everybody's heart beating faster, and everybody's eyes on Mr. Tobiasch: was this strange new gentleman worried? Was he going to fix everything all right in the same brisk way he began?

It was soon plain that he could fix nothing. For a whole stretch of track suddenly blew sky-high just ahead of them, stopping the train completely. With one hundred and eighty children at his heels, still counting noses and still counting chances to get his charges home some longer way around, Mr. Tobiasch started off across meadows. But more bombings, more crashes, more holes opening in the earth at their feet meant further detours until his one hour of escort had lengthened into ten, then twelve. And the first thing the poor man knew, days later, he and all his charges had detoured way up into Russia itself.

Because these Polish children were from a Soviet portion of Poland, Russian policemen were friendly enough to pile them on trains leading into greater safety; but after a whole month of changing cars and riding farther each day, Mr. Tobiasch was surprised to reach Siberia; and it was August.

He counted noses again. Still one hundred and eighty! He breathed a sigh of relief, for it is curious business to offer an hour's service and see it stretch into two months. But obviously there was still more of such stretching ahead; and he settled down for the duration of the war in a colony near Lake Baikal. Russian peasant women brought milk and butter every day from near-by farms; for anybody could see that one hundred and eighty children would certainly get hungry, with only one poor man to look after them— and he in no way related to a single child.

The Soviet authorities offered to let the children go to school in town. But as the war went on, year after year after year, Mr. Tobiasch was unhappy to notice that all his little Poles were talking Russian all day long, and forgetting their own language. "This will never do!" he decided, and talked nothing but Polish to them himself; putting them to bed with Polish folk tales sounding in their ears, and the Polish words *"Do branco"* their necessary way to say *"Good night."*

He picked out all the choicest Polish proverbs to create pride in their past—"God has given all to all, and not all to one." "Who hasn't seen a church, bows before a fireplace." "God gives the wideness of the mouth according to the bigness of the spoon." "We cannot divide beauty into money." It was a good day for him if any of his one hundred and eighty children quoted one of them back at him; like the child willing at last to go to church, and using the old Polish proverb: "In want we learn to pray!"

This Siberian life went on for three years. Then the war was over. Poland was freed. Whereupon there were certain wonderful Wednesdays every week when letters would come by mail. But at once it was painfully clear that not a single Jewish child was ever receiving a letter. All his other little Poles would be dancing around on both feet in wild excitement over news from home; all his little Jews standing stockstill, feet rooted on the post office floor. Sometimes he caught them pretending that old letters from 1941 had just come.

No matter how much your hat has been off to Mr. Tobiasch up to this point, from now on you will probably want to hold it reverently in your hand out of sheer respect. For this man who had supposed he was taking one hundred and eighty children on an hour's ride, and had now had them on his hands over three years, arranged to take his fifty-six forlorn Jewish children back to Poland, the other boys and girls being claimed by their own families.

So with fifty-six miserable children at his heels they went to all the Jewish homes in their town in Poland. Not a single parent or relative was left. Moreover, Jacob Tobiasch made the heartbreaking discovery that his own children and his wife had also died in Nazi gas chambers.

At this, with a swift embrace, he managed to enfold all his fifty-six orphans: "*You* are my family!" he cried, and tried to console himself. But since there was no longer any spot in Europe where they would not need to go wandering from one refugee camp to another, he decided to take them all with him to the Promised Land, where the Jews of the whole world were gathering to make a new Hebrew homeland.

But this was another terrifying trip. Eight weeks to get from Poland to Paris, still counting noses, counting money, counting miles. Quite literally he saw that he was turning himself into a half-forgotten Polish saying: "To believe with certainty, we must begin with doubting." But finally from Paris he collected enough cash and enough official permissions to get his fifty-six charges down to Rome. Here it seemed sensible to have them learn farming, now that their new life in Palestine would be entirely agricultural.

"Has Poland an old maxim to fit farming, too?" a Jewish boy asked one morning, as he tried to learn the difference between spades and ploughshares.

Jacob Tobiasch laughed heartily and brought out of his memory the proper national quotation: "God will help a ploughing man!"

By this time, of course, his new babes are in old woods: but no longer lost. If indeed they were ever lost, with someone so resourceful to set their imagination working.

❦

PHANCIE PUT METALL
INTO THEIR LEGGES

A Gentilmanne, having led a Companie of children beyond their usual Journeye, they began to wearie & joyntly cryed unto him to carrie them, which because of their Multitude he cd. not do, but told them he wd. provide them Horses to ride on. Then, cutting lyttel Wands out of ye Hedge as Nagges for them, & a great Stake as a Gelding for himselve, thus

mounted, Phancie put Metall into their Legges, & they rode
cheerfullie Home.

From an old English document

27

WARMER WEATHER FOR THE WOODEN

WEDDING

People used to say in Amsterdam: "Do look quickly! There goes
that wonderful Dutch couple who rescued all those Jewish
orphans!"

They were well worth looking at. But what happened right
after their wedding five years earlier, sounded like something out
of this world. Our world, anyhow. Our safe, sane world: where a
theolog, all set to sail on a wedding journey to Java with a bride,
sails! Where the words "for better for worse; for richer for poorer;
in sickness and in health" get said about some dim and distant date,
but are never expected to be tested on almost the same day. But
you may recall how quickly Hitler dashed his armies across
Europe? In no time at all Belgium was lost, then Holland was lost.
The Gestapo moved in, and everybody else moved into an underground movement, so that any groom gave up at once all thought
of going places with his bride, remaining literally "frozen" in the
Netherlands for the duration. But not necessarily icebound and
frigid.

For when you met them and asked: "How was it, anyhow? And
what on earth is this I hear about rescuing Jewish orphans? How
did you ever happen to begin?"

She folded her hands reminiscently and smiled at Hans: "Well,
like this. Hans und I just married, not so long. But we could not sail
for mission work in Java; nay. Nothing doing in Netherlands,
neither. So one day we walk down street, und I poke Hans on the

arm as we pass little alley—you know these little dark crooked not-so-wide alley, down town in Amsterdam? Well, I say to Hans: 'I saw little Christ-Child run into this alley!' So then we better go in, too; und what we find is little bit of Jewish boy crying soft, like his heart would break in two. So tiny he was; not even so high up as my hip. 'Where is mother?' I ask him. But he say he no can tell now, for men came und took her off in big wagon. So I stoop down und put arms around him, und say: 'How you like be my little boy, now?' Und he say: 'O.K.!' Only in the Dutch language, you understand!"

Smiling over this memory, she added: "But if anybody had told me, then, that this would be first of 450 Jewish orphans Hans und I would adopt, I would not believe him!"

You did not believe her, yourself, of course! You decided she must have meant four or five orphans. But she cried out excitedly: "Nay! Nay! I mean four-five-o orphans!" and wrote it down on a piece of paper—450, as plain as day.

"But that is so many!" you gasped.

"Ja!" she echoed. "It is so many!"

"But where in the world did you hide them? I understand the Nazis forbade anybody to hide even one Jew; so how could you conceal so many noisy children, and where did you find them?"

"Ja, first we must go find them. Und this is easy. Maybe one day it as if God say: 'Railroad station!' So we go there und look maybe under bench. Ja! there is little Jewish child, hiding. Or maybe we just look in any alley; often we could find little child, very easy. So! One by one, we find them. But then one by one we must find new home, new mother; und this is not so easy. You know how Holland look—nice flat green meadow, blue canal, maybe? With cows, maybe? With windmill, maybe? With farmhouse, maybe? Well, I must take little Jewish child by hand and go knock. Comes the farmer's wife to the door. I must say: 'Look—it is the little Christ-Child in need of room once more.' Real quick she say: 'Nay! Nay! Cannot feed another mouth under this roof—those Nazis they have stolen all the foodstuffs, all the cows, all the bedding, all the seeds for the spring planting, all the clothes. Nay! Nay! cannot take another hungry one!' So then I must look sternly at this woman:

'But can you say again to little Christ-Child: 'No room? No room?'
And when she looked down at little Jewish orphan, she find she
cannot harden the heart. So, one by one, we place somewhere each
child we find. But it was hard work."

You began to admire her more than ever: "Terrific!" was the
word you chose. "Colossal!" came a little later. Then you asked
curiously: "Didn't it almost stagger you, at times?"

She pointed to her husband: "Please look at Hans. He did it with
his head!"

You looked at Hans's head; a crew cut, high cheekbones, clear
blue eyes: "What am I supposed to see?" you asked naïvely.

"In his head my Hans he must remember all the names of all his
450 Jewish orphans. Never must he write them in list on paper, for
fear Gestapo find this list. So in the head is only safe place for
names."

"Oh my!" you gasped; wondering if you yourself had ever known
450 persons by name.

"It is too soon to say 'Oh my!' For my poor Hans, he must also
keep in his head the 450 names of these 450 new foster mothers!"

"Oh my!" you sighed, for now the count was suddenly 900 names
to remember; and you looked at Hans's head with even greater
respect.

"Still it is too soon to say: 'Oh my!' For he must also keep in his
head the 450 *addresses* of these 450 foster mothers."

"Oh my! Oh my! Oh my!" you groaned, as if you could never
stop.

"Ja!" she boasted. "Ja! Und why must Hans keep all these names
in his head? Because in Holland we had two ration books each
month; for how could any little orphan eat unless my Hans give
foster mother new ration book twice a month? Und I must tell you,
each time each book cost $50 in your money."

"But my dear girl, that would be $100 per child; or $45,000 for all
of them, each month! I can't think where you found any such
staggering sums of money every month."

"Now *that!* That one was the only easy thing. You see, we had
Christian printer in Resistance Movement!"

She waited triumphantly for this marvel to sink in; but you

asked in a still small voice: "You aren't implying that he forged 450 ration books twice a month, are you?"

"Sure! Why not?"

"But *forging?* Isn't that dreadfully . . . well, at least, we have always been taught . . . good gracious, over in America we have been brought up to think . . ."

She watched you flounder, with surprise; and then looked you straight in the eye to ask bluntly: "So you wouldn't forge to force a cruel enemy to keep all those hundreds of little *Christ-Childs* alive?"

The weight of the entire 450 was suddenly around your neck like a millstone. Biblically! And you astonished yourself by saying: "Oh, but I could! Indeed, I could!"

"Ja, I should hope so!" She nodded. "For always you pray, when you go look for this little lost child. Then you find him, and you pray some more. By and by, you must pray: 'God, make this hard woman give this little boy houseroom!' Then next you must pray, night after night: 'Lord God, let not the enemy find this little boy, ever!' So when you do all this, how could it not be right feeding him in the only way left in Holland, all that time when we are all so terribly hungry?"

In the middle of this spiritual adventure, a short silence fell, as you realized with a sharp sense of reverence that you had never known two persons who undertook such a stupendous task all of their own accord, unrequested; right on top of a wedding, with neither salary, committee, nor denominational funds behind them. Just the Spirit of God making them dare each new danger. "But were you never caught?" you asked.

"Ja! Oh Ja! Which one shall we tell her, Hans?"

"How about when they kicked me out?" Hans suggested.

"Ja, that was very good, that one! Like this—maybe you know that in wartime you must walk on the street very carefully, with Gestapo everywhere. You come to street corner. You should wait for somebody to come round that corner safely. Then you say: 'Please, are *they* there?' Should he answer 'Nay!' then you just believe him, und go around the corner. But this time when we believe stranger, we go around the corner straight into police. They pull

Hans to Gestapo headquarters. That big officer who sits by the desk, the one with epaulets on the shoulders, *that one,* he yell at my Hans: 'You this fellow hiding Jewish kids?' Hans opens his eyes very wide und blue, und says, innocent-like: 'Who, me? But I am so young!' "

A sudden panic came over you and you said to this lovely serene girl: "Imagine standing there and seeing Hans in danger! What on earth did you do?"

She clasped her hands symbolically: "I closed my eyes. I prayed: 'Father in Heaven, could you please make Hans look younger and dumber than this'!"

"But could God possibly do it?" you asked, for Hans is so highly intelligent.

"Ja! Ja! Right off God did it. For Hans had the good idea, why not drop the lower jaw way, way down—Hans, show the lady! See, how stupid he looks, like idiot? that man by the desk, he shouted: 'Kick him out! He's crazy!' So they kick Hans out on the sidewalk—isn't God *wonderful?*"

"Isn't he?" you agreed.

But now that the year of their *tin* wedding draws near, now that the world is again a puzzling place, now that nobody trusts anybody around any street corner anywhere on earth, *now* you hope that wherever this wonderful couple are, they may have a child of their own growing up: a literal copybook of all their valor. For whenever you think of them you quote Shakespeare:

> O brave new world
> That has such people in it!

And it is your prayer that their tribe may increase.

"Would to God" is the mother of all prayer.
                                        Dutch proverb
Do small things like big ones, because the majesty of Jesus Christ is in us, Who lives our life, and the big ones like small and easy ones, because of His omnipotence.
                                        Blaise Pascal

28

THE GREAT GRAB

There never was a grab like it in the history of man. It was unbelievable, staggering, depressing! Yet, if the man himself had not said that the grab could take place, it would never have occurred; at least, not on such an overwhelming scale. One by one, perhaps, the things might have disappeared just as they had been disappearing for four years—black feet would tiptoe secretly into the hut, and black hands would close covetously on a much-envied object: but that was theft, and everyone knew it; whereas this other greater grab the man himself permitted—it was unbelievable, staggering, amusing. How people laughed! Long and low and guttural, at first; then in high glee. The little stars winked down in sheer surprise. Had such very special laughing ever risen from that jungle village in all the history of man? Never!

You will be wanting to know all about it, for there is wonder in it, and dismay, and glee, and a happy ending. Moreover, every bit of it actually happened.

When he first came, he was better than a circus would be to you, like a continuous side show to the people in that village on the Congo.

"What a lot of trouble he is to himself!" everybody thought, for he was surrounded by the most peculiar set of objects. Not a person in that village could guess what anything was. Surely this man was foolish above all men, for he took a little stick with stiff bristles on one end, and with these bristles and some water he scrubbed his teeth. The very babies gurgled over such absurdity.

"He must be very proud of his teeth!" people chuckled, nudging one another. But by and by it was whispered in awe: "He has gold teeth. Not all. But some!"

Now nobody in all that tribe had ever had a gold tooth. People stopped laughing at the stick-with-bristles. They accepted it as necessary for the proper respect due to precious gold teeth. But although they accepted the toothbrush, there were still the hundred and one other queer belongings. For instance, he sat on specially prepared pieces of wood, raised up in the air on legs.

"As if the ground weren't made to sit on," people said, their eyebrows raised.

"It is those tight pieces of cloth he puts his legs into! Can a man sit just *anywhere* when his body is sheathed in such stuff as he wears?"

In fact, his clothes caused talk for a whole year. Shoes, for instance. What atrocities they were! Why should any sensible mortal want to wedge five toes into one big round leather toe—stiff and tight and airless?

The only possible answer was: His feet are white. White feet must be very soft and tender. White bodies must be very sensitive, they evidently needed all sorts of nonsensical things: clothes, peculiar sticks of wood to sleep on—for a bed was the prize surprise, there was so much trouble to it! The funny legs, the queer mattress, the punchable pillows, the white sheets. All absolutely unbelievable, except, of course, that one could see and feel and handle with one's own eyes and hands. Or even steal these unbelievable things, when fortunate enough to succeed.

Here then was a man who was a great deal of trouble to himself. But otherwise quite harmless. He seemed to have come to live among them forever. Also, he seemed to have no other purpose than to talk.

Well, talk was a good thing. There was always plenty of time to sit in circles around him on the ground and let him talk. But their eyes were busy with his belongings. So that for a long time his talk went in one ear and out the other. They would interrupt him frequently with their deep questions:

"Are you really white all over?"

"Can a black man grow gold teeth?"

All this time the man talked. It was good talking. About someone called God the Father. It took four years to tell them over and over how God the Father said, "Don't do this!" and "Don't do that!"

They always nodded their black heads at the appropriate times: yes, this was a good talking. Yes, this was a wise talking. Yes, they had no doubt that it was all true. But the man became discouraged when he saw that they kept right on being the same kind of people —black feet still crept on tiptoe into his hut, black hands still closed covetously around much envied objects, in spite of that well-known "Don't" of God the Father: "Thou shalt not steal."

The Man began to think. He thought very hard. He decided that "Don't" is a very cold part of the Bible; he decided that there was something warmer in it—the warmth of the Lord Jesus Christ to whom little children ran gladly, and for whom great men had left profitable businesses to give back dishonestly earned gain.

"I will try love on them," he said. And so, after four years of "Don't," he began that very day with the really fascinating book of Luke. Every day he translated twelve verses into the dialect of that tribe, and the black people sat in circles on the ground around him listening with the first interest they had ever shown, for these stories were very real. All about a baby—shepherds—presents. These were things a person liked.

All went well, therefore, until one day the man came to the sixth chapter and the thirtieth verse of that chapter. Put yourself in his place and see if you would want to read it to such a circle of listeners: "Give to every man that asketh of thee; and of him that taketh away thy goods ask them not again."

How dared he translate those words? Would not all the feet that had stealthily crept into his hut, now come openly and—grab? Of course, he dared not translate. Moreover, he felt sure that God would understand why he skipped that verse. He would know that his missionaries needed proper equipment to carry on the work, and sufficient simple comforts to keep them well and strong. Of course it was only right to omit the thirtieth verse.

But you know how it is with us; there's that something inside that talks back at us. And conscience began to talk back at the man: what business had he to decide what to skip and what not to skip? Was it not all God's Word? It took him days and days—I think he probably had review lessons to pass away the time while he debated—debated. The terrible indecision!

But there came a day when he stood in the usual spot with the usual crowd around him, and on the amazed ears of those listening people fell the thrilling words: "Give to every man that asketh of thee," etc.

If the man's heart beat faster than usual, consider how theirs beat! The bliss of it! The wild bliss! Would he never stop talking? For nobody was listening now; there was that momentous question to decide; what to take? What to take?

But when the Great Grab finally began, it was no longer a question of what to take, for everybody wanted everything, and the problem was to keep the thing you grabbed.

Picture it to yourself: the tropical sun beating down on palm trees, on bare black bodies bustling here and there, grabbing. See the strut of pride that young black brave displays as he sallies off with an umbrella, grinning from ear to ear. For of all things, an umbrella is the most laughable. In dry weather, a mere stick; in wet weather, behold it spread out its black branches like some strange palm tree! Hitherto in the rainy season, it had been sufficient to tear off a huge banana leaf and balance it on the head; what style, therefore, to carry this collapsible bit of magic! He held it tight—clasped in his arms, and no one could pry it loose, although there were many who tried.

The grab went merrily on.

There was a general rush for that comical little round gleaming thing with a white face, which ticked inside as a tiger's kitten purrs, and slowly moved its two black whiskers over its face. Impossible as it was to believe, it was with this thing that the man had been telling the time of day for four long years—no matter whether the sun rose visible or invisible. Now surely this was something to grab! It was grabbed! You would have thought it a Harvard-Yale football match, the way each new owner ran for home, tackled on all sides by rough hands, now tumbling down, now hurtling forward.

How tell of that congregation? Of the women who took boots for their bare feet? Handkerchiefs for their black noses? Spoons and forks—when hitherto fingers had been plenty good enough? How tell of the desperate pillow fights? The mattress match? The awful pom-pom-pull-away of which each chair became the center?

As for the bed, it was envied by whole families, who pummeled each other lustily over it; and the books—the food in tin cans—the dishes—the table—the pencils—who did not take what he could?

The Great Grab kept up for hours; and articles which belonged to one person one minute, belonged to another person another minute; for the muscles of some were better than the muscles of others. The girl who prinked into the mirror amazed at her own loveliness, prinked only a minute, for a warrior who needed to know how he looked as much as she, grabbed it from her. For the fiercer one's war paint, the more startled one's enemy.

Yes, the Great Grab went on.

Down every little forest trail the man saw his possessions disappearing in a whirl of flying arms and scurrying legs.

There never was a Bible verse so upsetting—so devastating. At nightfall he walked into his hut, and it was just a hut. Just a roof, like other roofs, thatched with palm leaves; woven walls; a floor. It held nothing else; nothing.

The man lay down to sleep that night, with nothing but the floor. Yet surely he remembered that when the Lord Jesus was here among men, He had no place to lay His head, either. But the loneliness of it seeped into his very bones. Feel his utter dismay. What was he to do now, dear God? What, indeed!

And all this time there was wild laughter in the other huts. The little stars winked down in sheer surprise. There was the family with the umbrella, bent nearly double with laughter as they did the simple trick which made a foolish stick spread its black branches in the air above them. The mattress family rolled on the mattress—bounced up and down—proved a hundred times how soft it was! How shockproof! They laughed and laughed.

The spoon family practiced eating; the fork family also. They couldn't do it! They spilled things. They dropped things. They seemed all thumbs. "Here, let me try it!" ordered a vainglorious father, only to be doused with the spoonful of liquid or spotted with the drippings from the fork. Laughter! As for the clothes family, their problems were legion: where to wear the various articles? How to climb in? How to walk in them? Which was front? Which back? How to climb out?

In fact, all over that kraal and far out in the deep black forest, the same mirth had seized everyone. The Great Grab had been a complete success. Even the surprised little stars could see that.

The man could hear the sounds of it. The angels may have covered their faces with their wings. But God the Father is patient, He knows how to help heroes. And sinners.

Mirth had to die down some time. And one by one the gay persons lay down on their floors to rest. And then, the high excitement over, a curious thing happened. That little something inside that talks back began to talk back to them, too.

"Selfish person," it said to each one's soul, "how about that White Man? A long way from his brothers in the tribe of White Men is he. He must be low in his heart, always, missing his father, his brothers. And what did he come for? To teach you the things of God the Father. To make your children wise enough to read the magic medicine. Yet think of him tonight—no bed, no pillows, no sheet, no candle, no table, no chair, no food, no book, no clothes— nothing. You have made him uncomfortable; he, used to the soft things of white men. His heart is low within him. Yet what word did he say to stop you?"

There is nothing like such inner conversations. They twist a man and turn a man. He writhes. He denies. He stands up for himself. But black men and white men have a hard time of it when consciences begin to talk back at them. Even in the depth of an African jungle. Such a hard time of it, that toward morning down the forest trails came the soft patter of stealthy footfalls—somebody bringing a mattress—somebody bringing a pillow—somebody bringing a chair—a table—a mirror—books—spoons—clothes—

"This must be Nzambi's man," these somebodies whispered, awed. "We must not rob God's man."

If they had learned a lesson, God's man had also, in the morning, when he saw the stack of his possessions at his door.

With a new joy in his face he read them the other chapters in Luke's Gospel, and the people listened earnestly. They wept as if their hearts would break when he came to the death of the Lord Jesus; but when they heard about the first Easter, it was as if Christ himself had risen in at least one heart, for the first convert came forward—Lutate was his name. He had to be hidden in the

White Man's house for safeguarding, for his enemies tried to poison him. Then the chief's son was converted, and before long there were ten eager believers.

The Man took all ten of them with him on a trip through the surrounding forest villages, telling the story of Jesus. The ten grew to be a hundred. The hundred, two hundred. The two hundred, five hundred. The five hundred, eight hundred. More. More. Then a thousand.

But it all dated back to the Great Grab.

News of this marvelous revival reached America: the man who was just "White Man" to the African was known by name in America as Mr. Henry M. Richards. It became known that there was no church on the Congo big enough for those thousand persons and a beautiful thing happened. The members of Dr. A. J. Gordon's church in Boston decided to send a chapel to Mr. Richards! It was in many sections, all ready to be put together. In the course of time, these sections arrived at the end of all transportation facilities, which was exactly sixty long, hard, rough miles from Banza Manteke where Mr. Richards lived. What were miles to those new Christians? They wanted that chapel! Therefore, they volunteered their services and walked those sixty miles there and sixty miles back carrying the entire chapel on their heads, in seven hundred separate loads. Each trip took a week, yet some of them made that rough and tedious journey five times—their faces glowing with a new love and happiness—a happiness which had kept on growing ever since the Great Grab.

I see Africa and Asiatic towns,
I see Algiers, Tripoli, Derne, Mogadore, Timbuctoo,
*   Monrovia,*
I see the swarms of Pekin, Canton, Benares, Delhi, Cal-
*   cutta, Tokyo;*
I see the Kruman in his hut, the Dahoman and
*   Ashantee-man in their huts;*
I see the Turm smoking opium in Aleppo,
I see the picturesque crowds at the fairs of Khiva and
*   those of Herat;*

I see Teheran, I see Muscat and Medina, and the inter-
vening sands;
I see the caravans toiling onward.
. . . I mix,
I see ranks, colors, barbarisms, civilizations; I go among
them, indiscriminately,
And I salute all the inhabitants of the earth.

Walt Whitman

*It was in West Africa in 1927 that a blood specimen was
taken from a black native named Asibi who was sick with yellow fever. This specimen was inoculated into a rhesus monkey
which had just been received from India. Asibi recovered
but the monkey died of the disease. All the vaccine manu-
factured since 1927 both by the Rockefeller Foundation and
government and other agencies as well derives from the original strain of virus obtained from this humble native. Carried
down to the present day from one laboratory to another,
through repeated cultures and by enormous multiplication,
it has offered immunity to yellow fever to millions of people
in many countries. Wherever today in yellow fever areas the
armed forces of the Allied nations are stationed, they are
protected from the disease by vaccination from this same
strain. Through the creative imagination of science, the blood
of one man in West Africa has been made to serve the whole
human race.*

The Rockefeller Foundation Report for 1943

29

THE LEAVES WERE FOR THE HEALING

You may have heard Dr. Brown tell the story. How he looked up
while preaching one Sunday morning in his California church, and
saw in the back of the room a most surprising man, wearing an
immense sombrero, and leaning nonchalantly against the door-

jamb, as if sitting down might seem too permanent. The next Sunday the stranger was there again, still standing, and still under the big brim. Dr. Brown managed to reach him at the end of the service, and as they shook hands, Dr. Brown said: "I couldn't help but spot you, my friend, since you were the only man in the congregation wearing a hat."

"Oh, don't they wear them?" the stranger asked, looking around curiously. "O.K., parson, I won't do it again."

A few Sundays later, when he shook hands, he left a small envelope in Dr. Brown's palm, in which he found a check for ten thousand dollars, and a short note requesting that half of this amount be given to the Methodist Women's Foreign Missionary Society, and the other half given to the Presbyterian Women's Foreign Missionary Society.

Most ministers never have such thrilling things happen; and Dr. Brown used to wonder, years later, why he never took time off to call on this peculiar person, who lived some distance away, on a ranch, and rode to church on horseback. But the demands of a large parish were relentless; and in the end he moved East—possibly it was the call to become Dean of the Yale Divinity School.

In any case, one day he heard from a lawyer in California, who informed him that a certain miner had died, and had left the Reverend Charles R. Brown a considerable amount of money in his will. Could he arrange to come West for the settling of this legacy?

When his vacation came, Dr. Brown was to be in California; and found that the miner had left him one hundred and ten thousand dollars; and that there was a written request that half of the amount should be given to the Presbyterian Women's Foreign Missionary Society, the other half to the Methodist Women's Foreign Missionary Society.

And then Dr. Brown did what he had not done earlier: he rode out to visit the mine and the ranch. It proved to be a long uncomfortable trip; down a gulch, up a hill, through a canyon. With every foot of the journey he grew more impressed that the miner had cared about coming so far to church, over roads so rough.

On reaching the mine he said to the miner's mate: "Your partner must have been very much interested in religion."

"Well now, I can't say that *that* ever struck me about him!" the mate drawled in honest surprise.

"But look how generously he gave to missions," Dr. Brown explained.

"Oh *that! That!* Well, *that* was due entirely to the Chinese cook we had! I reckon I shouldn't speak ill of the dead, but my mate sure could swear; and he used to take it out on our Chinese cook. Yes siree, he sure could make the air blue with cusses. But that cook, he didn't know no English to speak of, so he would just sort of grunt-like, in a gentle kind of way. And that was mighty maddening to my mate, and he surely let loose more mouthfuls. Until one night—say now, come to think of it, that was sorta funny. Him and me were just sorta walking around the place, talking our blooming heads off, when we come to the cookhouse. We looked in the window, and seen the cook sitting under the hanging lamp, reading. My mate he says: 'Don't tell me that dumb cluck can *read!*' So in he goes and booms in his cross way: 'What you reading, Sam?' And blest if that cook he don't hold out the Good Book itself, with all the print in heathen Chinee flyspecks, so a Christian couldn't hardly tell was it right side up or not. But the cook says the one word: 'Bible!' My mate is fit to be tied, he is *that* surprised. 'Where in the H—— did it come from?' he asks. '*China!*' says the cook, and he points his thumb over the Pacific Ocean-like. Well siree, if my mate doesn't press the point: 'And how did it get here, Sam?' Sam points his thumb downward-like, and he grunts: '*Trunk!*' But my mate he ain't through with this funny business, so he thinks him up some more questions: 'And who packs it in the trunk, Sam?' The cook he looks mighty mournful-like: 'Mother!' says he. 'And was your mother a Christian?' '*Ungh-Ungh!*' grunts Sam. 'You like the Bible?' Sam, he touches the Book sorta gentle-like: '*Ungh-Ungh!*' Then blest if my mate he don't say: 'And is it the Bible makes you so quiet when I bawl you out and cuss you out?' And dashed if that cook he don't sorta smile up his yellow face into a mighty pleasant grin, but all he could say was just another: '*Ungh-Ungh!*' Funny story, ain't it?"

Dr. Brown asked if that was all that happened.

"Yep!" said the miner. "Excepting that on our way back to the ranch house, my mate says to me: 'Don't that beat all? For here I just remember how my pappy used to bawl out my mammy over giving her money to the heathen Chinee and foreign missions, in the which my pappy didn't have no belief at all. But I'm thinking stranger things than this has happened—supposing my mammy's money bought that Chinese Bible over in China, and turned Sam's mammy into a Christian. Then supposing she packs that there Bible into a trunk, and Sam he brings it straight to this here camp. And all my mammy's son does is to cuss him out, and cuss him out, and cuss him out. While all *he* does is read his Bible and forgive me like any honest-to-goodness Christian had ought to do. The whole point being, I can't for the life of me remember—was my mammy Methodist? or Presbyterian?' "

The sandalwood tree imparts its fragrance even to the axe that cuts it down.

Chinese proverb

FELLING THE TREES
On the trees go the blows cheng cheng,
And the birds cry out ying ying,
One removes from the dark valley
And removes to the lofty tree,
While ying goes its cry
Seeking with its voice its companion.
Look at the bird,
Bird as it is, seeking with its voice
its companion.
And shall a man
Not seek to have his friends?
Spiritual beings will then harken to him,
He shall have harmony and peace.

Old Chinese folk song

For every star in the heavens there is a man upon earth, and for every man upon earth there is a star in the heavens.

Chinese proverb

30

MORE LITTLE GRAY HOMES IN THE WEST

(BREAD CAST UPON THE WATERS IN CHINA RETURNS AFTER MANY YEARS, IN CALIFORNIA—3,000 MILES AWAY!)

This is going to be a devastating story to read through if you happen to be over sixty; or poor; or have even once conjured up a little dream house in the West—gray, perhaps; or white, perhaps. With rambler roses running riot over the doorway; with everything inside more modern than tomorrow morning; bristling with buttons to push, to save every ounce of energy; with every known gadget to keep things spick and span; with wide picture windows to bring the entire outdoors indoors to the parlor sofa. And not only *one* such superlative Last Word in Houses, but a dozen or more just as good—all to be given away for love. In case you qualify! Which makes the whole thing maddening, for the likelihood is, you won't do; whereas the house is the exact fairy tale where you could live happily ever after.

So, what about qualifications?

First of all—*Presbyterian?* Harder yet: have you ever been Presbyterian preacher? teacher? doctor? nurse? professor? director of? superintendent of? dean of? etc., etc. some foreign work for this denomination? Have you given all your adult waking hours to the Kingdom of God on earth in the Orient, Africa, South America? Have you so shared your friendship and skill, for instance, with one Chinese boy growing up in Cheefoo that he finds you are really the salt of his earth? Have you trained him so thoroughly in your Presbyterian school that he knows every modern business technique? Have you helped him secure his first job with an excellent British-American firm? Have you meanwhile led him to Christ, so that he has started practicing privately all that you publicly preach? Have you built his life so deep in the church that nothing whatever can shake him—neither wars nor Japanese soldiers nor Communist Reds? Have you seen him rise as high in his British-American Tobacco Company as a Chinese could get in those seventeen years? Have you watched him during the war turn into an almost sensational trader—buying whole shiploads of merchandise, selling things off to advantage? Amassing a fortune?

Have you realized how far-flung and important the sweep of his enterprise was, dealing in crude rubber now, opening offices for his firm in Hong Kong, Singapore, London, New York? Have you seen him adopting four Chinese orphans—three little girls and one boy? Have you seen him meet and then marry a successful young Chinese woman, head of a Presbyterian Mission School? Have you sighed as you saw him leave China, when Communists took charge of affairs, because he refused to do business with them? Have you watched him settling in the United States choosing a suburb near Near York, joining a Presbyterian church, sending his four little orphans to an excellent private school?

Have you figured out what a Chinese millionaire thinks as he looks over his life, picking out this one or that one who mattered most to his destiny? Have you shivered with joy to sense his gratitude rising and rising? beyond Cheefoo? beyond Hong Kong? beyond China? Beyond? Beyond? Beyond? Have you thanked your God that in whatever land your church has been planted, he has delighted to discover other men and other women doing identical kindnesses to other boys? Have you rejoiced that in his own wealth, he worried somewhat over the size of mission salaries, wondering if they might not be rather uncomfortably small? Have you liked it that he worried, too, over the years of retirement— would anybody have *enough* from pensions? Have you felt his enthusiasm mounting for missionaries who had made his own life wiser and wider and wealthier? Have you seen him wondering what on earth a man could do to bring absolute joy and contentment—at once—to persons, known and unknown, whom he admired so enormously?

In case you have passed the Final Examination thus far, then you will know all the answers about who qualifies for more little gray homes in the West—built from Mr. Frank M. S. Shu's magnificent gift of one million dollars, to tell to the foreign missionaries in his denomination that here are their garden-homes in Duarte, California: now that they are retired: now that they have given their best to the world, he gives back his best to them. Modern? Yes! But built on the ancient Chinese custom of veneration for old age, and tangible tribute to one's elders. He even has more dream houses of his own in mind: for when China settles down into some semblance of her former reasonableness, then he hopes to build similar homes in similar Chinese gardens for the retired Chinese ministers in his own country.

So this is a Chinese fairy story, pure and simple. Yet not so simple. Since this is really bread cast upon the waters in China three thousand miles away, returning after many years in the form of charming dwelling places in California. This is the prince who began collecting orphans whom he had seen and then began collecting the elderly whom he had not seen, so that every single one of them might live happily ever afterward. All this. And heaven too. Something besides the form, something beyond the sound!

I would not paint a face, a rock,
*   nor brooks nor trees,*
Mere semblances of things, but
*   something more than these.*
I would not play a tune upon the
*   sheng or lute,*
Something that did not sing meanings
*   that else were mute.*
That art is best which to the soul's range
*   gives no bound,*
Something besides the form, something
*   beyond the sound.*

                                 Li Po, eighth century

Clay is fashioned into vessels; it is on their empty hollowness that their use depends. Doors and windows are cut out to

make a dwelling, and on the empty space within its usefulness
depends. Thus, while the existence of things may be good, it
is the non-existent in them that makes them serviceable.

Lao-tse, 604 B.C.

31

THE PROPER BOSTONIAN BOOKSHELVES

You have heard of The Proper Bostonians, of course. How high
hat! how incorruptibly correct! how discreetly disciplined! But
judge for yourself how proper John Deferrari was; for eventually
the Beacon Hill dowagers themselves were far too dazed to decide.

His fedora, to be sure, was undeniably high hat—worn with the
crown full-blown, since he always felt that a dent down the center
was step number one toward rapid deterioration. But under that
hat dwelt a dozen disciplines so demanding that all Boston stopped
dead in its tracks to read in the paper that he had never had serv-
ant, housekeeper, nor cook; neither secretary, agent nor repairman
to keep up all those countless small properties which he had been
buying secretly from time to time, here and there on Beacon Hill,
or over on his own north side of Boston. His own two hands had
seemed proper enough to paint, plaster, paper, or patch up the
plumbing.

He had never had a housekeeper, either; nor wasted rent on a
safe-deposit box—all his fabulous financial transactions had been
carried around inside the busy brain up under that full-blown
high hat; and the investments themselves were properly pinned
inside his pockets; even the flaps of the outside pockets he fastened
in the most unfashionable fashion with big blanket safety pins.

His only address was: "General Delivery, Boston." But he rarely
answered his mail, partly to save postage, but mostly because it
seemed a more proper precaution to appraise his correspondents
face to face. He never wasted five cents on subway, bus, or ele-

vated, if he could walk. He never had a telephone, nor an automobile. And in eighty-four years he never had a doctor, safeguarding his health as properly as his pennies—"I eat baked apples, I eat good grapes, especially I eat ripe oranges. I am fruit man! I know!"

He never went to a theater, movie, concert, nor ball game. And, needless to say, he never married; not having had time to pick out a proper girl: somebody who would have had to be poor enough to pinch pennies, and provident enough never to dip into principal.

Proper or improper, John Deferrari had always dreamed a dream. "Dope things out," was his own phrase for it. And he had been at it ever since he was nine years old, day in and day out. Mr. Deferrari could become very enthusiastic about it, seizing his own ears and tugging them gleefully: "My own affairs are my life! They are my business, my pleasure, hey?" And his blue eyes would burn.

The day his picture came out in all the Boston papers with his dramatic news, the cop on the corner gave one astonished look, as he gasped: "What? That old Eyetalian? Seen him up and down this street for years! Thought he probably ran a hurdy-gurdy or something!"

The story began with an apple.

His father had eight other children; and when times grew hard in his fruit-peddling business, he took John out of school, placed a chip basket on his arm, and sent him out to peddle penny apples in their North End slums. But the boy soon doped it out: why not sell in a richer neighborhood?

When once down on State Street, in the financial district, he watched all the proper Bostonian gentlemen busy being bankers and brokers. Envy of obvious importance made him begin asking questions to dope out how they got that way. Before long he bought a pushcart. Not content with this step up in the world, he bought a horse and wagon; attending to the horse, himself. Next came a small store of his own. Then the whole building of which his store was a part. At twenty-six, he had doped out the way to run a wholesale fruit business and even a fashionable shop dealing only in imported delicacies. This shop was near the Boston Public Library. Man and boy, he had formed the proper Bostonian habit of going in there, night after night, reading about fruit until closing time. He began falling in love with the dream of fancy fruit from Spain—grapes, lemons, oranges, figs, almonds! Before long he began buying such fruit, going after hotel and restaurant trade; selling also to housekeepers and butlers all over Beacon Hill.

But always haunting the Library. When fruit was an old story, he tackled the bookshelves on real estate law, economics, corporation reports, financial statistics; and, for play, he devoured the lives of all the great industrial leaders—trying to dope out how on earth they made their fortunes. Bit by bit, in this bank or that bank, he began his secret buying—never investing in any corporation not founded or headed "by a man who had fought his way up from a poor boy—like me!" Land seemed the safest investment of all; so he began buying small houses, improving them, himself; and renting out rooms.

In spite of his relentless discipline of himself, there was never anything at all heartless in his treatment of others. During the depression years, when many who rented his rooms were jobless, unable to pay a penny of rent, he let them stay on and on, with the most compassionate kind of understanding that the fault was not theirs, personally; but a national disaster which would pass. He always gave generously to St. Leonard's Catholic Church to which he belonged; and he was exceedingly good to his only sister, Emelia.

Meanwhile, the first apple had grown into a fabulous four million dollars. But not a banker in town guessed what investments were concealed under those absurd safety pins in his bulging coat pockets. But one day John Deferrari took the big step. He asked advice of a startled trust officer in a bank. Feeling himself a Proper Bostonian now that he was over eighty years old, Mr. Deferrari knew the proper thing was to leave his money properly; so what would the bank officer think was the proper way to give one million dollars at once to the Boston Public Library? When this official dropped his jaw, and stared, Mr. Deferrari defended his gift:

"Boston gave me what I have. I will give it back to Boston. I made it here, I will leave it here!" As the banker recovered his breath, there were other things John Deferrari added: that he wanted young Bostonians to realize, as he did, what America meant. Surely such a gift would be a proper way to do it, would it not? The banker agreed. But thinking the poor fellow might be simply daydreaming, asked what securities did he have in mind? Offhand, he listed more than four hundred securities. (Probably feeling this pocket or that!)

It was a proud day when he deposited the accurate stock of papers in the banker's office. Only one "string" went with the gift: that a wing or a room be named in his honor, with his picture on the wall, and a bronze plaque to tell how he wanted his gift to perpetuate his ideals for the solid development of character and success.

The Library set aside five thousand dollars for this portrait of the old gentleman with his pale Italian face, his sharp cheekbones, staring blue eyes, wispy mustache and fringe of silvering hair. The day that he presented to the Library trustees this largest gift in their entire history, Mr. Deferrari turned up wearing an uncomfortable new gray suit; but the pockets were pinned with the usual safety pins, as protection against pickpockets even in that celebrated assembly. He had immense financial shrewdness about the accumulation of the income until the first million should become a second million; when again an accumulating was to begin, so that the total gift could be three millions—with no restrictions.

He was posed for his portrait under the picture of another financier, Alexander Hamilton. When he was asked the secret of his success, John Deferrari merely said: "Hell, you've got to be smart!" But by this time you must have guessed that the actual answer was: "Heavens, how else could a Proper Bostonian act when he fell in love with bookshelves?"

They shall not grow old
As we that are left grow old.
Age shall not weary them
Nor the years condemn.
At the going down of the sun
And in the morning
We shall remember them.

Inscription on the British Museum

The man who does not read good books has no advantage over the man who can't read them.

Mark Twain

There are only four kinds of readers. The first is like the hour-glass; their reading being as the sand, it runs in and runs out, and leaves not a vestige behind. The second is like a sponge, which inbibes everything, and returns it in nearly the same state, only a little dirtier. A third is like a jelly-bag, allowing all that is pure to pass away, retaining only the refuse and dregs. And the fourth is like the slaves in diamond mines, who, casting aside all that is worthless, retain only pure gems.

Samuel T. Coleridge

32

FIFTEEN HUNDRED JAPANESE BABIES
NAMED FOR EARL

He was not the sort of man anybody expected things to happen to. Yet folks still talk about him down in Hattiesburg, and whom on earth all those Japanese soldiers would have named their babies for if Earl M. Finch hadn't come walking along the street that Saturday, past that particular drugstore with just that particular soldier reading the menu pasted on the glass. Funny what it all led to! Babies and all. But of course they came a lot later; and nobody gave them a single thought that first day.

It began tamely enough, the way things did with Earl. He just said to the G.I.: "Hungry, son?" And the Japanese soldier said: "You bet!"

But one friendly word led to another, so after Earl Finch found that there were a lot of Japanese soldiers training over at Camp Shelby, and that they weren't made welcome anywhere in town because of all those ultra-patriotic notions folks had about Japanese, why the Earl said: "How'd you-all like to bring a buddy or two out to my place tomorrow night for supper?"

It makes us wonder now what Mrs. Finch said about strangers being invited in on her that way, with no warning at all, you might say; and she more or less an invalid, you might say. But a more devoted mother you never did know; and you can see for yourself how Earl wasn't the kind of a son not to take most of the responsibility, his own self. For Earl M. Finch may be a plain man such as you might never turn to look at twice. But I reckon he had the warmest heart in Mississippi, judging by what he began doing that Sunday.

Although the Japanese took step number two, themselves; and I reckon everybody was right surprised. For when Earl got home on Monday night from the shop he owned, there sat both the Japanese soldiers calling on his mother, having bought out nearly every florist in town to "say it with flowers." Mrs. Finch had all the vases filled, and flowers left over. Well, in no time at all Earl began asking a hundred of the Japanese out to his place for a barbecue supper. Then he began talking to them about their Japanese parents, until boy after boy poured out the most homesick story. For I reckon you will recall what our Government did to all the Japanese—turning them out of their homes and interning them in our American kind of concentration camp; only we had a fancier name for them—"Relocation Centers," we called them.

Earl M. Finch wasn't proud of what he heard, for each of these boys had some kind of a private hell of his own, these days. So the first thing Earl knew he was saying: "Give me your mother's address; I would sure like to write and tell her what a joy it has been to have you here at my farm."

So it all began easy and simple, what with Earl asking them to meals, and then writing letters to folks he had never seen. None of us ever thought he would turn into the letter-writingest fellow in town! Some of those G.I.'S were from Hawaii, and Earl wrote *their* parents, too; and I don't believe that in all his born days he had ever sent a letter overseas before. But of course, in the end, that wasn't even half the story. For he kept on having batches of Japanese out at his place; until finally he rented the store down next to his own, and let them use it as a clubhouse of their own. We used to wonder how Earl got a stroke of business done, what with his letters and all. I think myself, *the Lord* prospered him!

Finally came the week when some of the Japanese were ready to be shipped overseas. Likely you recall they got sent to Italy? Well sir, if Earl Finch didn't go down to New Orleans when they went, and hire rooms at a hotel, and give them a nice party. He wasn't really what you could call a rich man; although he did well with his men's furnishing store, like I hinted above. But he found money to fling parties and dances, and treated them as loving as if he was their own daddy till they sailed.

Back in Hattiesburg once more, he went right on being the en-tertainingest friend you ever knew, until more batches of them sailed off; and new ones came in. With Earl Finch writing more and more letters to more and more parents, not to mention to the G.I.'s overseas. Over and over I've heard tell how he wrote way over fifteen thousand letters—it makes me dizzy just to think of all that ink, and all those stamps, not to mention all the time it took.

Then, of course, the sad side started. For every once in a while a soldier would get killed over in Italy; so what must Earl Finch do, but cross the whole U.S.A. to comfort the wives and mothers. So that, from a hometown boy who never went *anywhere,* he be-came the travelingest man in Hattiesburg.

Right here the real nice part starts. For Earl was not what you'd call a marrying man, yet all over this country, and over in Hawaii too, there would be Japanese babies named "Earl" in his honor. Most of us would feel pretty much set up, just to have three or four kids named for us. But you've simply got to believe me when I tell you that Earl's list grew to over fifteen hundred babies! I declare, it would wake me up at night to think I mattered that much, for parents to want their first baby to have my name! I guess Earl was sort of touched too. And his mother was real pleased; for that kind of thing is right unusual, of course.

But there's better yet to tell you. For just wait till you hear what happened the minute the war was over, and those Japanese soldiers got home to Hawaii. Right off, nothing would do but Mr. Earl M. Finch must be invited to Honolulu, where they made the biggest kind of a fuss over him. Down at the wharf, when he walked down the gangplank, the park band began playing at the head of a big parade of cars. They escorted Earl to the big park; and there, if you please, five thousand Japanese gave Earl Finch a barbecue dinner. He is a right modest sort of man, and back here in Hattiesburg we used to wonder how he ever stood the fame and all. They even hung ropes of orchids round his neck; the right name for them is *lei*. Governors, mayors and all sorts of Japanese made speeches. Parents whom he had never laid eyes on before, came up to say how he had meant everything on earth to them all those lonely years. And then, of course, they began bringing up the babies. One by one, the young couples would say: "We wanted to call our baby *'Earl,'* if you don't mind?" It was when he began adding up the separate babies that he began feeling like the biggest granddaddy on earth; for sometimes the parents thought they were the only ones to have such a bright idea, little guessing what a queer sort of fix it put Earl in! Could he afford fifteen hundred silver spoons or christening cups; or whatever Japanese give, if they aren't Christians?

Still and all, in spite of this fuss and feathers, it was right much of a surprise to have Earl Finch decide to go back to Hawaii a year later and live there for good. For men wear clothes in Honolulu, too; so he sells candy from the U.S.A., and fancy shirts made on the islands.

Every once in a while somebody back here in Hattiesburg will still say: "He was a plain sort of man, really. You might never give him a second look; but I reckon Earl M. Finch has more call to feel good through and through than anybody else in these parts, after doing such friendly things; so quiet and all. Like something out of the Bible. Almost a miracle sort of thing. Yet sometimes it hurts a little, thinking it all over, to realize there wasn't a single thing Earl Finch did which any of us couldn't have done, too, if we'd only set our minds to it, as he did.

Pinch yourself, and know how others feel.

Japanese proverb

The pen scratches, the paper is silent.

Russian proverb

*For there is hope of a tree, if it be cut down, that it will sprout
again, and that the tender branch thereof shall not cease.*

Job 14:7

Daylight will peep through a very small hole.

Japanese proverb

33

AWOL: MAN INTO PAPER DOLL

*And many of the disciples turned back and walked
with Him no more. . . . Will ye too go away?*

JOHN 6:66-67

It sounds flimsy. And it was flimsy: to let himself be blown AWOL
like a paper doll down any street by any idle wind of doctrine. But
of course the man justified himself by saying that after all what
was he but a statistic? He said that he had always been that way;
even when he was more than ready to be born he had to wait an
extra minute while his hurried mother filled out a filing card at the
receptionist's desk at the hospital, and his frantic father wrote out
a check to cover his birth and "all the normal expenses connected
therewith."

He said that next he became a Paper Numeral thumbtacked over
the headboard of his hospital crib, and a Feeding Formula thumbtacked on the footboard. In eight days he became a List of Es-
sentials Every Mother Should Have on Hand in the Household
after Returning Home with Baby.

By bad timing, that had been the month when the Government
first wrote him up in their national Census:

HEAD OF HOUSEHOLD...name...age...occupation...
WIFE, if any...name...age...occupation...
CHILDREN, if any...name...age...occupation...

Since ne was their only "*if any*," and his parents had not yet settled on his name (having fully expected a girl, because he lay so quiet in his prenatal state), only his age could be given—nine days. So that his patriotic blowing through life was begun as a nine-day wonder, nameless, and unemployed.

It was on this very day that his loyal father had entered the boy in his own Alma Mater, Brown University, and waggishly repeated to his mother the time-honored sentence: "Brown-bred men are the best bred man." At which the baby gave a yeasty little yawp, not unlike Walt Whitman's more poetic one, but on a more well-bred scale, suiting his 7 lbs. 8 oz. His mother lost no time in having him christened. She had meant to ponder long and tenderly throughout the ceremony so that everyone would say later: "That lovely, lovely Madonna face! Shall you ever forget the consecration of it?" But he himself had been in no mood for little drops of water, and had howled his head off; so that the only thing appearing on his mother's face had been an agonized blush and her lips pushed far out into a sibilant: "S'h! S'h! S'h!" And he kicked the baptismal certificate out of the preacher's hand as Act One of this long, long paper-doll career. Even when his mother entered him in a pre-nursery school, the real significance of this number one step into life was turned into a frequent Report Card: Parents Please Sign. He became merely dots on a line which someone filled in; and no matter what miracle he came home to report graphically to his mother, she said only: "U'mm! U'mm!" so much more fascinating was his statistical rating:

I.Q. ......
Reaction to unknown games: *hostile...eager...indifferent...*
Mixes: *easily...aggressively...passively...*
Prefers playing: *alone ... with others ... with boys ... with girls ...*
Eats: *too fast...too slow...refuses what is set before him...*
Temper: *mild...variable...violent...*
Clothes: *too few...too many...too fancy...*

Even when he needed spectacles to correct a small defect in his vision, he became two filing cards and one prescription slip, one for the oculist, one for the optician; plus immense letters and absurdly small letters to stare at on a remote placard. To the dentist he became a horrible grin showing all his teeth on a card; the dentist putting an "X" wherever he planned to tinker slightly. The orthopedic shoeman stood him up on a sheet of paper and outlined his feet with a pencil; which always meant special new shoes and a big check from his father.

This kind of thing was continued by the public school system with report blanks full of such alarming items as Deportment . . . Psychological Attitudes . . . All maddening enough; but the dancing school filed away the most disgraceful cards about the little swain, with the word *refuses . . . refuses . . . refuses . . .* alternating with *girl shy . . . awkward . . . no sense of rhythm.*

Meanwhile, the church had done little but turn him into statistics also. The cradle roll began it, with frolicsome kittens pawing forget-me-nots arriving to say: "Welcome, Little Stranger!" Sunday school was almost all paper work: crayon tulips on poster paper for the window; take-home-cards with things for mother to help him do before next Sunday. The church kept up through the years a statistical rhythm: *"Come!"* said one card, his name and address having been run impersonally on a stencil through a machine; *"Give!"* the pledge card would urge. Or, still later: *"Pardon this reminder if you have already sent in,"* etc. etc. In the end his main preparation for church lapsed into paper work, also: first, a check, then a buff envelope about 2 x 3½ into which the check was pushed, the flap licked; and as he put it into his Sunday vest pocket, he read again the printed words: *"The Lord Loveth a Cheerful Giver."* He never questioned it; yet he never really believed it, his own mood being too uncheerful and perfunctory.

The rest of his routine was just as paper-bound and card-indexed, if not more so. All his relationships with books were purely statistical: some librarian printed, in incredibly clear letters, his name, address, sponsor; then a numeral, a book title, a date. College was one long headache, filing himself away in all the proper cubbyholes: *Tuition* here; *Board Bills* there; *Marks* elsewhere; *Assignments* at every turn. Ending up in a diploma, *mirabile dictu.*

His automobile ran only with paper. Check. Driver's license.

Insurance. Road map. Credit cards for gas. A.A.A. card. His health was practically paper—from insurance policies to Blue Cross Hospitilization: Always Carry on Your Person. His office was paper from A to Z. File this in triplicate, please. Miss Vetter, take a letter: "Yours of the 15th received, contents noted; in reply would say . . ." Miss Vetter yawned. He would have like to, also; but it was essential to keep up a self-important front.

What was marriage but paper? The invitations; following his list of guests, and her list. Gifts in endless tissue paper. Gifts listed on filing cards. Buff, if acknowledged. Blue, if unacknowledged. The doctor's clean bill of health. The honeymoon reservations, entirely paper; tickets, timetables, menus, side trips worth seeing. Newspapers. Above all newspapers. With advertisements to impress a pattern on a paper doll: What the Well-Dressed Man Will Wear This Season, lower vest button best left unbuttoned. Trouser legs looser; turned up in cuffs. Socks to shock. Blest be the tie that binds at Easter. Hat brims with that subtle, subtle saucy slant as if saying: *What goes on here?*

At which the Paper Doll came to, with a start. What does go on here? Name in a phone book! Name in a city directory! Name on a church roll! Name on a letterhead! Name on a payroll!

Blown down every street. Stepped on by every passer-by. Dehumanized. Depersonalized. In a draughty world one's only hope the lucky lottery of getting blown up against somebody as eccentric as Evita Peron on her public appearances down in Argentina—when people toss at her feet little slips of paper with their names and addresses written on them. And should the Señora Presidente stop—and should the Señora stoop—then! Then dreams came true. Since Evita's picking up of the paper was the winning of a sweepstake, really; for an audience with her was assured; and any request would be granted—house! job! clothes! education! operation! Just tell Evita. Capricious Evita, who might or might not stoop; but if she stooped, the little sheet of paper was like heaven.

But that was South America. Up north the climate was colder and a paper doll was simple a paper doll, cut off from the general run of—well! What was he cut off from, anyhow? And what *was* paper, this stuff his life consisted of? Wood pulp, of course. And from a tree. In a sense, a family tree, perhaps. But how did he ever go AWOL in this haphazard way?

He let himself be blown to a paper factory, and had the shock of his life. For this was not flimsy stuff, now! This was a desperate dangerous row of dilemmas. In no time at all: a tree sawed into logs, 5 x 4 x 8. In no time at all: bark ripped off by desperate machinery in a desperate hurry. Logs run into a chipper. Cut up into inch square chips, moved on a belt to be blown through a pipe into a cooking room. Lime poured on; mixed with sodium carbonate. He grew sick as the lid was clamped down tight. His wife did that with her pressure cooker at home. Except that this mass of wood pulp was the most nauseating black stew. He found himself saying: "Mass man! Mass man!" Water had to wash and wash this disgusting glue. Chemicals had to be used to turn it snow white. Then a crusher. A shredder. Milky stuff flowing out on webbed wire cloth. Draining. Passing under driers. Crushed out. Ironed, wound on rollers. Paper. Waiting.

Out of nowhere came the sermon: *This is your life!*

Some preacher seemed to make a better point: *This is the Life of Christ!*

He reconsidered the process and agreed it was a vivid moving picture of that sacred life. Cut down. Crushed. Shoved around. Mistreated.

From nowhere came the text: *There were also many other things that Jesus did, which, if they were written in a book, I suppose even the world itself would not be large enough to contain them.*

He found himself saying: "I am one of those pages!"

It lent dignity to his futile blowing around. Suppose he were really a leaf from that book? With a message stamped on it? Not just anybody's rubber-heel prints. But Somebody's footprints.

Out of many Sundays came a deeper memory: "Apart from Me ye can do nothing!"

And that, of course, was just his state—apart; isolated; a sole leaf blown hither and yon by every idle wind of doctrine. Nothing printed on him but his own face, his own figure. "Him that overcometh . . . I will write My new name on him."

Imagine blowing around being a Document. A proxy for God: "Know all men by these presents . . ."

He recalled the great documents of history, to give himself status. Could he be some new Magna Carta—giving all the peasants of this earth their chance? Or some new Declaration of Independence giving all men an *equal* chance? Or some new Proclamation of Emancipation giving every slave the *same* chance as the home-born? Or could he be some new Declaration of Human Rights? "We the peoples . . ."

Great winds began blowing around the earth. He felt himself swaying, eddying, swirling. He remembered the poet who had said that a poem begins as a lump in the throat, a sense of wrong, a homesickness, a lovesickness.

"Then I must be a poet!" cried the Paper Doll. A lump in the throat, apart from the Tree he belonged to. Homesick, because he was AWOL. Lovesick, because he did not know how to write his love poem and throw it at God's feet.

And then he realized that it had been written deep into the tree itself. Once and for all. When God so loved! Until it was grain of the grain. Pulp of the pulp. Webbed into the paper. The Word was made flesh and dwelt among us, we beheld His glory; and He stooped to pick up every single one of us. Every single one, to put us back in His Book of Life made of the Tree of Life.

The dignity of mankind is given into your hands; it falls with you and with you it may rise again.

Johann Schiller

A good poem goes about the world offering itself to reasonable men, who read it with joy and carry it to their reasonable neighbors.

Ralph Waldo Emerson

My journal is that of me which would else spill over and run to waste. It is a leaf which hangs over my head in the·path. I bend the twig and write my prayers on it, then letting it go, the bough springs up and shows my scrawl to heaven . . . The

*crow, the goose, the eagle carry my quill, and the wind blows
the leaves as far as I go.*

Henry D. Thoreau

*The Church is catholic, universal; so are all her actions; for
all mankind is of one Author, and is one volume; when one
man dies, one chapter is not torn out of the book, but translated into a better language; and every chapter must be so
translated. God employs several translators: some pieces are
translated by age, some by sickness, some by war, some by
justice; but God's hand is in every translation, and His hand
shall bind up all our scattered leaves again for that library
where every book shall lie open to one another.*

John Donne

34

RESPECTFULLY HAVE PITY ON PRINTED
PAPER

The very wastebaskets at the street corners were one vast hint,
if only she had been able to see her calling. But old Grandmother
Gatewoman was one of the foolish things of this world whom God
has chosen to confound the wise: only it would take a great deal
more terror by night and destruction by day before she could get
it into her simple old head that she was really a whole Psalm in herself; she, who could neither read nor write; and had already lost
all her family.

In the excitement of the Enemy's arriving, she often found herself thinking that a thousand had fallen at her side, and fully ten
thousand at her right hand; but that it still had not come near her.
Indeed, lying on her brick k'ang at night, she used to put herself to
sleep with the ninety-first Psalm, which was the only part of the
Bible she had ever managed to learn by heart through her long

years of churchgoing; and it was an immense comfort to her, now that all the noisy verses had come true in China, to discover that all the comfortable verses were true also.

"Here He is—giving His angels charge over me *again!*" she would think, almost with a chuckle, wondering why God should set His love upon her to deliver her from miseries which everybody else had to suffer.

Nobody wanted to tell her the truth, of course—that she seemed beneath notice, a stupid old creature with no wits, no cash, no job. Just this occasional locking and unlocking of the big gate in exchange for her bed and board of thin soup. Both neighbors and newcomers overlooked her in the rigors of readjustment. When nobody else in town knew quite where they stood with the Enemy, she went right on standing just where she had always stood—at the big gate, to lock it or unlock it. "I will deliver him and honor him. With long life will I satisfy him, and show him my salvation," she used to say before she went to sleep. Always remembering to add a big "Thank you" for God's goodness.

But before long she began to feel almost too protected, and she fell to praying that maybe God could please think up some little special simple thing which a dumb person like herself could do for Him in return. Now that nothing openly Christian was safe. Now that church people were being called out, questioned, fined, imprisoned—some of them tortured. Some of them even killed. She hoped God need not go quite that far in His answer! But had He no secret simple need of her, perhaps?

The response came soon. And she recognized it at once as God's voice, even though it was just the deacon from her church who did the actual talking. And the secret need he had of her was a big clumsy secret; for he brought her the pulpit Bible to hide: "The Enemy has taken over our church for their office; they were planning to burn up the Bible to heat their stove; but I hid it under my coat. I am a marked man, and it is no longer safe in my home, even though I have ripped off the heavy black covers. So I thought of you, Grandmother Gatewoman—they will hardly come here, to search you; so have you some secret corner for God's Book?"

"I live all day in the secret place of the Most High," she told him proudly; "my Psalm promises me that comfort."

The deacon looked at her, somewhat troubled. Poor old soul, what curious things uneducated people could say! But he was thankful to pull the heavy Bible out from under his long padded coat and see her stuff it hastily inside her old jacket.

"It is on my body!" she pledged him, in the very words which coolies always used when employed to carry burdens.

Just as he turned to go, old Grandmother Gatewoman asked the deacon, curiously: "Brother, what is your favorite Bible verse?"

He looked at her gently, as he whispered: "I have almost come to believe that the only thing left to us now in China is John 3:8—do you remember how it says that 'the wind bloweth where it listeth, and thou hearest the sound thereof, but canst not tell whence it cometh, and whither it goeth?' Well, Jesus adds, everyone born of the Spirit is just like that. Free as air!"

"How sensibly God always talks!" the old lady said with high pleasure. "Please honor me by saying it again, brother."

He repeated the words slowly and added: "The wind is all that is still the same, these days."

"The wind and the wastebaskets!" she chuckled. "Have you noticed that *They* have left them still standing at the street corners?"

"True enough!" the deacon nodded, and turned to look at the large woven basket near by. He read its sign aloud: "RESPECTFULLY HAVE PITY ON PRINTED PAPER."

"What's that you are saying?" she asked, suspiciously.

"But, Grandmother! You have lived here all your life beside this basket!"

"Yes! But how could I know that it *said* anything? Tell me what those words mean?"

"How dumb she is!" he thought. But in words of one syllable he explained patiently that Chinese people had always felt a deep respect for printed paper, and never let it fall to the ground to be stepped on; and that was why wastebaskets stood ready at street corners . . .

"That's proper! That's polite! Is it some new idea that *They* thought up, maybe? I didn't know the enemy had so much common sense!"

"No, it's an old idea in China—older than you are. Other cities have wastebaskets and signs, also."

"How I like having my street corner bringing up people politely! Please read me again what it says."

He read it once more. Then knew it was wiser to be on his way; nowadays it was never safe to be seen talking too long with anyone with whom one shared a secret.

"Go slowly! Go slowly!" she called.

So now let me ask you: have you ever lived with a pulpit Bible strapped around your waist secretly? The first ten minutes you may have felt honored by the trust: *"This is on my body"*—the pledge of a coolie to protect a burden with his very life. But a pulpit Bible is bulky and not at all flexible. Grandmother Gatewoman had trouble with it at once. But she had no other secret hiding place than her own patched jacket.

"This is going to keep me nice and warm!" she began by saying; but more to convince herself that this would be an endurable trust. "But so sharp at the corners!" she added, wincing. For even under the Enemy, life still consisted of downsittings and uprisings; and whatever torture a hairshirt may have brought to medieval saints, the Bible began bringing to her—standing at her gate all day, locking it, unlocking it. Between times, holding her sides in a state of suspense.

"That old gatewoman does not get younger," people would say, in passing, wagging their heads.

She began invoking her guardian angels: "Father God, You promised they would bear me up in their hands? So would You mind letting them deliver me just a little from this shield and buckler You sent me? I know I prayed for You to send me something. But I did not expect such a big one!"

When no angels appeared, she would clump wearily indoors on her wooden shoes, to lie down on her hard brick bed—loosening the straps; thus answering her own prayer, for a blessed interval of relief.

Then gradually her slow old brain began putting two and two together: now that no church gatherings were permitted, now that no Bibles were allowed in any homes, now that she alone was guardian of all these precious words of life, now that they were literally breaking her back, now that a big wind was blowing where it listed, now that the wastebaskets at the street corners still said: "RESPECTFULLY HAVE PITY", why not lighten this intolerable load by sending afloat through her gate—tonight—just a few pages of printed paper for somebody to pick up respectfully?

She was so honest a soul that she hardly knew whether this brain storm was *temptation* or *inspiration*. So she lived through another uncomfortable day in prayer about it, finally striking a nice bargain with God: "Father God, it's Your old Grandmother Gate-woman speaking. If You would be pleased to send a big wind down my street after dark tonight, would it bother You if I let a few pages blow out of my gate?"

That evening she wet her finger and held it up: Yes, God had sent a beautiful breeze! She detached only three pages, feeling that it might be wrong to make herself more comfortable too quickly. One by one she released them. And although the loss of only three sheets could make no possible difference in the total bulk tied around her body, so fascinated was her mind by this new plan that she felt no pain at all as she stood praying, passionately: "Now Father God, Ai ya! Quickly—quickly, Father God, could You send out my angel to see that somebody picks up that page of Your Book! Softly—softly, Father God, what winds you do have! Gently—gently, God, do please make the doctrine precious tonight to somebody new! People don't have time to waste nowadays, with the Enemy watching. Please, Father God, it's still Your old Gate-woman talking about that page of Your Book. It must be way down the street by this time. If it isn't too much to ask, could somebody please be born of the Spirit tonight? Gently—gently, God! My, but You certainly know how to blow! So perhaps You will forgive me if I go in to lie down now. Thank you very, very much for blowing so hard!"

Nothing delighted her more in the morning than discovering that no pages had stuck in crevices on her street. Whenever she

dared, she wandered to the corner wastebasket to look in, anxiously; picking through its contents.

She could hardly wait for nightfall. Neither could she endure the
balmy, breathless evenings. She would even scold God about them
in no uncertain terms: "Father God, can't You hear all sorts of
people passing this gate? If it would suit You to send some wind,
then maybe we could convert a few of them with pages from Your
Book. You know, Father God, it needn't be a great big gale. Just
a little breath of air would do, this once."

One night she even whistled for the wind, the way the Chinese
sailors did. She knew it was a very heathen custom; but maybe
God was so busy with the Enemy just then that He would not care
too much if a foolish Gatewoman did a wicked thing. Since it did
not work, anyhow, she grew discouraged over God. Was He losing
out to the Enemy, perhaps? But when He made up for His breathless nights by a whole row of violently windy ones, she could not
bear to go to bed at all; but let loose, at long intervals, the leaves of
her hidden treasure.

In the end, of course, the war was over. The Enemy went home.
The missionaries came back, and churches were opened. But when
the deacon called for the pulpit Bible it was a sight to behold—
shapeless, and wrinkled and bent; even looking far less large.
Grandmother Gatewoman was forced to explain what she and God
and the wind had been up to!

It was then that the deacon became one of the foolish things of
this world. For he handed the Bible to the missionary saying in
despair: "That silly old woman has ruined it!"

"Not at all!" said the missionary. "She has *used* it!" And suggested that the entire congregation start conversations wherever
they went, by asking: "During the war years, did you ever pick up
a page of the Bible on the street?"

A notice was even pinned on the town bulletin board, inviting
all who had found such pages to come to the church for a special
celebration. It was Grandmother Gatewoman's proudest moment
to see actual flesh-and-blood persons walking in, shaking their
hands in congratulations as they met her.

When the missionary asked her to speak, she said in her thin, cracked old voice: "I am so glad you did what the wastebasket told you to do: 'RESPECTFULLY HAVE PITY ON PRINTED PAPER' "!

It may not have been much of a speech, but it proved that God could use the foolish things of this world to confound the wise.

Then the missionary made his speech. He said that he had always liked the well-known Chinese saying: "May the five desirables come to your gate"—happiness, official honors, long life, joy, riches! And he felt that all five had really come to Grandmother Gatewoman's gate, just as Isaiah once promised: "For as the rain cometh down from heaven, and returneth not thither, but watereth the earth, and maketh it to bring forth and bud . . . so shall my word be that goeth forth out of my mouth: it shall not return unto me void, but it shall accomplish that which I please, and it shall prosper in the thing whereto I sent it. For ye shall go out with joy, and be led forth with peace: the mountains and the hills shall break forth before you into singing, and all the trees of the field shall clap their hands."

Which made the entire congregation clap *their* hands; and break forth into singing; and go out with joy; and be led forth with peace.

The only trouble was that in no time at all another Enemy had moved in, right on the heels of the one which had moved out; so that nobody broke forth into singing—the Communists forbade it. Nobody clapped his hands—the Communists would want to know exactly what this Christian applause meant. Nobody went out with joy. Nobody was led forth with peace. For only the wind was still free to blow where it listed in China. And only the wastebaskets said: "RESPECTFULLY HAVE PITY ON PRINTED PAPER."

But if Grandmother Gatewoman is still alive, it may be that God and the wind can find some other way for her to use paper: now that she knows it can never return to Him "void"!

The way is one, the winds blow together.

Chinese proverb

Only the hands that give away the flowers of their plucking retain the fragrance thereof.

Chinese proverb

May your children live in an historic epoch!
                                An old Chinese curse

When one leaf trembles, the whole bough moves.
                                Chinese proverb

> *If life is a tree*
> *Joy is its leaf.*
> *Leaves bud; leaves grow; leaves fall . . .*
> *If life is a tree*
> *Its roots are sorrows . . .*
> *Long after the leaves are bare,*
> *The roots cling fast*
> *Deep in the Earth-Mother's bosom.*

                                Kwei Chen

35

FROM CELLAR TO ATTIC AND OUT
ON THE STOOP

From time to time we too have been known to *paper the town:*
Vote for So-and-So! Invest in the Best Vest in the West! See Our
Super-Colossal Movie! You Can't Top Our Pop!

And somewhere men are making millions this minute sitting in
chairs to think up far worse slogans than these to stop us dead in
our tracks, and turn us right-about-face toward their places of
business. But as far as is known only three cities on earth have
deliberately papered their towns in a purely domestic fashion,
from cellar to attic and out on the stoop: as if charity, and Christianity too, begin at home.

It happened in Finland during the war. The places on the
Karolinian peninsula lay in the path which the Russian army was
sure to take. Therefore, they began to prepare for the day of

evacuation with more vivid Christian imagination than most of us can stir up even in three hundred and sixty-five safer days, staying at home.

For these Finnish Lutherans sent to their Bible Society in Helsinki and bought up all the Russian Bibles available. They cut the New Testament, page by page, neatly. And then waited. Waited for the inevitable moment when sirens would blow and radios would blare out the bad news: "The Russians are coming! Get out quickly! There isn't a moment to lose! Quickly! Quickly! The Russians are coming! No time to lose!"

But the Christian households did lose time. For each of them had spent the weeks of waiting in looking over every room for every flat surface sure to meet the eye instantly, or that could be opened, searched and pounced on curiously. And so it happened that when the sirens blew and the radios blared, there was an instant scurrying around under every Christian roof. For on every doorsill somebody laid a page from *The Sermon on the Mount,* and on every windowsill also. On each tread of the stairs to the second floor a page of the New Testament was laid; as well as inside each bureau drawer, on every shelf in bedroom, bathroom or clothespress. Other pages were put on every pillow, on top of each bedspread, under each sheet. While out in the kitchen and pantry, both oven and shelves were papered with the Word of Life; cellar steps; coal bins. These people jeopardized their safety as they flew around these familiar rooms which they might never see again. But their dream was to make sure that the enemy so soon to possess these premises might be startled at the sight of all this paper—just curious enough to pick it up, just tired enough to sit down, just fascinated enough to read it.

And then, please God, just moved enough to start believing! Maybe they would never know what was happening under their roofs; but as they hurried to catch up with their equally exiled neighbors—all of them burdened with bundles from home—a certain prayer would catch in their minds; and neighbor would say to neighbor: "Do you suppose they have read any of it yet?"

They seemed to tramp to the homemade litany of hope and remembrance:

God of the windowsill, doorsill and stoop,
God of the pantry ledge, staircase and bed,
God of the tabletop, bookshelf and desk—
Bless Thou the enemy within our front doors this day!

If anyone said: "But where do we go?" someone could quote from a page of St. John left on the threshold: *"Ya esme pute."*

"What does that mean?" the other person would ask, not knowing Russian, of course. And the answer would be: *"Mina olen tie."*

But because you do not know Finnish, you are referred to John 14:6, where the words appear: *"I am the way."*

Even across the years and the miles, you can almost overhear what a moment it was when a snatch of music from "Finlandia" made everyone burst forth into the ancient words of a Lutheran nun:

Be still, my soul! Thy God doth undertake
To guide the future as He has the past.
Thy hope, thy confidence, let nothing shake;
All now mysterious shall be bright at last.
Be still, my soul: the winds and waves still know
His voice who ruled them while He dwelt below.

This is the law of the house—the whole limit thereof shall be made most holy. Behold this is the law of the house. I looked and behold! the glory of the Lord filled the house.

Ezekiel 43:12

FINNISH PROVERBS

It is best to do business with God, He has two hands, and both are of equal warmth.

Walking through doubts the way to heaven is long.

God is not yet going on crutches.

A new day can change everything.

36

NOT A FEATHER FALLS TO THE GROUND

Since so few of us can ever hope to be bishops—and a lady, never, of course—it is always consoling to discover the very human ways in which they differ only a feather's weight from other clergymen. And indeed on many astonishing occasions, hardly act like bishops at all (with the world, the flesh and the devil all under control) but seem to be small boys, playing hookey; yet casually altering entire continents and influencing several million women for centuries to come.

Such was the day when a certain bishop was walking by himself in India, and a feather fell out of the blue. Full many a lesser man is born to let a trivial item like that escape his notice. But it is written in the history of his denomination for all time and eternity, that this bishop picked up this feather, which was of a good size.

As far as a mere woman can re-establish a bishop's probable stream of consciousness, his thoughts ran somewhat like this: our ancestors used to write with these things . . . I suppose they had to whittle the end into pen points . . . I wonder how this quill would cut? Do I or don't I have my knife in my pocket? Here it is . . . How easily it pares off at the end . . . Looks shipshape, I must say . . . but will it work?

Turning home at once to find out, the bishop dipped his quill into an inkwell and made a meaningless doodle. It worked perfectly. The next step was normal enough: since it worked why not write a letter with it? Sensible enough. But to whom? A sister is always a safe choice; so the bishop dipped his pen purposefully and began briskly: "Dear Isabella."

So far, so good. But what next. He found he had nothing of moment to say to Isabella, after all. But one could always fall back on tenderness when distance lent enchantment; so his new pen wrote with utmost devotion: "Why don't you come over to India some day? I would surely be glad to see you, and there are plenty of things you could do here."

It is astonishing to discover that because of this feather neither Isabella nor India were ever quite the same again. Nor the denomination. For the letter rocked all the Methodist women from Boston to Birmingham as news flew around the country that Bishop Thoburn sadly needed Isabella Thoburn over in India, and there wasn't a moment to lose. But where enough money was coming from, nobody knew; and yet, such is the magical power of bishops that when they speak, the deaf hear; and the lame know they ought to start walking. It rained torrents the day that certain Massachusetts Methodist women planned a meeting; only six women dared come out in such a tempest. But the six were enough to supplement the feather, for one of them stood up and said that she would rather walk the streets of Boston in calico than to disappoint Bishop Thoburn when he wanted our Miss Isabella. Everyone everywhere began giving two cents a day; and although it may sound like a mere feather's weight, enough pennies and enough weeks earned plenty to transport Miss Thoburn to India.

It has been said that the bishop was somewhat upset when such a casual note brought forth this embarrassing moment as he wondered what on earth to do with this number one unmarried missionary now that here she was!

But he need not have worried. For the Thoburn temperament was as experimental in Isabella as in the bishop, and she started right in by opening the first school ever held for girls in India. It was hard work to persuade these shy little creatures to come. All six of them wept hard, since everybody said it was impossible to teach a woman anything: "As well try to educate a cow or a hen!" said their fathers.

"Nonsense!" said Miss Thoburn firmly. "Look at me! I read! I write!"

A good-sized boy was employed to sit outside the front door to safeguard these reluctant little scholars. All day he sat there with a club on his knees, in case parents or neighbors grew abusive. But in the course of years that small schoolroom turned into the magnificent Isabella Thoburn College—the first woman's college in all Asia; and the graduates began fanning out all over India as Christian teachers, doctors, evangelists, homemakers.

One of the best-known graduates, Lilivati Singh, used to sit and gaze admiringly at Miss Thoburn as she sighed: "The dream of my life is to be like her." And when she too began to kindle and re-kindle this light all over India, it was God at work again. For if no sparrow falls to the ground without our Heavenly Father's knowledge, think with what perfect care He chose a bishop in a light-hearted mood! For not a feather in all history ever did more for women in a more momentous fashion: organizing them in America, educating them in India.

No leaf falleth but He knoweth it; neither is there a seed in darkness of the earth, nor a thing green or withered, but lo! it is noted in a distant writing.

Qur'an 6:59

If all the trees on earth were pens and if there were seven oceans full of ink, they would not suffice to describe the wonders of the Almighty.

from the Koran

A sentence should be read as if its author, had he held a plow instead of a pen, could have drawn a furrow deep and straight to the end.

Henry D. Thoreau

When the pupil is ready the teacher will come.

Hindu proverb

37

THE PENCIL OF THE HOLY GHOST
ALWAYS WRITES IN SHORTHAND

It is not only in church that the pencil of the Holy Ghost writes in shorthand. For there is always more than meets the eye in anything a man sees or hears. Plato called this the world of the eyeball: that perception of things seen, interpreted by a remembrance of things past, still painted on the retina. Or, in Thomas à Kempis's words: "Blessed be the ears that heed not outward speech, but hear the whisper of God."

This conversation might well concern the whole law of the universe written in his members, so that a man in the pew could take one phrase from the Bible and read into it whole pages of physics and chemistry. For example, such a familiar phrase as the one where it is written: "And Jesus, knowing that He came from God and was going to God, humbled Himself, and knelt, and washed the disciples' feet"—for there the Holy Ghost has also written the whole cycle of water: *from God to God.* The heavens are telling it! The entire Atlantic and Pacific Oceans are telling it! Even that small mud puddle on the sidewalk is telling it! The sun forever drawing these bodies of water upward; the clouds holding these waters a little while, then returning them to water the earth.

The man's own body, 90 per cent water. His own blood observing the same tide as the oceans—one drop of blood making the circuit of his entire body from his heart and back to his heart in a matter of three minutes, pumped by a faithful organ which serves him from cradle to grave, whose rhythm ought to beat some nobler hymn of praise into his system.

St. Francis could sense all this when he wrote in his *Canticle to the Sun:* "Our Sister Water, humble and serviceable, and precious, and very clean." Ralph Waldo Emerson could sense this reverence also: "When I watch that flowing river, which, out of regions I know not, pours for a season its streams into me, I see that I am a pensioner." And Walt Whitman saying it this way: "I see letters of God dropped in the street; and every one is signed by God's name." To which Kagawa has added a Japanese footnote, even richer: "Science books are letters from God, telling how He runs His universe."

A man in the pew might well substitute for a prayer book the science books of his school days, for one hour of worship at least! For there he will discover that the shorthand for water is H_2O. The world of his eyeball retains enough memory of this symbol to recall that water is actually the home of two terrifying sons of thunder—Hydrogen in a double dose, to each part of Oxygen. He gasps with shock of this memory as applied to Jesus Christ, however, for hydrogen is the most explosive gas: he remembers that Zeppelin called *The Hindenburg* which crossed the Atlantic, powered only by the H; and, just over Lakehurst, New Jersey, exploding into a mass of flames; while oxygen is the gas without which there can be no combustion. Could it possibly have been H_2O which our Lord had in mind when He said: "I am the Water of Life"? If the churchgoer could be quickened by the Holy Spirit, he might look up the Lord's own hint of His explosive possibilities when He said: "I *could* call twelve legions of angels . . ." enough to wipe My enemies off the face of the earth . . . I could fight back . . . I could use the atom, known to Me since the foundation of the world, and blow this earth to Kingdom Come . . . I could . . . Instead of which, inspired by the Holy Spirit, the gospel writer wrote: "knowing that He came from God and was going to God, He humbled Himself, and knelt, and washed . . ." As if H_2O were His shorthand for showing that this orderly combination of forces in each drop of water meant that even one drop of water could put out one exploding match; two drops of water could put out two exploding matches; and enough water would put out all the fires. His sole aim in coming to earth having been to create a safe home for all the children of men.

Every name which Jesus chose for Himself holds similar physical mysteries in shorthand and similar patterns of spiritual meanings to be painted on the world of the eyeball. *Bread,* for instance! What is it but the home of the "lump" and the "leaven"? Three parts of meal to one part of that nudging excitement called yeast. The yeast with its nasty nuisance value, forever pushing and prodding the lump: "Come on and get up!" The lump forever yawning lazily: "Let me alone, will you? I don't want to get up!"

But the nature of the leaven is nudging; and the nature of the lump is resisting every inch of its inevitable rise, up and up. For all the work of the farmer in his field, all the work of the cook in her kitchen, was planned toward this one loaf of bread to feed the children of men. From God to God.

The trouble with the churchgoer is that just when the commercial world has gone further and further into the use of shorthand and trademarks and symbols, the religious world has used them less and less. So that it is possible nowadays for the eyeball of even the saintliest Christian to know from advertisements in buses just whose "Ale" has three interlaced circles, with no notion whatever that it is sheer sacrilege to use this as a trademark, when, from the days of earliest Christendom this threefold interlocking of circles stood for the Trinity only. St. Patrick using a shamrock—one leaf each for Father, Son and Holy Spirit; so that it spoke for itself an ancient Gaelic frith to avert evil: "I am going out on Thy path; God be behind me; God be before me: God be in my foot steps."

"The word of the cross is to them that perish foolishness; but unto us who are saved it is the power of God unto salvation." But not to know how to interpret the thing seen, cuts off the man in the pew from his long, long Christian heritage, back to his past in the Catacombs when the earliest Christians used symbols as passwords —the fish, for instance, which would mean nothing to the pagan, but to the secret church member meant that the Greek word for fish, *ixthus,* was an acrostic containing the initials of Christ's names:"Jesus Christ, God's Son, Saviour." The same with the little ships; just a ship to the pagan; but to the Christian it was a safe shorthand to say that whenever Christ had been on board Peter's boat, the disciples were safe; that the yardarms represented the cross; and the three waves underneath stood for Father, Son and Holy Ghost.

Then, in the days of the medieval church, when people were illiterate, and Latin was unknown to them, the carvings on their walls, the saints in their windows, the rise and fall of the liturgy spoke to the world of eyeball and ear, and was all the Bible they could read.

But now, in spite of all his education, the average churchgoer sits unconscious of the shorthand surrounding him:

> I love Thy church, O God,
> Her walls before Thee stand,
> Dear as the apple of Thy eye,
> And graven on Thy hand.

But if this never means Isaiah 49:16, then what a loss for a man to sit before those walls with no name graven in shorthand on his palm. For verses 5 through 17 are a jubilant combination of poetry, painting, music and architecture.

How exhilarating it would be some Sunday, if, instead of a sermon, the preacher should give his entire congregation some sort of a self-examination paper, with strangely searching symbols for his people to brood over! Deacons asked to describe in twelve dramatic words the major events in Christ's life—urged to choose vivid words, teeming with pictures; not exactly shorthand, but brief, sharp strokes to "tell all"! Suppose some one man, more agile with crossword puzzles, should manage to achieve an answer like this:

Annunciation ... Nativity ... Flight ... Boyhood ... Baptism ... Ministry ... Chalice ... Agony ... Betrayal ... Cross ... Tomb ... Resurrection ...

Would the preacher be glad that at last this agility had been focused on something durable for all time and eternity?

Suppose that the Trustees were faced with dollar signs extending down the page, twenty-two different lines in a column, and were asked to name the twenty-two parables of Jesus in regard to the use of Po$$e$$ion$—

$_____
$_____
$_____
$_____
$_____etc., etc.

And if any of them should fall short of the quota of twenty-two, suppose that man had to stay after church and copy five times this "*Agreement*" which William Carey made with his two colleagues, Marshman and Ward (after forty years in Bengal, with no furlough home): "Let us give unreservedly to this glorious cause. Let us never think that our time, our gifts, our strength, our family, or even the clothes we wear are our own. Let us forever shut out the idea of laying up a farthing for ourselves and our children. Let us continually watch against a worldly spirit, and cultivate a Christian indifference toward every indulgence. Rather let us bear hardness as good soldiers of Jesus Christ." (No wonder that in front of his humble cobbler's home in England there is a rustic stone fence with William Carey's own words inscribed along the length of it: EXPECT GREAT THINGS FROM GOD; ATTEMPT GREAT THINGS FOR GOD.")

Would the preacher feel that since the $ sign is one bit of short-hand which Trustees know how to interpret between Sundays, that this Sabbath stint might give the Holy Ghost a chance to write on the stub of their checkbooks also?

Since any insect or tool is merely shorthand for some special type of activity, suppose that the preacher had planned a young people's page edged with ants, spiders and bees on one side, with chisels, pencils and pens on the other, with the following quotations to be translated into French or German or Spanish:

Francis Bacon in his "*Novum Organum*" divided men of science into three groups: those like the *ant,* which collects and uses at once; the *spider,* which spins cobwebs out of his own substance; the *bee,* which gathers all her material from flowers, but digests them and transforms them into sweetness by some inner power: surely a hint in shorthand, which the author of "Tristram Shandy" put into the field of the four arts: "How do the slight touches of the chisel, the pencil, the pen, the fiddle stick, etc.—give the true swell, which gives the true pleasure! O my countrymen! be nice!—be cautious of your language; and never, O never let it be forgotten upon what small particles your eloquence and your fame depends."

To which the prophet Joel would surely have read from his second chapter: "And it shall come to pass afterward, that I will pour out my Spirit upon all flesh; and your sons and your daughters shall prophesy, your old men shall dream dreams, your young men shall see visions; and also upon the servants and the handmaids in those days will I pour out my Spirit."

The laborious twisting of another tongue around these un-churchly words of Bacon and Sterne might help a young church-man to realize that there is more to visions and dreams than meets the eye! (And it might help the preacher to dare to dismiss them as jubilantly as James Barrie once dismissed graduates from his college in England: "One hopes that you are leaving Oxford feeling that you are hearing a thousand nightingales, could eat all the elephants in Hindustan, and pick your teeth with the spire of the Cologne Cathedral. That's the spirit!")

And then, of course, the ladies' examination—suppose this took the form of a letter, saying: "To the Women in Our Congregation: There was a little girl learning to write, to whom her teacher said: 'But where is the dot that belongs over the letter i?' To which the child made a wise reply: 'I'm afraid the dot is still in the pencil!' For that is always the trouble with our little i's: their dots are so apt to stay in the pencil. For the truth is that the Christian life is learning to copy the handwriting of the Holy Spirit; and from an old gabled city in Germany named Lübeck we bring you an ancient inscription from the beautiful thirteenth century Cathedral. In order that you may surely read between the lines in your own handwriting, you will see the row of dots waiting for your personal row of i's to challenge you as you copy the message, line by line:

> Ye call me Master, and obey me not.
> . . . .
> Ye call me Light, and see me not.
> . . . .
> Ye call me Way, and walk me not.
> . . . .
> Ye call me Life, and desire me not.
> . . . .
> Ye call me Wise, and follow me not.
> . . . .
> Ye call me Fair, and love me not.

. . . .
Ye call me Rich, and ask me not.
. . . .
Ye call me Eternal, and seek me not.
. . . .
Ye call me Gracious, and trust me not.
. . . .
Ye call me Noble, and serve me not.
. . . .
Ye call me Mighty, and honor me not.
. . . .
Ye call me Just, and fear me not.
. . . .
If I condemn you, blame me not.
. . . .

To which medieval message can now be added a modern miracle
from Lübeck! For in 1942 the R.A.F. dropped bombs on that city,
with no least intention of hurting the lovely old church, but fire
gutted the interior, and the terrible heat warped the whitewash.
No sooner did repairmen get to work than they found, under this
peeling whitewash, perfect patches of Gothic frescoes. Only too
obviously, somewhere about the fifteenth century, sober churchmen thought these startling saints and vivid virgins were much too
exciting for walls of a sanctuary. And as for all the little beasts
from Aesop's fables, they, of course, were absolutely inappropriate!
So, for five hundred years, all this glorious beauty lay whitewashed
over, until September, 1951, when the restored treasures were
shown to the admiring public which came to attend the seven
hundredth anniversary of the church.

It is nineteen hundred years since there lived on earth the most
amazingly colorful personality of all time, whom men called Master! Light! Way! Life! Fair! The pencil of the Holy Ghost has
always been at work restoring this lost beauty for those with eyes
to see . . .

*A Poet, a Painter, an Architect, a Musician—the man or
woman who is not one of these is not a Christian!*

William Blake

POET

Some folk as can afford,
So I've heard say,
Set up a sort of cross
Right in the garden way
To mind 'em of the Lord.
But I when I do see
Thik apple tree
An' stoopin' limb
All spread wi' moss,
I think of Him
An' how He talks wi' me.
He never pushed the garden door,
He left no footmark on the floor;
I never heard 'Un stir nor tread,
And yet His Hand do bless my head,
And when 'tis time for work to start
I takes Him with me in my heart.

Anna Bunston De Bary

PAINTER

The church do zeem a touchen zight,
When vo'k a-comen in at door,
Do softly tread the long-aïled vloor
Below the pillar'd arches' height,
Wi' bells a-pealen
Vo'k a-kneelen,
Hearts a-healen, wi' the love
An' Peäce a-zent em vrom above.

W. Barnes, in Dorsetshire dialect

ARCHITECT

The builders have died; but they have
left us their adoration.

John Ruskin

MUSICIAN

Consider it well: each tone in our
scale in itself is naught,
It is everywhere in the world—

loud, soft, and all is said:
Give it to me to use! I mix it
with two in my thought:
And there! Ye have heard and seen:
consider and bow the head.

Robert Browning

The pencil of the Holy Ghost has labored more in describing
the afflictions of Job than the felicities of Solomon.

Francis Bacon, 1561-1626

38

IN SEARCH OF A PORTABLE PROTESTANT

Not a man had dreamed that on this dreadful day when he was about to lose everything dear on earth, his pew could somehow go along with him on the dark journey ahead. Not the literal wood, of course. But the freedom and voice and message of the pew could easily be transported, the preacher said—provided he could fit it in his luggage! Whole families groaned aloud where they sat when this was first mentioned: for they knew that limited luggage by heart! The size the Nazis said it must be, the shape they said it must be, the weight they said it must be. Did the preacher think luggage had flexible sides and collapsible contents, perhaps?

There was hardly a dry eye in all Holland that Sunday. For the Nazis were commandeering every able-bodied man over sixteen and under sixty for slave labor in Germany. Not a congregation in any Dutch Reformed Church but held its quota of these future slaves; and women could hardly sing the old familiar Netherlands hymn that morning:

We gather together to ask the Lord's blessing,
He hastens and chastens His will to make known . . .

But who could know the "will" of God in wartime? With the Enemy on every street, and about to reach inside every front door for some beloved man or boy? Surely that could not be God's "will"?

The preachers in Holland had one answer which began to redeem a small share of their despair: this curious Christian thing which a man could hide in his luggage.

In every church in Holland on that final Sunday practically the same story was told and retold in practically the same words—

"My good friends, let me tell you that over in New York this year, the American Bible Society found that it had large piles of Russian Bibles—but very few Russians to buy them. So they shipped all those Bibles to Geneva, to the headquarters of the World Council of Churches—although they knew there were very few Russians in Switzerland to buy them. But the World Council had its ear to the ground; and they heard about our Dutch tragedy—how men would be forced into slave labor in Germany this coming week; so they shipped the Russian Bibles here to Holland; and I stand here on this pulpit surrounded by them. For the thing which the World Council knew, which now we know also, is that the Nazis are also conscripting Russians for slave labor in Germany. It may very well be, therefore, that as you work in mine or field or factory, you will work beside a Russian."

A strange shiver shook the pews: for this was news nobody had known before. And everybody listened for their preacher's next words—

"Now you have heard for a long time about Russia: that the things you hold dear about church and pew and Bible, they have been taught to despise. You have probably been sorry to hear how they have grown into an irreligious people. You have shuddered to think what tomorrow will be like if all Russians grow up cruel and godless. You have heard that no one under sixteen can be taught religion, that the owning of Bibles is forbidden; and you may have thought that there was nothing on earth which you could do about it! But now there is everything on earth for you to do: since of all the people in Holland, you, and you alone, will probably meet a Russian. May I ask all of you to stand who are about to leave this week?"

These men stood up. It was a heartbreaking moment. If their

own faces were white and haunted, the faces of their families were sadder, twisted in deep misery over this parting.

"Good friends, let me remind you how often in the Bible God has used His 'saving remnant' to redeem a bad situation—some little handful of forlorn men in the Old Testament, some persecuted exiles in the New Testament: scattered all over the map; but living witnesses to the light that was in them, wherever they went! It can happen again, through you! Now of course I know that the Nazis have told you exactly how much your bundles should weigh. I know that you have been packing and repacking them every day, trying to decide whether an extra pair of shoes might be wiser than a heavy quilt. But here I stand on this platform, surrounded by Russian Bibles which can only get into Germany if you leave something precious at home. Do you mean to tell me that Christianity has meant nothing to you worth passing on? Has this pew never brought you any message, Sunday after Sunday, to make you the Christian you now are? Have you never prayed that God would find some way to Christianize the Russian people and get the forbidden Bible back into Russian hands? Then who but you can take care of that prayer? Since only your own baggage can carry your answer? The Bible says that 'the Word of God is not bound'— but it is within your power to bind it and limit it all the rest of this year if you refuse to let it start working. So I ask you—here in the sight of God and man: what will you leave at home in order that these Bibles may surely travel with you?"

The silence was terrifying. They could have heard a pin drop. Each man stood as if petrified. Then one by one they turned to look down at a wife or mother: did she think anything could possibly be spared? One by one the women shook their heads in warning: remember how freezing the nights may be! Remember how endless the year may be! Remember that luggage is not flexible, contents are not collapsible! It was alarming, therefore, to have the preacher say:

"I see that once again the Word of God is quick and powerful, sharper than any two-edged sword, rightly dividing the thoughts and intents of Dutch hearts! So let me tell you that sixty years ago when other Russians were being sent off into other slave labor, in

Siberia, Feodor Dostoevski was walking with them in despair; but as they passed a certain peasant woman's hut, she rushed indoors and brought out her Bible, thrusting it into Dostoevski's hands. In the long loneliness of his twelve years in exile, when he had nothing else to read, Dostoevski fell completely in love with Jesus Christ. He began dreaming deep dreams of how he could pass on this love to the Russian people, if ever he reached home again. He began thinking up magnificent plots which could present Jesus Christ in novels dramatic and searching! Well, many of you may know that his very dreams saved him from the perils of that long exile; and he did reach Russia again; and the books which he wrote became famous the whole world over. His one theme was that 'each of us bears the guilt of all and of everything on earth, not merely the general world-guilt, but each one individually for all and each on the earth!" How do you know that you may not be working in exile beside another Dostoevski? Think how tremendous it could be through all eternity to know that you were the person who gave Dostoevski the Bible which caused him to say: 'I believe there is nothing lovelier, deeper, more sympathetic and more perfect than the Saviour; I say to myself with jealous love that not only is there no one else like Him, but that there could be no one.... There is in the world only one figure of absolute beauty: Christ. That infinitely lovely figure is as a matter of course an infinite marvel!' Would you not like to help discover another Russian like that Russian? The Bibles lie here on the pulpit around me. And I ask you once more: is there really nothing you can leave at home in order that these Bibles may surely get into Germany?"

This time it was the women who nudged their menfolks. But this time the men needed no prompting. This time the Word of God was so quick and powerful that the men came down the church aisles; and it is a fact that not a single Russian Bible in all Holland was left untaken or unpacked that Sunday!

It was said by Thomas Macaulay of Thomas Carlyle that he knew how to pack truth close, and make it portable.

Who builds a church within his heart,
 And takes it with him everywhere
Is holier far than he whose church
 Is but a one-day house of prayer.

         George Herbert

39

PIN-UP GIRL

It must have been tantalizing to sit on the women's side in the Early Christian Church meetings and hear which Pin-Up Girls had caught the fancy of two Apostles writing letters. More scandalous, really, than if Southern preachers should unanimously choose Mary McLeod Bethune as the one outstanding lady living below the Mason and Dixon line; or Northern parsons should vote for Sacajawea as the only woman contributing significantly to the nation. (Undoubtedly admirable arguments could be advanced for each viewpoint; at the very least, both of these women had been honorably married! And in spite of their dark color—or maybe even because of it—had carried conspicuous projects through to success in the face of all sorts of difficulties.)

Take the case of the Apostle James, Bishop of Jerusalem, writing to displaced Jewish Christians scattered abroad. Who would suppose that so good a man in so high a position would dwell with such obvious approval on a woman who was certainly no better than she ought to be—to put it mildly. If a bishop *had* to pin up a woman on a church wall, why not have chosen Miriam, for instance? Look what a resourceful little baby-sitter she proved to be when the infant Moses was floating around in the bulrushes. Think how cleverly she recommended her own mother as a proper nurse, when the princess happened along, and decided to adopt the child. And always remember how contagiously she did her song-and-dance down on the sands of the Red Sea, until everybody simply went wild with enthusiasm over the abandon of her act.

If any of this complaint ever came to his ears, the bishop would probably have taken pen in hand to reply: Respected sisters of the church which is scattered abroad, your mumbling words have come to my ears. Permit me to call your attention to the book of Numbers, chapter twelve, and you will soon discover the reason why Miriam cannot possibly qualify in my pastoral letter on public morals and the private use of one's tongue. In twelve clear verses the author tells us how Miriam had murmured against Moses for having married an Ethiopian woman. Decide for yourselves, ladies, why she objected to sharing leadership in the family circle with a woman of another race and color. But the fact is that God came down and said: "I heard you murmuring!" and found her conduct so shocking that leprosy broke out all over her—in Old Testament days this was, as I feel sure you recall, a sign of divine disapproval. She had to be shut out from camp the required seven days. And will you please read for yourselves in the fifteenth verse the penalty this imposed on everybody else, as a private prejudice always does —for in that verse it says: *The children of Israel could not journey forward till Miriam was well again.* Surely you would not expect your bishop to hold up before you with approval a woman who, through jealousy and prejudice, held back her entire nation?

So now kindly permit me to explain to you my completely proper fascination for Rahab the harlot. In the first place, ladies, she was not a Jew. Yet you can read for yourselves in the book of Joshua that she went dead against every *social custom* of her own city by housing men of my race who were aliens and enemies. She outraged every public opinion regarding *patriotism* by hiding men who were spies in her nation. She was ingenious enough to use every shred of their gratitude, because of her protecting them, to bargain shrewdly for the safety of her own household—was this not tenderness at its most feminine? And so, beyond custom, beyond creed, beyond local race prejudice, she created sanctuary for strangers she believed in; she became a safe dwelling-place for the children of God. Actually a preliminary "city of refuge," ahead of the six such famous cities which our Jewish ancestors built at God's command. Do you recall that they were to be on high places, easy to spot in the landscape when a man needed a place at once? And where did Rahab live but high on the high city wall?

Now that Jesus is no longer here among men, sometimes I ask myself—was it because Rahab once lived in Jericho that our Lord deliberately chose the road from Jerusalem to Jericho as the scene for His greatest parable about neighborliness? Was it because Rahab was not a Jew that He made His hero a Good *Samaritan* instead of a Good Jew? It galled all of us, at the time, to think how easily he could have let a Jew save the man who fell among thieves, when it would have seemed so much more sensible to let the *thieves* and *robbers* be Samaritans! But no! He had to go piling compliment on compliment about the Samaritan's loan of his beast; the Samaritan's generous gift of oil; the Samaritan's skill in rubbing in that oil; rubbing it on himself; the Samaritan's rental of a room in the inn for a total stranger; the Samaritan's lavish handing over his purse to the landlord, promising as much more as might be needed. Some of the disciples felt, at the time, that our Lord certainly was going a little too far in outpraising an alien! But of course, ever since Pentecost, we have all seen clearly that the Kingdom of God is everybody everywhere. This Kingdom can have no nationality, no kindred, no race, no tribe. And Rahab knew enough to start practicing it centuries before we blind disciples dared try it!

In a way, she was God's first Christian convert before there were any Christians. She just felt what it could mean. She was our first shelter in a time of storm. Our first refugee camp for those scattered abroad. She was our first underground movement.

I hate to notice that in your own rigid rectitude and respectability you ladies are looking only at Rahab's profession. And thinking the worst! Has it never occurred to you that possibly it was in memory of Rahab's profession that our Lord welcomed the chance to talk with a sinful Samaritan woman at Jacob's well, in Sychar? He shared with her one of His very richest thoughts, maybe because she was not of His race. Maybe because she did not accept His way of worship. Maybe because where He was so pure she was so impure. But the moment she heard something supremely deep and spiritual she turned on her heels, hurrying back to town, calling: "Come! Hear a man who told me ..."

It startles me now to think that perhaps this is the regular

Samaritan practice! Do you ladies recall that when Jesus cured ten lepers, it was only the Samaritan leper who hurried back to say "Thank you!" Do you remember in the book of Second Kings, how, during the siege of Samaria, four Samaritan lepers from a starving city found the deserted tents of the enemy stored full of food, and cried at once: "What do we here? We do not well, this is a day of good tidings, and we hold our peace!" So they hurried back to their city of famine with their news of food. In short, those *not* Jews do a great deal of wonderful hurrying to do a great deal of wonderful good.

Then, too, if I must justify my reasons further, think what historical precedent I have in holding her up as a suitable picture for any man's wall, since the Psalmist himself pinned her up as a model of hospitality. It distresses me to think that you have overlooked Psalm 87, apparently. Let me recommend it as your Book-of-the-Month choice: "The Lord shall count, when He writeth up the people, that this man was born here . . . I will make mention of Rahab to them that know me . . . this man was born here!"

And lastly, since I understand many of you have joined local chapters of such national organizations as Daughters of This or That, your membership depending on your family tree, let me remind you that Rahab married a Jew, eventually, and in that line of descent came Ruth and Boaz, Jesse and David; and Rahab is therefore an ancestress of mine and of my Brother, the Lord Jesus Christ. And I have never heard that it was in any way amiss for a man to hang his own great-great-grandmother's picture on the wall!

It would have been a wholesome letter to get from a bishop. But since St. James never wrote it, he was contented to let these scattered ladies of the scattered tribes read between the line of what he *did* write: "For if any be a bearer of the word and not a doer, he is like unto a man beholding his natural face in a glass; for he beholdeth himself, and goeth his way, and straightway forgetteth what manner of man he is. . . . Pure religion and undefiled before God and the Father is this, to visit the fatherless and widows in their affliction and keep himself unspotted from the world." Which, with all of the next chapters, is a powerful preamble for

Mary McLeod Bethune down in Daytona, Florida, and for Saca-jawea guiding the Lewis and Clark Expedition through our entire Northwest.

For landscapes may differ from hot to cold, from seashore to Rocky Mountain trails, but their pure religion was the same, and also their keeping of themselves unspotted from the world.

In Mary Bethune's case, the fatherless majored! For she saw them on every street in Florida—black children growing up with-out proper books or proper schools or proper chances to get ahead in life unless somebody raised some money and started a special school. So she set out to start it, herself.

Then everyone in the neighborhood put his foot down hard, and said: "But not here!"

She traveled east and west with her big persuasive voice and her wonderful black face. Men pinned her up in their memories! "How splendid for America if only there were more Negroes eactly like her!" Money came in slowly. And she started her school.

"Not here! Not here! Not here!" the people of Daytona said.

"Here!" she pleaded persuasively; and they must have looked in their mirrors one Sunday morning, and decided to be doers of the word instead of hearers only, for today it is hard to find a Christian in Daytona who has not pinned her up with pride: "Mary McLeod Bethune? Why, that wonderful woman was born here!" But the Lord should count, when He writeth up the nation, that Bethune-Cookman College is the real picture of her true religion—with its wide green lawns, its large and beautiful buildings, and the hun-dreds of Negro students with their earnest eager faces.

As for Sacajawea, whom Lewis and Clark engaged as an Indian guide for their long Northwest expedition, her story is earlier in time, and totally different in emphasis. For she was married to a Frenchman, and on one of the most strenuous stretches of their travel, he would go evening after evening to this man or that man saying, secretly: "My wife, I will loan her to you for tonight, if you want her." But evening after evening each man would think of his own wife back home and answer firmly: "No! No, thank you!"

Finally the party reached the most treacherous part of the Rockies where pack horses were essential; but when Lewis and

Clark went to an Indian chief to ask for this loan, the chief refused, vigorously: "White man no good. All time cheat Red man!"

After several more refusals, Sacajawea stepped forward: "But these White men—you do not know as I know them. They have all kept faith with squaws back home. Good? That Frenchman, my husband, each night he offer me to them. But each man say: 'No! No thank you!' These White men, they keep faith!"

The Indian chief nodded approvingly: "Good!" For a woman of his own race had said a thing difficult to tell. Believing her, he loaned horses and scouts to get Lewis and Clark across the Rockies; and, after that, on to the Pacific itself. In its way, it is Rahab and the Promised Land in reverse and with variations. But the Apostle James would have known how to appraise hard and lonely men on a hard and lonely expedition, with pure religion, undefiled before God and man, keeping themselves unspotted from the world. With the result that the great northwest corner of our own Promised Land was opened up to us because of one woman's frank decision—against custom, against prejudice, caught up in a vision of a new day on this continent.

This main-miracle, that thou art thou
With power on thine own act and on the world.
Alfred Tennyson

You say the little efforts that I make will do no good;
They never will prevail to tip the hovering scale
When justice hangs in the balance.
*   I don't think*
I ever thought they would.
But I am prejudiced beyond debate
In favor of my right to choose which side
Shall feel the stubborn ounces of my weight.
Bonaro W. Overstreet

40

LETTER TO THE ANGEL
IN PHILADELPHIA, PA.

*(AN APOSTOLATE OF AFFECTION AMONG ALL THE
UNDERLOVED)*

Dear...?

If I had ever been secretary of an organization in our church, perhaps I might know how to address you suitably; for *"Dear Sir"* sounds stiff and formal, and *"Your Honor"* sounds as if you belonged to the government down at City Hall. Once, in the newspaper, I saw the most gorgeous religious title—*"Your Beatitude"*— only to discover that the prelate was Greek; and while I am at sea about your own nationality, I am thinking of you as more or less Anglo-Saxon, since God assigned you to us. So I hope you won't take it amiss if I simply call you *"Dearly Beloved"*—our pastor uses those two words every once in a while in a sermon, and they surely make a person think twice; does he mean me, or is he lumping a lot of us together?

Personally I have never been able to think of you, for instance, as lumped with all "the angels and archangels and the whole company of heaven and earth"; for while it is a perfectly thrilling sentence and makes my hair stand straight up out of its natural curl, still it does push you off into some dim tomorrow when we will join that blessed company of all true believers. But what I find so satisfying about you is that God seems to have assigned you to us, today: *"Unto the angel of the church at Philadelphia, write."*

But as far as I can tell, nobody at all has bothered to write you in years and years. In looking up dates, for instance, I find that our

King James Bible came out in 1611; that was only seventy-one years before William Penn first came over to Pennsylvania and started his Holy Experiment. So I presume that maybe you knew him? For angels don't grow old as we do, probably; although when I read up about angels in the Bible it said that some of you had "fallen." I hope you weren't around that day, for it is in regard to falling that I feel I should write to you now, Dearly Beloved; and I wouldn't want to embarrass you if the word still makes you as self-conscious as it makes me when I think of our church. For we keep falling down on our obvious job, Dearly Beloved; and it seems high time that somebody made you an annual report—the way our treasurer does at the end of the church year: how much new money we take in, what we used it for, and then a lot of tripe about the way our wonderful trustees never touched a red cent of our blooming old Endowment Fund. Why should anyone clap over that silly old statistic? But our best families all do. Not our pastor, though! I tell him he looks just like St. Sebastian: you know, the one so full of arrows that you marvel he can look so pleasant? (Our pastor thinks my Roman Catholic mother gave me a lot of lively notions, which my Quaker father somehow never managed to cancel out—but look at the denomination I belong to *now!*)

Here I am wandering from the point, as usual. The one unanimously unmentionable point about our church which the book of Revelation made such a point of mentioning to you, is: "Behold I have set before thee an open door, and no man can close it."

But the wicked truth is: our men *have* closed it!

You know the door I mean, don't you? The door on our side street? When our neighborhood began to run down, and our rich members didn't like to park their cars along that side any more, why then, my goodness, the janitor was ordered to bolt the side door and put up bars: "so those street urchins can't break in, some dark night."

Dearly Beloved, we don't have street urchins on our street. Every single child had a long string of the heavenliest names; they just ripple along and along like something out of Dante. I am the one that ought to know, for I live on that side street, myself; and the children come in to see me a lot, and run my errands; on ac-

count of my crutches. (You may have noticed yourself that a
crutch makes you seem awfully little and young, to a child?) And
they aren't urchins. They are Cristoforo Colombo, and Luis
Agusto, and Herculo Bartolomeo, and even a little St. Jean Baptiste. Also I can report to you that he is the only bad child we have;
he thrives on wild locusts, wild honey, and wild everything else.
But I use him for my errands, and he is so dependable it hurts. He
pops his head in and shouts: "I done it!" So I am supposed to pop
something into his mouth if I have it handy. If I don't he keeps
track! (We call it "Wild Honey"!)

But you know as well as I do that our side door ought to be open
all day, so that he and Beppo and Tony and Chris could have a
better game room than the gutter, upstairs in that locked room.
Our pastor dreams about it. I believe myself that we are killing
him, inch by inch, on account of our side door. He says that every
time he shuts his eyes he sees that game room, complete to the
last checkerboard, etched on his eyeballs. For he adores children.
And he calls out the funniest sentences as soon as he sees them.
They drop everything, flat, and tag at his heels. *Pied Piper,* all over
again. But can he budge our trustees! "Could I fix up that upstairs
room for the children of our neighborhood, gentlemen?" They turn
into stone figgers, like those stiffs in museums—Rameses and his
seven sons; Ptolemy I, II and III. So then he tackles them on the
aged. Had they noticed that the cheap boardinghouses were at-
tracting an unusual number of forlorn old folks? Even their backs
were touching: stooped over, gabled up, rather like the rooftops
down our way? Now these poor souls would not jeopardize our
premises . . . But no; Rameses I shook his head. Ptolemy III looked
down his nose. Parsons were such visionary fellows.

Our pastor came to call on me later that afternoon. I think I am
a Tonic; for although I live on our side street, and am as poor as a
church mouse, and have a crutch, I haven't always been any of this.
So he lets loose his thunderbolts on me. Such as:

"The other day I dreamed up a club room in our basement for
all the old ladies and gentlemen! I painted the walls daffodil yellow, and the bookcases tulip red. I had sofas as green as grass. And
a small gas burner in the corner with a mess of jolly cups and

saucers, so that anybody could make a cup of tea whenever the notion took him. Like the idea, lassie?"

I could hardly breathe it was so perfect: "Fairy tale!" I cried, delightedly.

"Precisely! By the Grimm Brothers. Both of them quite, quite dead!"

So you see we are crushing the poor man, upstairs and downstairs. We lock up our unused rooms. We padlock our interesting doors. We won't spend a red cent of our crazy Endowment—that E should be a lot bigger capital; but I have no outsizes handy just now; and little St. Jean Baptiste is in school. I hope.

Dearly Beloved, are you the angel to bear our pastor up when he strikes his foot against a stone wall? He needs you at every turn. I can't think why he sticks to us, when he gets called to plenty of wideawake parishes, where he need not break his heart between Sundays. But, you know, he probably is so in love with our dreadful side street that he will never leave us until even Ptolemy walks out of his pew in our Museum and adopts this whole street as his family and every child as his child. (I stagger a lot to think what he will do with the little Mr. St. Jean B.! But maybe God will give me grace enough to hint that enough "Wild Honey" sweetens that saint . . . pro tem.)

And now, Dearly Beloved, I want to confess the next *irregular* thing I catch myself doing regularly in church. I got the idea from one of my own Quaker forbears who took part in William Penn's Holy Experiment. It seems that although the King of England gave William Penn all this land here in Pennsylvania in payment of a debt, Mr. Penn felt he had no real right to it unless he bought it from the Indians. Do you know the story? How he measured the land by laying pairs of breeches end to end, in the presence of the Indians, and paying them for every inch. The Indians loved his honesty. They called him their Big White Brother; and swore that "Lenni-Lenape shall live together in love so long as creeks and rivers run and while the sun and moon endure."

So the rather un-Holy Experiment I try in church is counting the number of gentlemen worshiping in pews that Sunday; then I figure out how far down our street their breeches would reach, *from our closed side door?* Then I pray and pray that God will please persuade these particular men to reach *that* far down our street—please, oh please! But I can't imagine how any of our prayers ever sieve through the ceiling and up through our lovely closed room, then through that ceiling to God.

George Fox once said that "one man raised by God's power to stand and live in the same spirit the prophets and apostles were in can shake the country ten miles around."

But I'd be satisfied, pro tem, with the extent of our men's breeches! George Fox used to say also: "This I know experimentally"; and it has long been my most stirring quotation. But last Sunday God spoke to me—straight through our mansard roof, our closed room, our sanctuary ceiling, and all that thick fog of prayers floating around up there, God spoke. And as clear as day He said: "*What* do you know experimentally, little Miss Bridget Fox, you deaf and dumb and blind girl, you?"

It was the particular moment on Sunday morning when the purple light stops coming through our stained-glass window to tamper with Mr. Rameses' whiskers, and the deep, deep blue light falls on Mrs. Ptolemy's feathers.

"Blue!" I thought to myself. "Blue what?"

And because it was March, I thought of St. Bridget's blue homespun cape. I am named for that blessed woman, and have grown up knowing that when she tried to wheedle land for her first religious building, the king said that he would give her as much as her cape could cover. I can't think how the clever darling ever swung it so far and wide, but it covered an *immense* lot of land; and the king was upset. But he gave it to her. And she called it Kildare: The Cell of the Oak. And Ireland began to be just as much blessed by what Bridget did as by what St. Patrick did.

So I thought to myself: Why do you bother with the un-Holy Experiment over the length the men's breeches will go down the street? What about using your own blue homespun cape to see how far you can measure? So "This I know experimentally"—

It is a simple thing, really: it is just an apostolate of affection among all the underloved; each of us doing for one another what Our Betters refuse to do.

I must admit it would have been a lot easier if God had only made me rich and influential and provocative; it would be such immense fun to be the kind of lovely creature men simply swoon over if you make a request: "But certainly, my love, certainly! Anything! Anything at all!"

But then I looked at my cell of a room (downstairs on account of my crutches) and I nicknamed it "Kildare." It's a challenging sort of word to have flying at you, both entering and leaving. And the miracle started weaving when I remembered a really devastating thing that Albert Schweitzer once said, that if you *opened your eyes and looked for a human being or some work devoted to human welfare which needed a little time or friendliness, a little compassion, or sociability, or work, there might be a recluse . . . an invalid . . . an old man or a child; or some good work needing volunteers who could offer a free evening, or run errands. Who could enumerate the many ways in which that costly piece of fixed capital, a human being, might be employed! More of him is wanted everywhere! Hunt, then, for some situation in which your humanity might be used!*

Dearly Beloved, can you see what a funny sentence that is: hunt an invalid? When I am one! Then I must have flung St. Bridget's cape! For suddenly I remembered that dreary old soul always up in the fourth-floor window across the street, in her gloomy old shawl. I don't wear shawls, myself. Not yet, anyhow. But in my Christmas box from the Church Benevolence Committee there had been a bright red sweater.

At the moment it was really all I had to send her. But I needed it myself, since this rented room is cold as Greenland's Icy Mountains all day, while everybody else is out working.

Then I had an inspiration. A note. And swapping sweater for shawl. I took a chance on her knowing English; for the more our street runs down the more we get foreign-born neighbors. So I just wrote briefly: "May I please say Hello to you, dear friend across the street, up there at the fourth-floor window. I'm the girl with crutches, at the first-floor window. I would love to call on you, but you may have noticed how awkward a critter I am, just on my own two front steps. So I am sending my red sweater to call instead! I thought how jolly if you could wear it, and then wave your arms at me; and it would really be my arms waving, too! Suppose you keep it two days; but how about sending your tan shawl for me to wear? My room is like Iceland! Is yours? My dear young friend St. Jean Baptiste will run these errands between us. He is my legs! He acts like a villain, but is an absolute treasure. So do wave my own red arm at me if you think this is a friendly idea! With loving greetings, Bridget Fox."

St. Jean Baptiste took six peanuts as "Wild Honey" for this errand. And in no time at all my red arm was waving and waving at me.

St. Jean Baptiste came back as sour as a lemon: "I done it! Rotten old woman, that one!" he said as he gave me her shawl. And when I showed him how gaily she was waving, he used language I dare not repeat to an angel.

So even if our church door is padlocked, Dearly Beloved, the miracle has begun on our street. As my Irish mother used to say, quoting a proverb from the Old Country: "God never closes a door but He opens a window." For when my red sweater came back to me, I had a bonanza to return with her shawl; so I wrote to her: "The jolliest thing has just happened; a woman in my church, who has two windows, got tired of both her yellow curtains and sent them to me. But I have only one window, and you have only one window; so I thought how friendly it would be if my fellow invalid across the street could be even more of a twin. Then we can pick out each other even quicker, and our curtains can wave at each other all day. My little St. Jean will put them up for you. Does the yellow remind you of sunshine? or daffodils? or the long gold braids of our new little German refugee, down at Number 12? When she jumps rope her braids are like Dutch windmills! With love, B. F."

I bribed the hungry young Baptiste with raisins; and when my curtains were up, he crossed the street to do the old lady's.

It was at this point that our pastor came calling: "Look!" I said with quite a gesture. "The Van Gogh room you dream about—yellow curtains, red sweater on invalid; old lady across the street. It's coming true!"

He looked at me in the strangest way: "Nucleus!" he cried. "You are nothing but a nucleus!"

"Cell!" I corrected him. "This is a cell, and its name is Kildare."

Now although I am poor as a church mouse, and live on an impossible street, I am a bone fide member of our monumental church; in good and regular standing. So what did our pastor do but report to the Benevolence Committee that poor Miss Fox was confined to the dingiest bedroom in Philadelphia; that it was a gloomy old dump; that he had discovered she had a lifelong yen for yellow walls, bright green spread, a red bookcase and some blue cups and saucers. The Benevolence Committee voted that I was entirely worthy of this outlay of money, and the janitor himself volunteered to come over and do the painting. It was almost alarming to see what a touch of color can do to glamorize even an ugly girl like me. And of course my room became our pastor's club for old folks. He parceled me out, at so many hours apiece, as so-and-so's charge to take care of: "Could you do me a favor?" he would begin. "Could you spare the time to step down the street from three to four this afternoon, and look in on our little Miss Fox? You know, that nice girl with the crutches?"

We overlapped my elderly caretakers as tactfully as possible; so that two or three congenial souls could meet and chat and share my cups of tea, and walk away together, arm in arm. We discovered who would be marvelous as baby-sitters for this or that young mother. We even found two retired schoolteachers willing to open a day nursery. But before very long I myself was being "loved" nearly to pieces: "I am being over-cared-for!" I confided in one old lady. "Since you live on the ground floor, too, why won't you come and sit in my room every Wednesday and take care of my callers, while I sit in your room and rest?"

"My goodness! My goodness! My goodness!" she chuckled and chuckled. "Will people just pop in? Or must I ask them?"

"Both pop and ask! Then by and by they may ask *you*. We aren't a very friendly street yet!"

"Why, I think we're a *wonderful* street! I can always feel something special the minute I round the corner and see the church. Somehow, I think a church adds a lot to a street, don't you?"

"Yes," I said, and asked her to come to sit with me next Sunday. She said she'd love to, except that she didn't have a thing to wear to a rich church like that—one that took up so much *land!*

Dearly Beloved, the land is our trouble. Once I saw our deed in which the lawyer assured us that he has "granted, bargained, sold, alienated, enfeoffed, released, and confirmed, and by these presents do grant, bargain, sell, aliene, enfeoff, release and confirm the following parcel of land as described hereunder, to wit."

Terrific, isn't it? And shows how we are indeed sitting pretty, with our big Endowment all tidy, too, in case God ever sees fit to call any of our first families above, to Himself.

Did you know that lawyers have another sort of permanent phrase: "he who owns the soil owns up to the sky." It may be O.K. for *lawyers* to feel convincement, as the Quakers say; but as an ex-Quaker, I can't be sure that any prayer can ever ever ever ever percolate through such sheer selfishness as our unused room, then on up to God. Now of course, in our small apostolate of love and laughter between neighbors, we are really only makeshifting and meanwhile-ing and pinch-hitting along, doing in Lilliputian ways what we ought to be doing in and out of our locked church door. I wouldn't be at all surprised to hear that, from heaven, we look like good baby bacteria working their blooming heads off just to cancel out the same number of bad baby bacteria running around loose on a slide, under a microscope. When what I long to do is to shine like the stars forever and ever from our big room upstairs, so that even the scientists way out at the Palomar Observatory will buzz with the marvel of *what is it* shining in the sky over Philadelphia, Pa.?

I know that the Bible says life does not consist in the number of things a person possesses. But hardly any of us here own anything at all! So when I saw how promptly the loan of my red sweater worked, I wondered if "Lending Baskets" might be a nice notion. I lured our corner grocer into giving me a lot of old grape baskets with wire handles. My lively St. Jean helped paint them, each a different color, so that I need never mix up my dear shut-ins by letting a lady get "Green" twice over! The whole point is that it changes the atmosphere of a stupid old room to have something fresh hanging on the wall or sitting on the table. Baskets are only keepable for a week; then returnable, and exchangeable. I loan absolutely everything I own except my crutches and my toothbrush—pictures, books, vases, even my mother's necklace with the little Cross; it goes in the Blue Lending Basket, and St. Jean says to me: "Gosh, that old dame in Number 19, she been Blue for three times already." She wrote me a little note and said: "I like Cross. It sleep in my hand all the night." I feel sure my mother will not mind; for although the little Cross was blessed by the Pope, *that* Pope is in heaven now, too, and I am sure she has fixed up this other irregular thing her daughter is doing, so that he won't mind the comfort it is giving to a Protestant.

Our pastor said I was a bit on the limp side about Lending Baskets for men, so he filled up a few, himself, with all sorts of gentlemanly gadgets—whiskbrooms, neckties, mufflers, paper weights, shaving cream, and a lot of sort of funny magazines for any minister to have—one on Deep Sea Fishing, one on Travel, one on How to Handle a Catboat; or maybe these were pamphlets. Anyhow, the old men out of work got a big kick out of it. And when our pastor comes to call they never need to bother about the weather, but can start right in on shareable careable items.

Another beautiful blessing is that now our pastor has all the flowers from up front sent straight over to me by the janitor, early Monday morning; and I have the millionaire joy of "saying it with flowers," a posy apiece, to all the shut-ins. I scribble little special notes to go along, on Sunday afternoons; for I can sit in church and gauge pretty well about how many to expect. Our people may not be too bright, but nobody ever misses what Tertullian meant when he said: "If I give you a rose you won't doubt about God any more." It makes them stop by to ask who this Mr. Tertullian is, please? When I say he's the man who said about Christianity: "It is impossible, therefore, it is certain!" they usually smile softly: "That Mr. Tertullian, he very deep man!"

Dearly Beloved, it is all as inconsequential as this; and there can't be *much* joy among the angels of God over what we keep doing on our street; but I do feel that from now on it is up to you to do something absolutely angelic to our men-of-affairs, so that they will entertain you unawares. How do the other angels manage with their overelaborate churches in underloved corners, these days? They must have side streets and empty rooms, too; and of course these endlessly lonely single people walking around "where cross the crowded ways of life," just exactly as the hymn says. All we can do now is to "wish them off" on each other, one gloomy mortal asked to go in to bring cheer to another . . . "and could you take him this bag of peanuts, please?" As futile as that. And as loving.

But back in the days of Zacharias, look what an angel did to change *him!* I wouldn't really want our Rameses to be struck dumb; but if he wrote on a slate the word "John" I should send him my little St. Jean on the doublequick! And I might remind you that when Balaam simply would not take a hint, then his angel worked excitingly through a little dumb creature. So I write rather desperately about that side door: for every day we are all getting more and more ready to walk right through it; but can't.

Or would it appeal to you to edge everybody gently into joining a church out on the Main Line where they keep moving, in that suburb called Laodicea? For I very much doubt if we still own all the way up to the sky any more, down here. (Or is this the time when fools rush in where angels fear to tread?)

The soul wherein God dwells—
What church could holier be?
Becomes a walking tent
Of heavenly majesty.

Johannes Scheffler

Where there is no love, put love, and you will find love.
St. John of the Cross

Who can doubt that we exist only to love? Disguise it, in fact,
as we will, we love without intermission. Where we seem most
effectually to shut out love, it lies covert and concealed; we
live not a moment exempt from its influence.

Blaise Pascal

Love cannot be idle.

John Ruysbroeck

Note: This chapter has been presented effectively by two readers: (1) a young woman in a red sweater, seated at a table, reading her letter as she is in the act of writing it; (2) someone at the rear of the audience who reads Rev. 3:14-20, at the end everybody singing: "Where Cross the Crowded Ways of Life."

41

THE BISHOP'S SHADOW BLESSED LIKE
PETER'S

In no time at all the whole ward buzzed with the warning: "Celebrity calling!"

Patients who braced themselves against every such ordeal, braced themselves; and hoped the celebrity's eye need not light on them. The more nonchalant were resigned to whatever celebrities did, especially when they heard that today's caller was a clergyman; their mood being: "O.K., Padre, O.K.! Just show this bunch of terribly crippled guys what you've got to make such a fuss about, Rev. Celebrity!"

Actually he put on no airs at all; not even a clerical collar buttoned behind; but everybody there knew about his cathedral, and watched him curiously as he went from bed to bed—remembering not to shake hands with the armless, or to suggest unlikely achievements to the hopelessly lame. But in an easy fashion he asked the right question here, the right question there, until somebody called out: "Speech, Bishop! Speech!"

Men who braced themselves against speeches, braced themselves. The more nonchalant sank a little deeper into their beds: "O.K., Padre, tell us! Tell us what's ahead for guys like us!"

It was a very good talk—earnest; graphic; right. So everyone listened. But down in his heart every bishop knows when men only listen because they are there: caught on the spot, with no chance to escape. So he plunged into an even more compelling plea for them to consider Jesus Christ—He too had been wounded, and for their sakes; stricken, smitten, afflicted; and by His stripes we are healed; as a root out of a dry ground, He has no form or comeliness; yet when we shall see Him, there is no beauty that we should desire Him. He made this magnificent quotation his starting place to prove the Lord's full understanding of men caught in similar hopelessness to His own. But any bishop knows when men are only listening because there they are—a bed is a bed. No hope is no hope. No future is no future.

Before leaving, he poured out his whole soul in intercession; not a ready-made prayer from his Prayer Book, but one for the men in that room; stricken, smitten, afflicted. But even as he said "Amen," he knew that he had failed to register any clue to a divine life for their mortal state. This had been just another visit! It had not changed a thing in their gloom about tomorrow!

But at the door he turned suddenly, and walked back into the room. They all thought he had forgotten something. But the fact is, he had remembered something.

For he took off his coat, and let it fall to the floor. He took off his vest, and let that fall, also. He took off his collar, his necktie, his shirt. He peeled off his undershirt. Things lay in a pile at his feet. Spellbound, the patients saw how slow and painful all these motions had had to be. Then he took off his trousers; his shorts; his shoes; his hose. And everyone saw plainly that each part of his maimed, deformed body was strapped together by an endless number of complicated braces and pulleys and belts.

He looked around at them then in an unself-conscious, compassionate fashion. After which he began struggling slowly back into his clothes. Nobody said a word during the silent Ritual for the Robing of a Bishop. But when he was dressed, he could feel a deep sense of kinship stirring, almost as the shadow of Peter had once had power to fall with healing on the sick. At the door he completed this sacrament of suffering by raising his hand in benediction: "Now unto Him who is able to keep you from falling, and to present you faultless before the presence of His glory with exceeding joy, to the only wise God, our Saviour, be glory and majesty, dominion and power, both now and evermore. Amen."

The seed of God is in us. Given a hard-working farmer, it will thrive and grow up to God whose seed it is; and accordingly its fruits will be God-Nature. Pear seeds grow into pear-trees, nut seeds into nut-trees, and God seeds into God.

Meister Eckhart

Life is a piece of Duty conjoint to a piece of mystery.

Abbé Bremond

42

HUMPTY DUMPTY DOES HIS DAILY DOZEN

*Greater than an army with banners is an idea
whose time has come.*
VICTOR HUGO

He had given himself this name. For what else was more right for an air pilot who had bailed out, sat on a wall of atmosphere, had a great fall, and could not possibly get up again? All of this in wartime. And all of this so seriously that when the surgeons saved his life, they could not leave either arms or legs with which to live that life. So he lay in his hospital bed filled with despair, rebelling against the very idea of enduring the impossible fate of being a helpless body to the end of his days.

But a new idea can always drive out an old idea. And valor is as much a part of a pilot's paraphernalia as his plane or his parachute. So that when the new idea grew its own legs and its own arms, able to walk through the hospital, he found the plan so engrossing and his new love so absorbing, that he saw he could do a dozen times a day a job nobody else could do as convincingly as a chap completely crippled.

For suppose somebody stopped by his bed to cheer him up. What more natural than to say: "Do me a favor, will you, please? Reach in my locker and get me that little blue Book in there, and find me the place called John 3:16, and read me what it says."

The nurse had to reach in the locker, and read it. The interne had to reach in, and read it. The orderly had to reach in, and read it. The matron had to reach in, and read it. The patients one by one, had to reach in, and read it. The neighbors, who called from his home town, had to reach in, and read it. Everybody fumbling through his Book, to find his text, and hear the story which Humpty Dumpty told them of the super day of his super joy when the Padre had come along and read it to him first. And the reading he could not possibly do alone without legs to walk to his locker, or arms to reach in and get it out and open, everybody else did gladly a dozen times a day.

The next week the surgeon could hardly believe his eyes: "Man alive!" he cried. "You're better!"

"Yes sir, I'm doing fine now, thank you."

"But what on earth has changed you?"

Humpty Dumpty was waiting for this, and practice had made him perfect: "Would you kindly reach in my locker, sir, and lift out the little blue Book?"

The surgeon looked at it curiously.

"And now if you would kindly turn to John 3:16, and read me what it says, then you can see what's been happening to me, sir."

The surgeon found himself reading the words: "For God so loved the world, that He gave His only begotten Son, that whosoever believeth in Him should not perish, but have everlasting life."

The pilot looked up eagerly: "I discovered I'm Whosoever! I believed every word of it! I realized I need not perish! And I'm better!"

It was at this point that something old and something new must have begun touching the surgeon's soul, too—boyhood memories of Sunday school, or his mother's Bible, perhaps; young manhood memories of his glowing motives on graduating from medical school to go to the worst corner of the world and do something magnificent for all the miseries of mankind. This entire vision crowded back as he held a small blue Testament in his hands and saw that a greater Physician than himself had been at work with this cripple: the extra healing of a touch he recognized.

"Keep the Bible, please," Humpty Dumpty said. For he saw a mysterious healing at work in the surgeon, and was delighted to see the great man writing his name on the flyleaf.

The rest of the idea grew out of this wonderful moment. Why not have his locker stuffed with Testaments, enough to give every day to everyone who stopped to see him? Propped high on his pillows he became a Padre himself, with the constant checking up on all his friends, later: "What did you read this morning? What did it say? Would you mind finding it again, and reading it to me —I don't happen to know that place." Then, when the reading was over: "Isn't it simply tops? Every word of it clicks!"

Lost in this round of delight, his old despair had so vanished and his will to live had been so awakened that the doctors decided he had the grit to learn to use artificial arms and legs. The pilot heard this news in strange silence. Then he said slowly: "So! I can go places preaching! So! the rest of my life the Government must pay all my expenses and even give me a pension, while I go places preaching. And I'm the guy that dared to ask: 'Can He do anything for me?' Yet now I can go places preaching!"

He said it with such awe that it reminded people that once the original Humpty Dumpty had said: "When I make a word do a lot of work like that I always pay it extra." For obviously here was his double eager to pay extra for every inch of his hard new way through life.

Everything in creation has its appointed painter or poet, and remains in bondage like the princess in the fairy tale, till its appropriate liberator comes to set it free. The story of the Sleeping Beauty is more than a fairy tale, it is an allegory of the life of every human being who fights his way through life.
Ralph Waldo Emerson

I have resolved to run when I can, to go when I cannot run,
and to creep when I cannot go. As to the main, I thank Him
who loves me, I am fixed; my way is before me, my mind is
beyond the River that has no Bridge.

John Bunyan

43

INTOLERABLE COMPLIMENT

He used his pain to strengthen his personality.
SAID ABOUT VINCENT VAN GOGH

A short time ago somebody made a survey to discover what people
do in time of trouble. The answers fell into three categories—
"Jump in the car, step on the gas, and drive like hell." "Keep the
radio going full blast all day, so that I can't even hear myself
think." "Go to the movies and lose myself in somebody else's mess."

Curiously enough, the last half of the last answer is half of the
ideal solution for trouble—to lose oneself in somebody else's mess.
Only it should be a real mess, not a shadow moving on a screen,
with makeshift scenery and make-believe trials.

This book is full of true stories of people who have tried this—
Jacob Tobiasch losing himself in the mess of fifty-six Jewish children with no parents left in Poland, taking them to Palestine; the
young Dutch couple losing themselves in the mess of four hundred
and fifty Jewish orphans, during all the five years until their
wooden wedding; a Japanese woman losing herself in the mess of
Henry Bovenkirk's imprisonment, arriving with cupcakes; Frau
Forell losing herself in the mess of the horrible concentration camp
at Gurs, in order to save an insane woman; Yellapragada Subba-
Row losing himself in the mess of Hindus suffering from sprue, in
memory of his brother; Ethar Milliken, lying in bed in Maine but

losing himself in the mess of refugee misery in Europe and the use of his farm for their rescue; a Waldensian pastor hiding nine Jews in his church organ; Greek and Norwegian archbishops; Earl M. Finch in Mississippi, et cetera.

Startling and spectacular, all this was the noblest sort of sharing at moments of public crisis, making unexpected heroes out of the very impersonal mess. "Red courage," men call it.

But "gray courage" is purely private. A lump in the throat. An ache in the heart. A daily disappointment. Among other unforgettable sayings which C. S. Lewis has bequeathed us, his description of pain as *God's intolerable compliment* stings deep into everyone's misery.

Narcissa Whitman could have said: "Never mind the compliment, God; just give me back my baby!" For here was a heroine: wife of Marcus Whitman: first white woman to cross the Rockies: building that first crude home in the wilds of Oregon: helping her husband to translate the Bible for the Nez Perce Indians: bearing a baby in this uncivilized corner of our country, far from comfort and care. Surely this is enough of a compliment for one woman! But one day when her back was turned, this beloved child drowned. How shall a private woman take an intolerable compliment like that, out in lonely territory? Narcissa Whitman took it by asking into her home eleven demoralized little orphans from the tragic Donner expedition, which had been beating its way westward when hunger grew so desperate that parents gave what little food there was to their children. When this gave out, human flesh was eaten by the maddened men and women. When adult deaths mounted, and orphans finally began arriving—dazed and destitute—Narcissa Whitman laid away in the back of her heart the brief memory of her own sorrow, and gathered into her arms the eleven Donner children whose long slow agony was still written all over their tragic little faces. And in the end she could write: "We feel that the good Father has blessed us beyond our most sanguine expectations. It is good to feel that He is all I want, and if I had a thousand lives I would give them all to Him."

About this same year there was John Bright in England, destined to hold various posts high up in William Gladstone's government, later on; but now with his entire private sky darkened by the death of his adored wife. Day after day he would sit lost in a grief so profound that nothing else registered, until the moment when his friend Richard Cobden planted this new idea: "John, when this first wild surge of your sorrow is over, you and I will go through the streets of England and find millions of poor women suffering unfairly because of our unjust Corn Laws—and together you and I will throw ourselves into the job of repealing those Laws!" In his stricken state, any such service to suffering womanhood struck its own sympathetic chord. And from that day, these two men were the leading agitators in the Anti-Corn-Law League, finally getting the Corn Laws repealed in 1846, the year when the potato crop had failed in Ireland and the harvest had failed in England: and men were ready to vote more compassionately in Parliament—due to a man who "used his pain to strengthen his personality."

In his rich translation of 2 Corinthians 7:10, Dr. Moffatt makes St. Paul write: *"The pain God is allowed to guide ends in a saving repentance never to be regretted, whereas the world's pain ends in death."* And in his translation of Jeremiah 51:58 he writes: *"Pagans waste their pains"*—by merely doing ninety miles an hour in their cars! by merely hearing soap operas and jazz! by merely watching imaginary persons walk through motions on a silver screen!

People returning from Calcutta like to tell what the Lees did when all six of their children, at school in the cooler mountains at Darjeeling, were buried alive in a landslide, one night in a violent storm. How could parents face such a total sweeping away of everything precious—not a child left to dream about, to write to, to hear from; no short or long vacations when their home would break forth into singing; no clothes to lengthen, no buttons to sew on; no confidences to share; no puzzles to straighten out; no children! no children! no children!

But as missionaries, the Reverend Mr. and Mrs. Lee knew only too well that Calcutta was full of little underloved brown children of all sizes—underfed, unwanted, without any care or tenderness. Their need was for children, was it? They simply walked out on the streets of Calcutta and picked them up, making a home for more than three hundred of them; and for over thirty years let the endless variety of so many needs fill up their emptiness. "The pain God is allowed to guide"; "never to be regretted!"

As it was in Oregon, England and India, so it was also in Switzerland. Neither cold, nor fog, nor heat, nor snow could stop these couriers from the swift completion of their appointed rounds. But the story from Switzerland brings in a vicarious note of victory which entered into none of the others. For in this instance, there was a French couple whose children were at school when the bombers came. Nazi bombers; strafing. And when their plane left, the parents were living, but all of their children had been killed. Their hatred of all things German may have been bitter, at first. But when news came through that British and American obliteration bombings were coming over Germany each night, that uncounted German orphans were roaming the streets in gangs, fierce as little wolves; dirty; ragged; inhuman as little monsters . . . then the French couple began thinking: "It could have been that way with our children, if both of us had been taken, and they had been spared."

The next step was pity. The next, compassion. The next, God guiding their pain: why not have a Rest House in some safe place, to salvage these wild waifs, keeping them until they could be properly placed with some family? Switzerland was almost the only safe spot on the map of Europe just then; so they took a large house, and kept it full to the brim of the orphans of German parents who conceivably might have caused their own children's deaths: but through their kitchen—they found joy in having this hunger fed; through their furniture—they found relief in putting these children to bed. Eternity framed in domesticity!

In India, the Hitopadesa described this conduct, centuries ago: "Hospitality is to be shown even toward an enemy. The tree does not withdraw its shade, even from the woodcutter." And in Persia a proverb warns: "Kiss not thine own child if an orphan is standing by." While the Scottish proverb says: "Welcome is the best dish in the kitchen." But *who* is to be welcomed, their "Braid Scots" version of Matthew twelve describes:

"Noo there cam seeking Him His mither and His brithers; but they coudna win nar Him for the thrang. And it was said to Him:

'Yere mither and yere brithers are staunin oot-by, and wad see ye.' And raxing oot His hauns toward His disciples, He says: 'That be my mither and brithers! For wha sal do the wull o' my Faither Aboon, he is my brither, and sister, and mither?' Then quo Jesus: 'Tha birdies o' tha lift hae nests, and tha foxes hae holes where they may gang, but tha son o' Man no hae whaur He may lay doon His head in tha gloaming.'"

MISERERE PSALM

Have mercy uppon mee oo god
After thy grat mercy
Remember youre promys made yn baptym
And chrysts mercyfull bloudeshedyng,
By the wyche most holy sprynklyng
Off all youre syns youe have fre perdun.

Psalm 51, 1440 version

KING'S WAY OF THE HOLE CROSS

Thou canst not escape the cross. Whithersoever thou runnest, thou carriest thyself with thee, and thou shalt ever find thyself. Turn thyself outwards, turn thyself inwards, turn upwards, turn thyself downwards, everywhere thou shalt find it.

Thomas à Kempis

All great & honourable actions are accompanied with great difficulties, and must be both enterprised and overcome with answerable courages.

William Bradford, Plymouth, 1620

44

JUBILATE, AMEN

And he touched his eyes again, and he looked up; and saw all men, clearly.

MARK 8:25

A man took a walk one day, in his own woods.

And a woman took a walk on the same day, but you would never dream that it was in the same woods; for although they were side by side, she saw so much more in the estate on her side of the fence than he saw on his side. Yet actually she could see nothing at all!

The man felt the way men often feel, these days. What's the use? The world is going to the dogs, anyhow. His own business was one big headache. That man in the White House seemed set on doing all the wrong things. His own health was certainly nothing to brag about. And here was his estate going to rack and ruin, while he paid a caretaker good wages to keep things shipshape. Look at that fence sagging! Look at those dead limbs! So this was the way he walked along; half blind; seeing men as trees walking to their ruin.

The woman felt as only a woman can feel, unable to see a thing, whose caretaker had stretched a steel wire from the house through the woods to the river, so that—hand touching the wire—she could have the joy of walking alone through her woods, just as her neighbor could. And this was the way she was walking along; blind; but seeing God walking once more in a garden in the cool of the day.

The man stopped in his tracks to watch her, alarmed at the speed of her going. Should they let Helen Keller go skipping along out-of-doors that way with no one to guide her? Then he saw the steel

279

wire and relaxed—so *that's* how she manages, is it? But, even so, what spring in her heels! What lift to her chin! What bliss on her face! Then, to his astonishment, he saw her stop in her tracks, also. She knelt swiftly on the pine needles; and leaning far forward she cupped a small wintergreen plant in the palms of both hands. She smelled it. She laid her cheek against it. And then uttered a warm jubilate: "Thank you, God! Thank you!" After which she stood up, walking on . . .

And the man felt a spirit pass over his scalp (as with Job when he said: "The hair of my flesh stood up!") for his own eyes were suddenly opened, and he saw Helen Keller more clearly. So this was the secret of the spring in her heels, the lift in her chin? But how did she ever get that way? He began remembering her life— that small sightless, speechless, unhearing child, cross and rude and unruly. Then Anne Sullivan trying to teach her. Trying, indeed, to *reach* her. Pouring water all day on Helen's hands, then tapping out in her palm the word "Water"; more pouring of water; more tapping. Water. Tapping. Water. Tapping. More water. More tapping. Over and over, all day. Until suddenly the idea got through to the little girl's closed mind—there was some connection here; something outside was telling her something.

From that moment on she ran touching everything everywhere, holding out her palm eagerly: "Tell me! Tap it out quickly—what is it? How do you say it? What is it for?" That constant curiosity never leaving her! When Phillips Brooks told her about God, tapping it out in the palm of her hand, she nodded and said: "Yes, I have always felt there must be *Somebody!* So now I know His name!"

The man from next door could even recall how Helen Keller had said that it was very good of God to put so much of Himself in raised print out-of-doors, for blind people to read. And now he had seen her reading Braille in the little red raised dots of wintergreen berries!

All the world and his wife live next door to Helen Keller, these days. It is, therefore, to neighbors on the other side of her fence line that she calls in no uncertain voice: "I who am blind can give one hint to those who see—one admonition to those who would make full use of the gift of sight: use your eyes as if tomorrow you would be striken blind. And the same method can be applied to the other senses. Hear the music of voices, the song of a bird, the mighty strains of an orchestra as if you would be stricken deaf tomorrow. Touch every object you want to touch as if tomorrow your tactile sense would fail. Smell the perfume of flowers, taste with relish each morsel, as if tomorrow you could never smell nor taste again. Make the most of every sense; glory in all the facets of pleasure and beauty which the world reveals to you through the several means of contact which nature provides. But of all senses, I am sure that sight must be the most delightful."

Like Emily Dickinson, she is not going to heaven at last, she's going all along—

> The word of God came unto me
> Sitting alone among the multitudes;
> And my blind eyes were touched with light.
> And there was laid upon my lips a flame of fire.
> I laugh and shout for life is good,
> Though my feet are set in silent ways.
> In merry mood I leave the crowd
> To walk in my garden. Even as I walk
> I gather fruits and flowers in my hands.
> And with joyful heart I bless the sun
> That kindles all the place with radiant life.
> I run with playful winds that blow the scent
> Of rose and jasmine in eddying whirls.
> At last I come where tall lilies grow,
> Lifting their faces like white saints to God.
> While the lilies pray, I kneel upon the ground:
> I have strayed into the holy temple of the Lord.
>
> Helen Keller

He never wasted a leaf or a tree. Do you think He would squander souls?

Rudyard Kipling

For there is hope of a tree, if it be cut down, that it will sprout again, and that the tender branch thereof shall not cease. Though the root thereof wax old in the earth, and the stock thereof die in the ground; yet through the scent of water it will bud, and bring forth boughs like a plant.

JOB 14:7-9

Art and blue heaven,
April and God's larks,
Green reeds and sky-scattering river:
A stately music—
    Enter, God!

Robert Louis Stevenson